"Rick Richardson invites us to take our hands off the panic button and look at what the latest research is really telling us about the spiritual temperature of America. He says the data show that people are far more receptive to faith than we've been led to believe. And his own experience of engaging with unchurched people confirms it. *You Found Me* offers us fresh hope for launching missional communities that see genuine conversion growth. This book is fresh, inspiring, and deeply informed."

Michael Frost, Morling College, Sydney

"Based on research, Rick debunks the myths that say the sky is falling on the Christian faith in America, and instead, he convincingly shows that people are actually more open to talking about spirituality than we thought. Read this book and you'll find yourself receiving practical help on raising up leaders and communities that can welcome those who don't yet follow Jesus!"

James Choung, author of *True Story* and *Real Life*

"By living in the negative numbers over the past three decades, I have come to realize through Rick's research that I have been part of the problem. Evangelism can be difficult without the depressing narrative of negativity often shared about the unreceptive and unchurched. Read this book and join a growing movement of leaders who are convinced that, by God's grace, we can and will reach the unchurched of this generation! Rick has been helping lead evangelism cohorts with our Austin pastors, and the emphasis and practical steps to proclaim and demonstrate the gospel is making a difference in our church and community!"

Tim Hawks, senior pastor of Hill Country Bible Church, Austin, senior leadership team, Christ Together

"Jesus calls every local church to be a missional community of disciples who make disciples, experiencing growth primarily through the conversion of new disciples rather than the transfer of existing ones. Yet too many churches have given up hope that they can be missionally effective with today's emerging generation. Through rock-solid research and decades of on-the-ground experience, Rick reveals how the most fruitful churches of our time are effectively making and multiplying disciples in a rapidly changing culture, and he shows us exactly how we can do the same. This book is a must-read for every Christian leader."

Michelle Sanchez, executive minister of Make and Deepen Disciples, Evangelical Covenant Church

"At a time when many are assuming that the Christian movement across America is down for the count, Rick Richardson provides far more than a ray of hope. In his new book, *You Found Me*, Rick describes the strategies that the top 10 percent of churches growing through actual conversion (conversion communities) are using to make headway in evangelism, living out and joyfully sharing the good news. In my hometown of Portland, Oregon, a proudly progressive and unchurched place, we've seen great gospel progress through active engagement with our community, which is seeking to continually encourage and equip everyday believers to share their faith. Unchurched people are far more open than we give them credit for. There's so much more we can do to share in the harvest, which Jesus continues to assure us is ripe and ready!"

Kevin Palau, president and chief executive officer of the Luis Palau Association

"This message is something Rick lives, is constantly learning, and is experienced leading. Those stories make this message both personal and possible. I greatly value the partnership LifeWay Research has had with Rick and the Billy Graham Center to equip the church with insights into our culture today and the vital role of congregations."

Scott McConnell, executive director of LifeWay Research

"Let's be honest, those who have a passion for meticulous research and detailed data can end up writing books that are slow or dry (though often very helpful). This is not such a book! Rick Richardson writes with the heart of a pastor, the mind of a scholar, and the passion of an evangelist. It is rare to find a book with excellent research that is a page-turner, but this is such a book. As you read, you will learn information needed to reach out effectively, you will have your heart ignited for the gospel, and you will be equipped to mobilize others to bring the amazing good news of Jesus to our world."

Kevin G. Harney, founder of Organic Outreach International, lead pastor of Shoreline Community Church, author of the Organic Outreach trilogy

"There is no one I trust more as a guide for evangelism than my friend Rick Richardson. Rick and I have been in conversation for years about what it will take to reach people and disciple them in our contemporary culture. I am excited to see this book, based on wide-ranging, national research, come out. The spiritual sky is not falling. Rick will show you why. *You Found Me* will stimulate your imagination, enthuse and reshape your practice of spiritual conversations, and guide you to being simultaneously humble and fruitful."

Todd Hunter, author, professor, and Anglican Bishop

"God's people were made for more. The solid and insightful new research in this book will equip your church for more kingdom impact. Furthermore, if you want to understand what God is doing in our time here in the West, you need to read this book."

Rob Wegner, director of Kansas City Underground, author of *Made for More* and *Find Your Place*

"Rick Richardson is a true champion of the faith. His fire for evangelism and passion for the lost are inspiring. He has spent decades promoting evangelism among the students of Wheaton College as professor of evangelism and leadership, and he has blessed me personally with his care and concern for the lost, especially for the younger generation. I'm glad he wrote this book, and I pray it moves many to take a more active role in sharing their faith."

Luis Palau, evangelist and author

"This book is good news about the good news—people are much more open to the gospel than we've been told! With clarity, conviction, and carefully researched data, Rick Richardson provides inspiration and practical ideas to help us reach more and more people for Christ."

Mark Mittelberg, author of the Becoming a Contagious Christian course and *The Questions Christians Hope No One Will Ask (With Answers)*

"I love Rick's vision and his wisdom for helping create conversion communities, where the Holy Spirit moves powerfully and lives are transformed regularly. We are seeing this on college campuses across the country. Rick's impressive research is grounded in honest success and failure stories of local churches figuring this out as well. May God use this book to help churches everywhere experience more of God's ripe harvest in our lifetime."

Doug Schaupp, national director of evangelism, InterVarsity, coauthor of *I Once Was Lost*

"Few books have the potential to change the conversation like this book could. And for a church that has lost its sense of mission, I can't imagine a more important conversation to change. My prayer is that this book encourages many churches to reclaim their passion for the gospel and their voice to share it."

Mark Young, president, Denver Seminary

Foreword by Ed Stetzer

Rick Richardson

YOU FOUND ME

**New Research on
How Unchurched
Nones, Millennials,
and Irreligious Are
Surprisingly Open
to Christian Faith**

IVP Books

An imprint of InterVarsity Press
Downers Grove, Illinois

InterVarsity Press
P.O. Box 1400, Downers Grove, IL 60515-1426
ivpress.com
email@ivpress.com

InterVarsity Press® is the book-publishing division of InterVarsity Christian Fellowship/USA®, a movement
of students and faculty active on campus at hundreds of universities, colleges, and schools of nursing in the
United States of America, and a member movement of the International Fellowship of Evangelical Students.
For information about local and regional activities, visit intervarsity.org.

While any stories in this book are true, some names and identifying information may have been changed to
protect the privacy of individuals.

Cover design and image composite: David Fassett
Interior design: Daniel van Loon
Images: glittering gold paint: © MirageC / Moment / Getty Images
        defocused color background: © Sudhir Kumar / EyeEm / Getty Images
        abstract light watercolor: © lutavia / iStock / Getty Images Plus
        abstract blue wave: © oxygen / Moment / Getty Images

ISBN 978-0-8308-4154-7 (print)
ISBN 978-0-8308-6454-6 (digital)

Printed in the United States of America ∞

InterVarsity Press is committed to ecological stewardship and to the conservation of natural resources
in all our operations. This book was printed using sustainably sourced paper.

Library of Congress Cataloging-in-Publication Data
Names: Richardson, Rick, 1955- author.
Title: You found me : new research on how unchurched nones, millennials, and
    irreligious are surprisingly open to Christian faith / Rick Richardson.
Description: Downers Grove : InterVarsity Press, 2019. | Includes
    bibliographical references.
Identifiers: LCCN 2019007949 (print) | LCCN 2019012973 (ebook) | ISBN
    9780830864546 (eBook) | ISBN 9780830841547 (hardcover : alk. paper)
Subjects: LCSH: Non church-affiliated people—United States.. | Evangelistic
    work—United States.
Classification: LCC BV4921.3 (ebook) | LCC BV4921.3 .R53 2019 (print) | DDC
    269/.20973—dc23
LC record available at https://lccn.loc.gov/2019007949

P   25 24 23 22 21 20 19 18 17 16 15 14 13 12 11 10 9 8 7 6 5 4 3 2 1

Y   37 36 35 34 33 32 31 30 29 28 27 26 25 24 23 22 21 20 19

I dedicate this book to dear friends who sometimes had different

spiritual perspectives than I do but who have gone on a spiritual

and conversational journey of sharing their convictions

and asking about mine, and pursing the kind of friendship

in which we can learn from each other and mutually influence

one another. I especially think of Dick, Pat, Gerard, Nancy,

Jael, Marvin, and Chris.

Contents

Foreword

Ed Stetzer

American Christianity is dying.

Every few months this headline rings out in secular and religious newspapers, during the evening news, and on social media. Bolstered with studies that reveal Americans less willing to identify with traditional religious groups, Christians and non-Christians alike claim we are witnessing the long-awaited collapse of American Christianity.

These arguments were given full form in Robert Jones's controversial *The End of White Christian America*. Published in July 2017, the book weaves together historical themes and data out of the Public Religion Research Institute to prove that Christianity—by which Jones means evangelicalism—is dying. Jones points to a variety of factors, chief among them shifting demographics and moral attitudes of the broader culture. As evidence, Jones points to changes in religious self-identification/affiliation, concluding that America is turning its back on the Christian church.

Jones proved to be the voice that launched a thousand think pieces, each amplifying the volume and deepening the sense of impending evangelical collapse. As this was already a popular genre for religious and secular pundits alike, we have witnessed a deluge of pieces heralding the death of the Protestant church in America. This narrative is powerful in that it allows each author to supply their own rationale for the decline: the rise of the spiritual nones, a growing divergence between church social morality and culture, or simply that Western secularism has finally taken root.

The result of this constant bombardment is that we have reached a point where most *pastors and ministry leaders* accept his argument as given fact. No longer confined to clickbait headlines and social media posts, this thinking has begun to permeate our pews and pulpits. At the dinner table and elder meetings, Christians breathlessly whisper to one another about the impending doom of the American church. Equal parts urgency and panic, this attitude has sparked a veritable cottage industry of conferences and books. Each presents the same set of beliefs as gospel truth: the church is declining, people are leaving the church, and those outside the church are resistant to evangelism.

In this context, Dr. Rick Richardson's *You Found Me* is a breath of fresh air. Armed with research on the state of church outreach and the attitudes of the unchurched toward faith, Richardson charts a compelling vision for church outreach and evangelism in our new, post-Christian world. In the first section of the book, Richardson takes no prisoners in outlining how myths regarding the church's steep decline or the hostility of our culture to faith sharing can infect and damage our outreach. These myths prove self-fulfilling prophecies, discouraging Christians about the future of their faith and making them hesitant to engage their communities with the gospel. In laying the groundwork for how to engage effectively, Richardson unpacks why these myths do not hold up under close scrutiny and explores churches and ministries that are succeeding despite this narrative. As Richardson points out, it is crucial for pastors and ministry leaders to root out these myths both in their own thinking and in their organizations if they want to instill a culture of effective evangelism.

In the second and third sections, Richardson truly hits his stride through translating his research into practical advice for church leaders seeking to generate a culture of outreach. Through studying churches in the top 10 percent of evangelism, what the book terms *conversion communities*, Richardson identifies central practices, training, and perspectives that fuel successful evangelism cultures. As such, Richardson follows Paul's encouragement to the Corinthians to "imitate me, just as I imitate Christ" (1 Cor 11:1 NLT). Moreover, the book reclaims an identity for the church as a missional organization: a group of believers called to and embedded within a specific community for the purpose of serving and evangelizing. It is a return to a holistic understanding of outreach, seeing the needs of the community as a window to live out the gospel and frame spiritual conversations. Richardson gives a robust depiction of the church as not only a place where God's people are equipped but also as a hospital for the broken, an embassy out of which we are sent, a family table where all are welcome to share in the feast, and a temple where we worship King Jesus. As such, this book is likely to have a significant impact on our understanding of the state of the church as well as inspire Christians to reclaim our calling to go into the world to show and share the love of Jesus.

You Found Me marks the culmination of several years of research directed by Richardson through the Billy Graham Center Institute. It is fitting that Richardson, as director of the institute, should publish the first major research initiative of the center, setting the tone for future projects as advancing scholarly discussions through quality research while simultaneously focusing on equipping pastors and church leaders for the work of ministry. The strength of this research project is seen in part through its combination of quantitative national surveys and qualitative interviews. The result is a book that can draw connections between the broad, macro trends in American religion while digging into the stories and experiences of those who are living out their faith in churches and ministries across the country. *You Found Me* sets a high bar for future research from the institute and models to similar organizations how to leverage similar studies for the advancement of God's kingdom and the edification of his church.

Introduction

The Challenge Congregations Face in America

I love pastors and leaders of churches, and I also feel their pain and disappointment when things don't go well. I have been a pastor at various churches for some years, and even when I have not been on staff, I have almost always served as a leader in my church in some capacity. I think of a few of the pastors and leaders for whom I am praying these days. Let me tell you about one of them.

Pastor Nate is a loved and effective pastor. He is there when people are in crisis. He is a good communicator with a warm heart and pastoral understanding in his sermons. He is really likable and liked, even loved.

Nate also has a big heart for reaching people who don't know Jesus. He is Southern Baptist, after all. Part of why he went into ministry was his heart for neighbors and friends and family members who did not know Jesus. But over the years, the everyday demands of the church ministry he leads pushed out any time he might have had to reach out. He wasn't sharing his faith with his friends much and had started to give up on even trying, but his church didn't seem to mind. They liked having Nate all to themselves. Who wouldn't? Nate would not have put it this way, but his life was a parable of gradual mission drift over years. He had lost some of his passion and almost all of his personal practice of reaching out to people outside the church. His church was not growing, and it was even shrinking some, though not a lot. The church would certainly be able to go on for years, but something central was missing from Nate's life and ministry, and he knew it.

Lately Nate has been trying to make changes. He started reaching out himself to friends and neighbors. He is meeting with a few other pastors to share stories and keep himself accountable. He has told his elders he wants to change, and he has appointed a woman from his church, Shelley, to help him lead the change and get other people involved in reaching out.

There is a further problem that has derailed the effort. A few months after Nate began to make changes, he discovered that one of his church volunteers had abused kids in Sunday school. He and the church ended up in an article in the local newspaper. His church has had to pay legal fees. They have been caught up in controversy and pain. A few families have left. The staff person who headed the children's ministry needed to be reassigned. All of Nate's steps toward growing in outreach have now been swallowed up by the leadership crisis. And Shelley, who has so much passion to help Nate and the church make a difference, is frustrated and feeling helpless.

Nate and Shelley long to see friends and family members come to know God and to connect to a congregation. They long to see their church making an impact in the community. They long to grow as a church by reaching people who are unchurched, but presently these longings are going unfulfilled. Instead, the church is shrinking, the everyday business of the church consumes most of the energy of most of the leaders, and the additional crisis has consumed everything else.

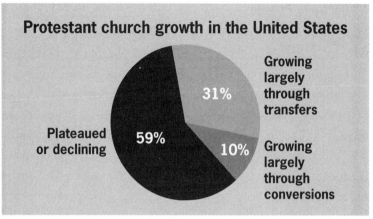

Figure 1.1. Protestant church growth in the United States

Nate and Shelley are not alone. As a whole, the church in America is struggling, and pastors and leaders and church people are feeling it. Eighty percent of all churches in America are plateaued and declining.[1] For Protestant churches in America, the numbers are better but still not good. Over the last three years, 59 percent of Protestant churches in America are plateaued or declining.[2]

In addition, 31 percent are growing but primarily through transfers, which come at the expense of the churches that are declining. Only 10 percent are growing primarily through reaching new people and therefore fit our definition of a conversion community.[3]

These healthy and vibrant churches are growing; attracting new, unchurched people; and making a difference in their communities. But for most churches, if trends and business as usual continue to characterize the American church context, churches will decline, people will drift away from any congregational involvement, and communities will experience increasing moral and social decline.

What can be done? Is the culture's drift away from church congregations inevitable?

A Few Good People

There is an intriguing interaction between Abraham and God in Genesis 18:20-33 that has a bearing on the decline of churches in America and what could be done about it. In the passage, the writer reports how God tells Abraham he is going to destroy the cities of Sodom and Gomorrah. Apparently, both cities have become so morally and socially degenerate and so devoid of any redeeming people that they are fit for nothing but destruction. Abraham takes issue with this and argues with God. Summoning his courage, Abraham asks whether God would spare the city if there were fifty righteous people. God says yes. In an odd scene, the two protagonists, God and Abraham, begin the Middle Eastern practice of bartering. Abraham slowly whittles God down to ten. If even ten righteous people can be found, would God spare the city? Yes.

Sadly, not even ten righteous people can be found.

interesting observation

It was not the presence of evil people, unjust relationships, or violence that doomed Sodom and Gomorrah. It was the lack of good people, bonded with one another, working for justice, compassion, and reconciliation. I will come back to this theme several times. The primary problem the church faces is not the shifting or hostile culture around us. The primary problem we face is us. Whenever the church recovers its quality of life and boldness of witness, it grows, even against immense cultural barriers. We *can* be the ten righteous who catalyze the sparing of Sodom and Gomorrah.

In 1867 British philosopher John Stuart Mill explained, "Bad men need nothing more to compass their ends, than that good men should look on and do nothing."[4] Almost one hundred years later, in 1963, Martin Luther King Jr. echoed that sentiment in his "Letter from a Birmingham Jail" when he wrote, "The ultimate tragedy of Birmingham was not the brutality of the bad people, but the silence of the good people."[5] When good people do nothing, communities deteriorate.

Congregations, including Christian congregations, keep communities alive and healthy.

Healthy congregations create communal bonds that build social connections of caring between people. They contribute to their community through civic involvement, social service, and concern for the hurting. Healthy congregations can make significant cultural contributions to communities related to music, or art, or architecture, or practicing positive relational presence. Healthy congregations host volunteer organizations, and members often volunteer for nonprofit service organizations that meet the needs of underresourced people. Healthy congregations reach new people and provide meaning and direction in life to many individuals who otherwise might merely live for themselves.

Consequences of Ineffective Conversion Growth

But most congregations today in America are struggling to be healthy and vibrant, and many are missing the mark. There are numerous consequences.

Pastors and leaders often feel like failures, and their efforts to make a difference feel futile. Pastors often go into ministry to lead a healthy, vibrant congregation that could reach people and influence communities. Instead, too many are presiding over congregations that are shrinking in numbers and impact, and they are often expected to do what feels impossible: turn it all around. Carrying that weight and not achieving success burns out many good people.

I think of Gary, who is a more effective preacher than many and is more loved by his people than most. Despite his gifts and vision, and the work he did over ten years, he watched his congregation go from 900 to 650, losing many leaders and members to the hot new church nearby. Every December he was overwhelmed with a feeling of desperation to meet budget. He knew that if the church didn't break even, he would have to cut church expenses and fire people, and he was always wondering when the axe might fall on him. Carrying this weight, his morale went down and his preaching suffered. He struggled to maintain his edge and freshness.

Then he entered a downward spiral in his relationship with the worship leader of the congregation. They didn't see eye to eye. The worship leader had decided that worship needed to be intense and designed for the really strong believers, and he was resistant to making any allowances or adjustments for newer people who were still seeking and merely curious about faith. As a result, the church stopped reaching new people, and church members felt as if they had to choose between the vision of the two leaders. Gary was much more concerned with remaining vibrant through reaching newer people, and the worship leader did not value that effort. In response, Gary asked the board chair whether he could let the worship leader go, as the conflict was undermining trust in Gary's leadership and unity in the direction of the church. The board chair said no, which left Gary feeling as if he had to choose between fighting and maybe even splitting the church or leaving on a good note, if that were still possible. He chose the latter. He left celebrated and thanked, but he was not interested in further congregational leadership opportunities. He took a different kind of job. Gary had lost hope and energy, and the congregation kept shrinking and turning inward.

Gary is certainly not an extreme example but a fairly typical one. This story represents so many who have lost hope and have left congregational leadership feeling like failures. Often lead pastors are judged on three main criteria: (1) Is the congregation growing? (2) Are we meeting budget? and (3) How was last week's sermon? By two of the three, most pastors in America feel as though they are not making it. Some feel that they are struggling with all three. Others feel that the list is a lot longer than three!

People without direction and connection stay that way. Most churches are not reaching new people or bringing in fresh vision, gifts, and contributions to the life of the congregation. Most Americans are trending away from congregational involvement. As the papers and studies have touted, the "nones" are on the rise! Nones are people who tell us on surveys that they have no preference for any particular religion and no allegiance to any religious group or organization. They include atheists, agnostics, and "nothing in particulars" on surveys. They are such a significant and growing group of congregationally disconnected people that I devote a major part of a chapter to reaching out to them. They also appear as supporting actors in many other chapters. Pew Research, the gold standard in this kind of research, tells us after surveying thirty-five thousand Americans in 2007 and then again in 2014 that the nones have grown from 16 percent of the population in 2007 to 23 percent of the population in 2014.[6] Even more alarming for the future of congregations, the percentage of nones from among older millennials (born 1981–1989) has risen from 25 percent to 34 percent in seven years, and for younger millennials (born 1990 to 1996) has risen to 36 percent.[7] Nones are the fastest-growing religious identification in the nation.

Now, let me say, the word *nones* probably does not mean what you think it means. We will explore how people often misunderstand what nones represent. They are not necessarily antireligious, anti-Christian, or even antichurch. Many are very spiritual, and more of them than you might expect are receptive to congregations and faith conversations. Nevertheless, it is a startling statistic signifying a stunning trend in American society. Churches and congregations are losing their influence and social status for an increasing percentage of Americans, particularly where there are the most consequences for congregations of the future—that is, among emerging adults.

Although I will bring a counterbalancing perspective in this book, we still must face the reality that the number of increasingly alienated people from churches and congregations is growing. Can it be turned around? How much should we in congregations even value connecting with people who feel disinterested or alienated from religious institutions in America?

Jesus consistently valued the alienated and the disconnected most. That was his point in three stories he told about a lost sheep, a lost coin, and a prodigal son (Lk 15). The alienated, those "lost" to religious life in Jesus' time, were profoundly valuable to Jesus, such that he sought them, loved them, healed them, and confronted every religious person who pushed them away. Congregations seeking to emulate Jesus and his values similarly have to be profoundly concerned at the loss of so many people and so much influence for good in their lives.

Congregations are feeling less and less successful in the mandate Jesus gave them, to make disciples (followers of Jesus) who make disciples. In other words, at the heart of Christian faith is the generative impulse to develop reproducers, people who come to faith and then pass that faith on to others, who pass it on to additional others. That is the basic pattern for how Christian faith went from being a tiny minority in a backwater country to being the largest religious movement in the world.

Rodney Stark, as a sociologist of religion, documents that growth in his book *The Rise of Christianity*.[8] His study of demographic growth and its cause led him to emphasize the combination of the message, lifestyle, and compassion for the hurting that led to explosive and viral growth. Ultimately the most powerful empire in the world forsook its pagan gods and turned to the Christian God. In some ways, winning the empire ended up changing Christians more than the empire. But there were also many good consequences, including the elevation of women, the incorporation of the Ten Commandments into the moral values of society, the restraining of the worst dimensions of despotism in the emperors, and the amelioration of the worst effects of slavery.

One of the compelling stories Stark reports on in *The Rise of Christianity* is that when plague hit Roman cities, Christians, unlike others, stayed and cared for both their own and others who were stricken. As a result, once plague had swept through the cities, these urban centers belonged to the Christian population, not through conquest but through self-sacrifice and service. Stark explains,

> For the Christian, there is an 80 percent probability that any one of his or her Christian friends and relatives survived the epidemic and remained in the city (as a result of the commitment to care for the sick and the results of this care). For the pagan, these odds are only 50 percent (since many fled and others died alone). The consequence of all this (the Christians who remained and the pagans who fled) is that pagan survivors faced greatly increased odds of conversion because of their increased attachments to Christians.[9]

Congregations today need to recover that focus on making followers of Jesus who reproduce themselves in faith and in the ethical and compassionate behaviors that imitate Jesus. But one of the problems is that too many pastors are consumed with running the organization rather than reproducing faith and action in people. As a result, many churches feel more and more marginalized, powerless, and aging. Rather than churches feeling that their influence is growing, most churches feel as though their influence is stagnant or shrinking.

Hope for the Future

But the picture is not all bleak. There are many signs of light and hope—signs that many more congregations could be seeing a different reality in their common life.

I think of a church in Colorado that is located less than a mile from a lower-income elementary school.[10] This church saw a need in its community, so it started a back-to-school outreach where it now sets up tables out in the parking lot and provides thousands of kids with school supplies, new clothes, and free haircuts. It partnered with Food for Hope, so every Wednesday it takes 140 bags of food to this lower-income elementary school so that the kids will have something to eat over the weekend. Other churches in the area are also involved with Food for Hope, which strengthens the broader witness of the church in this area. The church's primary intent is not to recruit people to church, but people have still committed their lives to God in the process.

Besides the church's outreach to the nearby elementary school, it also has a compassion fund that allows it to help people pay portions of their utility bills, rent, or mortgage. Pastor David says, "They often get single moms who come, and they're looking for help with their rent, and a lot of these ladies are battling addictions, so they're not spending their money wisely. And we'll help them." Because this pastor can relate to people in this situation, he is able to say, "I know what you're going through. I've been there, but there is a better way." Pastor David often has the opportunity to share about Jesus in a kind yet clear way.

The church is actively looking for ways to meet the needs of its community. It has a designated local missionary, constantly looking for outreach opportunities. Outreach is central to the heartbeat of the church. As David shared about the outreach opportunities his church is engaged in, he explained, "What I seem to notice is that when you can meet a need, people know and the community knows that you care about them." This care often is what builds bridges to faith among the unchurched people in their broader community. In one year, the church has seen 150 people come to faith in Christ.

We surveyed many churches that have served their communities but not grown through people making new commitments to Christ—but it does not have to be that way. We can reach people and see congregations grow. Many people and congregations show us a different future: one in which churches are vibrant, the alienated are connected, reproducers multiply, and society is seasoned with salt and seeing brighter light from churches.

Overview of Contributing Research Projects

This book is based on a study of such congregations. First, the Billy Graham Center Institute, in partnership with Lifeway Research, surveyed two thousand unchurched people to find out how they viewed American congregations, what they thought about faith, and what they would respond to as congregations seek to connect with them.[11] The Billy Graham Center Institute is the research arm of the Billy Graham Center at Wheaton College and is pursuing a number of research projects to help equip churches and Christians to engage culture, revitalize the church, and renew society. In our survey of two thousand unchurched people from across the United States, we found out some very surprising things, including that unchurched people are much more receptive and interested in spiritual conversations and invitations to congregations than we might think from reports in the media.

Then the Billy Graham Center Institute, in partnership with Lifeway Research, surveyed three thousand congregations across the country to find out how they are doing in overall conversion growth. We identified the top 10 percent that are growing successfully through conversion and found that the most effective churches consistently combine serving their communities and connecting to unchurched people. Conversion growth and community influence go together. We also interviewed fifty-seven pastors from those top-10-percent churches and forty-one previously unchurched people from those top-10-percent churches to find out what they're doing right.

Sprinkled throughout the book, I will also unpack the results from our Small Church Evangelism study. The Billy Graham Center Institute, in partnership with Lifeway Research, and the Caskey Center for Church Excellence surveyed fifteen hundred small churches (under 250 people) and discovered the top predictive factors for sustained church growth through reaching new people. The top predictive factor we found was hospitality to the unchurched. If there is a silver bullet, this is it. I will look at all the factors we identified.

This book distills the key findings from several different research projects, but it also builds on them by demonstrating how these ideas can be practically applied in church contexts. Even before our research, we were helping churches across the country turn outward. For the last seven years, we have been field-testing best outreach practices through our cohort leader labs. We have worked with over 182 churches to date. (The total number of churches includes 120 churches involved in cohorts that are led by the Church Evangelism Initiative of the Billy Graham Center as well as 62 churches involved in cohorts that are led by the Evangelical Covenant Church in partnership with the Church Evangelism Initiative.) Each cohort consists of six to twelve lead pastors and a key leader from each church who champions reaching out and making an impact. It has been profoundly rewarding to apply best practices and see churches change. Building the bridges between research and application in churches has created a very exciting synergy. Many churches that have adopted some of these practices have seen the results. And they have been all sizes—from ten thousand, to five thousand, to one thousand, to five hundred, to two hundred, to fifty.

We do an evaluation every year of what's happened in cohort churches, and after one year, 100 percent of pastors say they are personally reaching out more.[12] Once pastors start living what they are trying to lead, in this case outreach, they can become much more effective at leading. Most pastors feel very ineffective at leading outreach. We run cohorts for two years because we want to get churches to the tipping point of culture change, but it's encouraging to see such significant change within the first year. Whenever leaders want culture change, they have to start by modeling the change they want to see in their church or their people. So these results after a year are very exciting!

Our cohort churches are also developing reproducers. Again, after just one year in the cohort, 35 percent of churches begin to see new people coming to faith and inviting others into faith.[13] They are becoming reproducers! Why not 100 percent? Because churches adopt the practices we suggest at differing rates and therefore with differing levels of impact over time. One of our early adopters, Matthew Rogers, a pastor of a church in the Chicago area, jumped in right away. He started modeling reaching out, and then he quite quickly appointed an outreach champion to be the partner with him and begin leading the ministries in his church to integrate outreach in meaningful ways. Britta is Matthew's church champion for outreach, and she has seen her friend Kristin come to faith and come to church because of the new emphasis on developing reproducers within every ministry of the church. When asked about how this process has affected her personally, Kristin's voice was filled with emotion as she shared,

> I think that it has given me more purpose outside being a mother. I didn't realize that I was a mother-missionary! That's part of what God calls me to do. Not just raise my children, but there are all these moms just a stone's throw away from me. We can do something with that. I kind of always knew it, but I didn't know it in a purposeful way that's joyful and meaningful in my life.

Matthew, the lead pastor, would say he and his church are experiencing a culture change. Our churches often need a makeover, a culture change, in order to focus outward more.

What follows in this book is what we gave Matthew and now want to give you: a strong biblical foundation and best practices from congregations that are effectively reaching people and having an impact in their communities. These best practices were discovered through research and then applied in 182 churches across the country through pastor cohort leadership labs.

As you go on this journey and read this book, get a group of leaders from your church to read and apply it with you. Encourage one another and stimulate one another's creativity. Hold one another accountable by working through the discussion questions together. We have also provided resources and exercises for you online that you will be able to access after purchasing this book. See appendix one for more information. Begin to grow your morale, vision, and impact through outreach.

I believe—and have seen—that if you turn outward as a church, you can reach people and change your community. And after all, isn't this what we as people and congregations are meant for?

Overarching Structure

Here is a preview of what is to come:

Part one will analyze the serious problem mistaken of myths about the church and the receptivity of unchurched individuals to congregations. We will see that some church people are behaving badly with statistics. We will look at the false narrative many churches have adopted about the attitude of unchurched people to congregations and its negative consequences—making congregations and leaders pessimistic and passive about reaching new people and influencing their communities. There is a better and truer narrative about the degree to which unchurched people in America are receptive to congregations, and that narrative needs to be told. In particular, we found surprising receptivity among unchurched millennials (people born between 1981 and 1996), nones (people who say they have no religious preference on surveys), and the nominally religious. As we embrace and pursue a new narrative about the receptivity in all these groups, it will give us more hope, optimism, and activism when it comes to reaching new people and influencing communities.

Part two will sum up the major findings from our two studies of Protestant churches: one surveying three thousand churches and one surveying fifteen hundred churches for a total of forty-five hundred churches. These surveys have resulted in us identifying two key factors that you can pursue to become a conversion community that reaches and influences new people. Qualitatively, we define a conversion community as a congregation that is seeing changed lives and growing primarily through reaching new people rather than by adding already churched people from some other congregation. I will unpack later the key quantitative criteria I used for defining conversion communities. The term *conversion community* was suggested by my friend Doug Schaupp, who used it as a central concept in his book *Breaking the Huddle*. These two factors structure the whole change process we lay out in this book to revitalize your congregation through your mission. Part two explores the cluster of factors that is captured by this question: How do you get all your leaders participating in the mission of God to reach people and restore communities? Your leaders represent the DNA of your church. If your leaders have a missional DNA, your church and everyone who comes into your church will catch that DNA. This missional-leader development process is one half of what our research showed can revitalize your congregation.

Part three will unpack the other cluster of factors captured by this question: How do you develop a missional culture in your whole congregation? The results of our interviews with nearly sixty top-10-percent conversion-community churches showed us the key factors that characterize missional congregations. These factors have enabled them to grow by reaching new people and influencing their communities. In this part, we get to hear from both pastors and the previously unchurched, who tell us why they came to Christ and to a particular congregation. We found three simple practices that any church could adopt and adapt for becoming more missional and reaching more people. Parts two and three, then, are the heart of the vision we want to communicate that came out of our research and has been field tested. These two parts structure the book but also seek to pass on a vision for the kind of congregation your church could become and the kind of impact you could have.

I have had a front-row seat in seeing what I am presenting work. After ministering among college students for twenty-five years with InterVarsity Christian Fellowship, including time spent as national field director of evangelism, I became a pastor of evangelism and discipleship in an Anglican church and practiced what I will recommend in this book. After my time as a pastor at that church, I then helped with the first Willow Creek Church multisite campus, planted by Jim Tomberlin in DuPage County. I was the evangelism champion for that plant. We saw a number of people give their lives to Christ, and I was part of a larger church culture that made a difference in my community.

Since then I have been involved in Community Christian Church in Naperville, Illinois, with Dave and Jon Ferguson, and now I attend a small urban Anglican church plant called Cornerstone in Chicago's West Loop. I have also worked to establish a relational connection to my parish Catholic church, Old St. Mary's in the South Loop of Chicago, because of the wonderful impact they are making in my neighborhood. So I am not just a researcher; I am also a practitioner, and I love to bridge strong missional theology with good cultural analysis and church best practices to help churches and pastors thrive in their mission. I also must admit, I have learned just as much from my mistakes as I have from making wonderful progress. Our findings are based on Protestant churches because that is where my primary expertise lies, but they also have significant relevance for congregations in other wings of the church, like Catholic or Orthodox.

Not only am I a practitioner but I have also led the process of testing every one of these insights and best practices in local churches in many cities through our leadership cohorts. Pastors have seen their church DNA change, new people reached and retained, their congregation revitalized, and their communities influenced for good.

Keys To Recovering Missional Imagination

Jesus once said, "The harvest is plentiful, but the workers are few. Ask the Lord of the harvest, therefore, to send out workers" (Lk 10:2). Jesus had a vibrant and contagious missional imagination. As I talk to church leaders around the country, I often feel like I hear the opposite message: "The harvest is sparse, the workers are many, and the competition for the few interested unchurched people is intense. People in our culture just don't care about the gospel any more, and they don't like the church." Our team's research findings don't agree. I think Jesus' assessment and prayer are still relevant for America today. Imagine if churches and leaders around the country started to radiate hope that the message we have and the service we offer is needed, welcomed, and wanted by many, and can still affect the direction of the unchurched and the quality of life in our communities. Such a rooted and realistic hope could change a nation. That is the power of missional imagination.

I want to offer a few keys that are foundational to recovering a missional imagination for the harvest in North America. These are the underlying assumptions for this book. If you don't agree with them, you will at least know where I am starting from and why. The three key foundations for recovering missional imagination are:

- becoming reenchanted by the power and beauty of the mission of Jesus

- recovering the reality of the receptivity of the unchurched people in our culture and the ripeness of the harvest
- recapturing a vision for the church and its potential for being brighter light and stronger salt in our world

Here in the introduction I will say a few words about being re-enchanted by the mission of Jesus. Then the bulk of the book will focus on research that uncovers the reality of the receptivity of the unchurched in America and how we can recapture the church's potential for becoming brighter light and stronger salt in our world.

It can be very difficult for us to be reenchanted by the mission of Jesus since for many of us familiarity has bred a loss of wonder and awe. But I would suggest that is because we have lost sight of just how revolutionary, captivating, and unconventional Jesus' mission was. Jesus reached the lost, alienated, socially ostracized, and religiously discarded people of his day, and he did so with compassion and courage. I love the story recorded in Luke 19:1-10 as a paradigmatic example of why Jesus went to the towns and villages of ancient Palestine. Jesus says about a despised and discarded Jewish sellout to the Romans: he is why I came, to seek and to save the lost. His main detractors were among the righteous, respectable religious establishment. Jesus' typical convert would have echoed today's common refrain, "I am spiritual but not religious. As a matter of fact, religious people don't even like me or want me around." But Jesus did more than just reach the dregs of religious society. He also restored these broken and discarded people. After all, his most compelling (and enchanting) description of his mission is recorded in Luke 4:18-19:

> The Spirit of the Lord is on me,
>> because he has anointed me
>> to proclaim good news to the poor.

[handwritten margin note: unfortunately true sometimes]

He has sent me to proclaim freedom for the prisoners
   and recovery of sight for the blind,
to set the oppressed free,
   to proclaim the year of the Lord's favor.

How can you get more compelling and beautiful than such restorative work among the broken hearts and the bits and dregs of the world?

Jesus not only reached people and restored them; he also reproduced himself so that millions and ultimately billions could benefit from his heart and compassion. He did so by calling together twelve apprentices, modeling the life he wanted them to live and give away, and then sending them out with power and hope for the whole world. He reproduced his heart in the hearts of others. As a result, his movement was not for a moment but for millennia, and his mission was not to a few but to multitudes through all time. That is compelling and powerful and beautiful. When the church recaptures just a bit of this beauty and power, then people in it and in the world take notice.

Jesus also had a funny way of building his kingdom: he gave it away. "As the Father has sent me, I am sending you" (Jn 20:21). That was his way, to reproduce and then release laborers to the ends of the earth. He didn't build his own kingdom in his own time, maxing out his power and influence. He gave away his life to others, then released them to go everywhere to everyone to light a million little torches that could be carried to every nation.

What did Jesus do? He reached. He restored. He reproduced. He released. A strategy to change the world. And whenever we recover it, we once again join that world-changing movement and contribute to it. We start becoming brighter light and stronger salt.

I want to notice just a few things that stand out and speak to some of our current debates over the mission of Jesus.

Jesus did not come just to dialogue, accept, and understand. He came to influence. He came to announce good news. He came to change lives and create congregations or gatherings of his followers on mission.

In this book, I am unashamedly concerned to see the renewal of congregational life in America. Though I have the greatest respect for the research and writing of Elizabeth Drescher in *Choosing our Religion: The Spiritual Lives of American Nones*, and I deeply believe in respecting the religious and spiritual journeys of people who are very different from me, I only partly agree with her conclusion toward the end of the book, where she says,

> The energies of the majority of Americans who continue to affiliate with institutional religions, then, is best spent not in attempts to "recapture" Nones and draw them back into churches, synagogues, and mosques. It seems a far better spiritual investment to listen more deeply to their stories so that we can develop a richer, more complex story of the American spirit.[14]

I agree we must listen deeply, affirm and learn all we can, and so enrich the American conversation and culture. But in the end, I also believe in being deeply faithful to one's own tradition, Scripture, conscience, and God, and to communicating respectfully, thoughtfully, and with profound conviction one's sense of the truth and the vision of the good for all people. Only faith communities that have maintained such commitment, conviction, and clarity of communication have continually experienced renewal and vitality. The biblical word that captures this kind of passion and commitment is *evangelism*, which means communicating the good news of God's intervention through Christ in history to put right everything that has gone so wrong—not through conquest but through sacrifice, humility, love, and a death on a cross. Churches and denominations that lose the priority of this kind of vibrant communication and spiritual influence will dwindle and only ultimately feed the none-ing of America of which Drescher writes. So I am in this book and in my work and life a prioritist for evangelism, despite the fact that the word *evangelism* conjures up very negative images and associations for too many in America. As you will see, I want to reimagine and revitalize a chastened but courageous and clear evangelism, not discard or distance myself from such intentionality to influence.

I am also concerned to reimagine and revitalize the experience of conversion to faith in the context of congregations. Conversion can happen in a moment or over a long period of time.[15] But congregations that are not conversionist, and that do not offer the hope of vibrant change in life direction and in quality of life, will again have little to offer that cannot be found in the broader culture in any association one might join. It is the transformative power of the Christian message and of Christian congregations that will lead to the revitalization of religious, or at least Christian, life in America. No amount of strategy, structure, or civility can replace such vibrant generativity of life, hope, and faith in Christ that is lived out in communities. The greatest problem churches face is not the none-ing of America but rather the none-ing and secularizing of the church. When congregations recover the mission, passion, and conviction of their founder, culture shift and religious disaffection will not undermine or marginalize vibrant congregations. They will continue to grow and be bright light and savory salt in their communities. Our research across the country confirms that conviction.

Jesus may have said it best in Matthew 4:19 when inviting his first followers to join him: "Come, follow me, . . . and I will send you out to fish for people."

May we be reenchanted and then reignited by the mission of Jesus. With that foundation, we can look at our culture and its people and begin to have a missional imagination for them. Ready for the ride? Let's next look at the unchurched, why they are disconnected from congregations, and what we might be able to do about it. We will immediately begin to discover some real news about the unchurched but also some "Chicken Little" statistics that are getting in the way of our mission and ministry as congregations.

Questions for Discussion

1. Churches in America are plateaued or declining at a significant rate. Where do you see your church: plateaued, declining, or growing? What factors are affecting your congregation's trajectory?

2. Rick mentions several consequences of so many plateaued or declining churches, including a sense of discouragement or failure on the part of pastors and leaders, the disconnection of many people from the church, and the congregation feeling ineffective in the mission of being brighter light and stronger salt in its community. Among those consequences, where would you most like to see change in your congregation and why?

3. Rick mentions several keys to recovering a missional imagination, including becoming reenchanted by the power and beauty of the mission of Jesus, recovering a vision for the receptivity of the unchurched people in our culture, and recapturing a vision for the church and its potential for being brighter light and stronger salt in our world. Where do you feel your congregation is strong on missional imagination, and where do you need to revitalize?

Part 1

Recovering a Missional
Imagination for the
Unchurched in America

Exposing Common Myths
About Unchurched Americans

There are few things we like more than a startling statistic. Something eye-popping that will alarm us, make us laugh, or prove a point. Nothing helps create an enduring narrative in our culture faster than a statistic that can captivate our imagination. Sadly, this often leads us to latch onto false statistics and quickly pass them on to others. These false statistics and the accompanying narratives, or myths, are nearly impossible to root out, and even today many still believe they're true. Consider these myths you might have heard or even passed on:

- *Myth 1: Women over forty with a university degree are more likely to be killed by terrorists than get married.* The cause? A *Newsweek* cover in June 1986 declared an impending "marriage crunch," highlighted by the fact that women over forty had only a 2.6 percent chance of getting married.[1] The story was so bad and discredited so thoroughly by scholars that *Newsweek* went so far as to retract it twenty years later.[2] That didn't mean the myth wasn't popular as it was so enduring in American life that it was featured in the popular movie *Sleepless in Seattle* in which two characters argue over whether it is true.

- *Myth 2: Your soul weighs twenty-one grams on average.* This outlandish figure was first postulated by Dr. Duncan MacDougall of Haverhill, Massachusetts, in 1907. To support his thesis, MacDougall simply weighed terminally ill patients just before and then immediately after they died.[3] It was widely considered to be proof of the existence of the soul.

- *Myth 3: We use only 10 percent of our brains, and if we could just use our whole brains we could tap into untold powers (e.g., extrasensory perception, telekinesis, and advanced intelligence).* This myth is so old and widespread that researchers are not even sure where it originated.[4] Despite the best efforts of scientists to kill this myth, it has given rise to a whole cottage industry of science fiction books and television programs.

- *Myth 4: One in five kids has been approached by a sexual predator via the internet.* This statistic was reported in a 2000 study issued by the National Center for Missing and Exploited Children.[5] It pointed to an alarming crisis, especially in light of the amount of internet usage by American kids.

- *Myth 5: In America alone, about 150,000 teens die of anorexia nervosa each year.* This alarming statistic was reported in many feminist-authored books exploring the challenges of teen girls, notably in Naomi Wolf's bestseller *The Beauty Myth*.[6]

So what do all these myths have in common? To begin with, they are usually started by or at least cited by a credible news source. Because of this credibility boost, people implicitly accept the statistic and begin to share it widely. Over time, as this myth is repeated as reality across countless blogs, books and articles, it becomes common knowledge. At this point, it is nearly impossible for experts to set the record straight.

The truth?

Educated women over forty have a significantly higher chance of getting married than being killed by a terrorist, the chances of which are a tiny

0.002 percent.[7] While the soul's weight is indeterminate, MacDougall's methodology in arriving at his twenty-one grams was laughably deficient.[8] Scientists agree that we use 100 percent of the brain, supported by new technologies in brain mapping that show no inactive parts.[9] Although one in five kids annually receive unwanted online sexual solicitation, usually by a friend being suggestive, the report in question goes on to say that only one in four of those solicited received a solicitation that left them very upset or afraid.[10] While distressing incidents should not be minimized, headlines using the statistic glossed over important degrees of severity among these incidents to overemphasize worst-case scenarios. The American Anorexia and Bulimia Association confirms that it is actually 150,000 who *suffer* from anorexia rather than die from it annually.[11]

Before any fingers get pointed, though, Christians love using bad statistics too! In his article "Evangelicals Behaving Badly with Statistics," Notre Dame sociologist Christian Smith argues,

> American evangelicals, who profess to be committed to Truth, are among the worst abusers of simple descriptive statistics, which claim to represent the truth about reality, of any group I have ever seen. At stake in this misuse are evangelicals' own integrity, credibility with outsiders, and effectiveness in the world. It is an issue worth making a fuss over.[12]

Summarizing and building on Smith's conclusion, Ed Stetzer helpfully reflects, "Evangelical leaders and organizations routinely use descriptive statistics in sloppy, unwarranted, misrepresenting, and sometimes absolutely preposterous ways."[13]

But why? Why do evangelicals fall prey to false statistics when the truth of the gospel is already compelling? Just like society around us, many evangelicals simply like to create alarm to sell books and influence people. The more dire the crisis, the more likely people will pay attention, read an article, buy a book, or attend a conference. The more drama we can generate by scaring people, the more people will be willing to do something about it.

But there are hidden costs to our misuse of statistics. To illustrate the severity of these costs and the danger they present to the church, we need look no further than the story of Chicken Little.

Chicken Little Syndrome

In the story of Chicken Little, an acorn falls on the head of a young chicken, causing him to panic, feeling that the sky itself is falling.[14] Armed with this mistaken myth, Chicken Little sets off to systematically convince his friends that the world is ending. Each friend agrees to join the mission until eventually they meet Foxy Loxy. The fox promises Chicken Little and his friends that they can be safe in his den. Foolishly, the group enters the fox's den, never to be seen again. The fable ends with the point that all went wrong because of the foolish fright of Chicken Little.

Today few people have never heard of the story of Chicken Little or its moral about unjustified fear. In fact, *Merriam-Webster* defines Chicken Little as "one who warns of or predicts calamity, especially without justification" and tracks its first recorded usage to 1895.[15] It has become so ingrained in our lives that the phrase "the sky is falling" has become a common way to describe people who imagine or exaggerate an impending catastrophe. Scholars describe the results of fear mongering as Chicken Little Syndrome, in which near-apocalyptic warnings drive people to either crippling fear or disastrous action.[16] One scholar provides a helpful definition as "a sense of despair or passivity which blocks the audience from actions."[17] The term began appearing in the 1950s.[18]

In other words, disproportionate alarm can cause panic, misguided actions, passivity, withdrawal, a sense of powerlessness, and even disaster through the power of self-fulfilling prophecy. When we misread reality, we can apply inappropriate solutions to problems we have inflated, or we can withdraw from the field of action entirely. Great leadership starts with a good description of the reality we are trying to address and change, and alarmist and misleading statistics are therefore not good leadership.

When it comes to researching and reporting on the present state of faith in America and the attitude of most Americans toward the church, too many have fallen victim to Chicken Little Syndrome. We are too quick to listen to the voices proclaiming, "The sky is falling!" by overstating the decline and even near-term disappearance of the church in America. Just like Chicken Little's friends, we hear the alarm and apocalyptic language, buoyed by suspect statistics, and in our fear we buy their books and attend their conferences. In doing so, we inadvertently reinforce alarm instead of action, passivity instead of proclamation, and defeatism instead of hope.

In light of these dire warnings, many Christians have stopped sharing our faith, inviting people to church, and expecting God to convert many and renew the church in our time. A recent Barna study reports that three-fourths of self-identified Christians who have had a conversation about their faith have fewer than ten spiritual conversations a year.[19] That's less than one spiritual conversation per month. On top of that— or perhaps at the heart of it—48 percent of Christians say that most non-Christians have no interest in hearing about Jesus.[20] No wonder there aren't more Christians sharing their faith. It's difficult to offer good news to people if we're already convinced that they won't think it's good and that we will offend people and push them even further away if we are bold and direct about our faith.

The sad truth is that the American church has fostered Chicken Little Syndrome for several decades, and we are now confronting the negative consequences. Some have withdrawn into separate enclaves, suspicious of outsiders.[21] Our narrative has led to many people in churches becoming pessimistic about their witness and their future, which has given direction and legitimacy to their passivity. If this is going to change, we need to root out the mistaken myths that

Christians tell ourselves about the state of the church, replacing them with truth that gets us on mission for the gospel in our communities.

American Church Myths Exposed

So what are the false statistics that have created mistaken myths in the church? I use the phrase "mistaken myths" because myths are not always false. They can sometimes reflect and point to foundational realities like the best mythic tales often do, or alternatively they can create distorted pictures of reality and generate false narratives. What half-truths and alarming statistics do we regularly cite that reinforce a misleading cultural narrative about faith and the church in America?

Warning: difficult content ahead. Many of the statistics I list you may have had shared with you or—gasp!—you may have passed on. This is not an attempt to point the finger but rather to right the ship. All of us have contributed to the problem at one time or another. In the spirit of charity and knowing that our united goal is the advancement of Christ's kingdom, we need to rightly engage the serious issues we face in the church, and this begins with an accurate picture of reality.

In the rest of this chapter, I will explore four central mistaken myths about the American church and the misleading statistics that continue to breathe life into them.

- *Myth 1: America is becoming non- or anti–Christian, "a nation of nones,"* those who have no allegiance to any particular religion or religious body.

- *Myth 2: Millennials are leaving the church at an alarmingly high rate and rarely, if ever, returning.* Church has become irrelevant to the emerging generation.

- *Myth 3: The church is dwindling in America and will disappear in a generation.* The church has been on a decades-long free fall to the point of impending near-extinction.

- *Myth 4: Trust in the church is at an all–time low as fewer Americans have a history of church involvement, and those who do often define their experience as negative.* The result is a public inoculated against the church, Jesus, and faith.

Together these four myths create a narrative of church failure and decline. Yet when we peel back the layers we discover that they are misleading or flat-out wrong. As we survey each myth, we will consider not only how it dominates common views of the church but how putting the truth into perspective can empower Christians to once again serve in their churches and engage society with boldness.

Myth 1: America Is Becoming "a Nation of Nones"

As with any myth that people accept, there are echoes of truth that help to support the message. Recent data out of Pew Research, reflected in figure 2.1, highlights what this myth gets right.

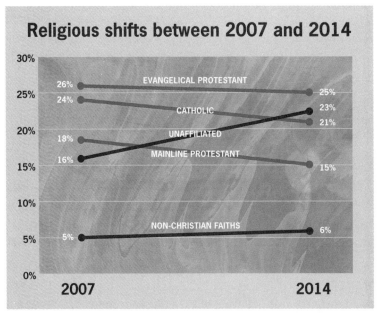

Religious shifts between 2007 and 2014

- EVANGELICAL PROTESTANT: 26% → 25%
- CATHOLIC: 24% → 23%
- UNAFFILIATED: 16% → 23%
- MAINLINE PROTESTANT: 18% → 15%
- NON-CHRISTIAN FAITHS: 5% → 6%

Source: "5 Key Findings About the Changing U.S. Religious Landscape," FactTank, Pew Research Center, May 12, 2015, www.pewresearch.org/fact-tank/2015/05/12/5-key-findings-u-s-religious-landscape/

Figure 2.1. Religious shifts between 2007 and 2014

There are several central takeaways we can glean from this data. First, between 2007 and 2014 the number of Americans who identify as Christian has dropped seven percentage points (78 to 71).[22] However, this data does not discriminate between nominal and committed Christians, and, as we will see later, this decline is overwhelmingly due to the former letting go of identification with Christian faith. Second, Catholics and mainline Protestants were hit particularly hard, with 3.1 percent and 3.4 percent declines, respectively. If this decline continues, one scholar estimates that mainline Protestantism has roughly twenty-three Easters left before complete collapse.[23] Finally, while fewer people identify as Christian, those identifying as religiously unaffiliated or "nones" has grown from 16 percent to 23 percent. This is a massive growth for only seven years, with millennials (ages eighteen to thirty-three in 2014) accounting for a significant portion of this shift (25 to 35 percent).[24] Looking only at the unchurched, those who identified as nones has risen to just over one-third (34 percent), again with millennials accounting for a significant share of this growth (43 percent of unchurched millennials identify as nones).[25] More critically, the percent of unchurched millennials who identify as nones *equals* the percent of unchurched millennials that identify as Christians. We have reached a tipping point.

Yet not all the news is bad. Digging deeper into the data uncovers several truths by which we can begin to sketch out a counternarrative that could empower more hope and more engagement. The most compelling of these is that Protestant evangelicals remain the largest religious group in America, surpassing nones and every other religious identification. Moreover, Protestant evangelicals have shown greater stability, with an increase in numbers, though a slight decrease in percentage of total population (-0.9 percent). In other words, the most evangelistically oriented wing of the Protestant church has remained stable, while significant losses have occurred in the least evangelistically oriented denominations.

One way to assess how non-Christian America has become is to look at the percentages of the ranks of the unchurched. For our research, we defined an unchurched person as anyone who has *not* attended church (or synagogue, temple, or mosque, for that matter) in the last six months, except for a wedding, funeral, or special event (e.g., holiday service). It is a fluid group, with some having just stopped attending six months previously and others having been away for years.

As of March 2016, there were *143 million* unchurched people (110 million, if we are just looking at adults) in the United States.[26] To put that number in perspective, if the unchurched formed their own country, it would be the tenth-largest nation on earth. That's ahead of Mexico or Japan! When we put this number in context up against those who still attend church (whether regularly or intermittently) and those who have since left the church, we can see the significance of this block of Americans.

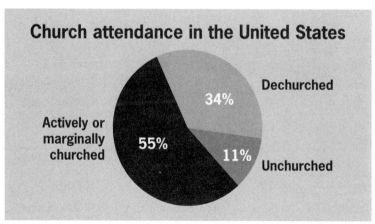

Source: "Unchurched Report," Billy Graham Center Institute and Lifeway Research, April 24, 2019, www.billygrahamcenter.com/youfoundme/research

Figure 2.2. Church attendance profile for people in the United States

Notice in figure 2.2 that, as of January 2016, 55 percent of Americans are somewhat or very churched. This is the *other* side of the coin.

Even as the unchurched population has grown, the majority of Americans are *still* churchgoers. By "actively churched," this study refers to those who attend more than once a month (about 45 percent), while the "marginally churched" are those who attended once a month or less. Thirty-four percent of Americans are dechurched, which means that they attended church regularly at some point in the past, either as a child, teen, or adult, but do so no longer. From the perspective of congregations, we had them once and we lost them. Finally, from our research, 11 percent are purely unchurched, having never regularly attended church at any time in their lives. In 2014, the Barna Group reported 10 percent as purely unchurched, so in the following two years this percentage has grown by about 1 percent.[27]

[handwritten margin note: I wonder, are unchurched or dechurched more to likely become/be interested in becoming church goers?]

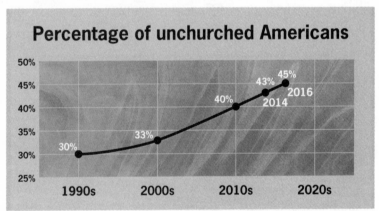

Percentage of unchurched Americans

- 30% — 1990s
- 33% — 2000s
- 40% — 2014
- 43%
- 45% — 2016
- 2010s
- 2020s

Source: George Barna and David Kinnaman, *Churchless: Understanding Today's Unchurched and How to Connect with Them* (Carol Stream, IL: Tyndale House, 2014), viii; "Unchurched Report," Billy Graham Center Institute and Lifeway Research, April 24, 2019, www.billygrahamcenter .com/youfoundme/research

Figure 2.3. Percentage of unchurched Americans

According to figure 2.3, not only are the unchurched a sizable demographic, but there is ample evidence that they have grown in the past generation. Beginning in the 1990s, only 30 percent of America was unchurched. While this grew slowly to one-third (33 percent) of Americans by the 2000s, it jumped to 43 percent by 2014 and again to 45 percent in 2016. This trend suggests that the unchurched percentage is currently growing by about 1 percent per year. In other words, the train is picking up momentum, not losing it. There is cause for concern. But panic? Alarm? Cause for trumpeting the marginalization and non-Christianization of America? No!

Let me offer three reasons why we shouldn't panic. First, any panic loses sight of the fact that 70.6 percent of Americans still identify as Christians.[28] Even as the trend line is going down by about 1 percent a year over the past seven years, it will still take more than twenty years before the majority of Americans no longer identify as Christian. More to the point, the percent of actively churched people has been consistent over the last decade.[29] The loss is among people who used to identify as Christian but were not active.

The second reason the church should not be overly alarmed by the rise in unchurched Americans is that even among those unchurched, the majority still *identify as Christian.* The black bars in figure 2.4 track the religious identification of *unchurched* people in America. According to our 2016 "Unchurched Report," 56 percent of unchurched individuals identify as Christians and 32 percent identify as nones.

[Handwritten margin notes: "indeed statistics are numerical values... we can't forget the extremely important value in even just one person who doesn't know Christ. Do I believe in that value? Do I live like it?"]

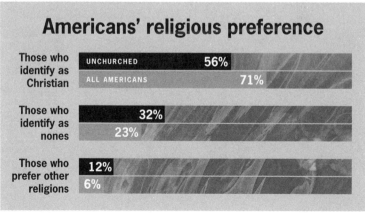

Americans' religious preference

Those who identify as Christian	UNCHURCHED 56%
	ALL AMERICANS 71%
Those who identify as nones	32%
	23%
Those who prefer other religions	12%
	6%

Source: "Unchurched Report," Billy Graham Center Institute and Lifeway Research, April 24, 2019, www.billygrahamcenter.com/youfoundme/research

Figure 2.4. Americans' religious preference[30]

What about the growing trend of the increase of the nones? Nones include atheists and agnostics (together only 7 percent of the American population; 3 percent growth between 2007 and 2014) and "nothings in particular" (16 percent of all Americans—4 percent growth between 2007 and 2014).[31] But catch this. Nones are not necessarily irreligious, by which I mean disconnected from any established or organized form of religion, or unspiritual. Spirituality is often defined in fluid and loose terms as referring to a feeling of connectedness to something larger than oneself, and that connectedness can happen through experiences with friends, pets, food, mind-expanding drugs, nature, God, or in many other ways that combine mind, body, and spirit.[32] Still, over two-thirds believe in God, 81 percent believe in a force or higher being that can be reached through prayer, most think churches benefit society by strengthening community bonds and aiding the poor, more than a third describe themselves as spiritual, and 20 percent pray daily.[33] Even nones are more spiritual, religious, and receptive than we might expect.

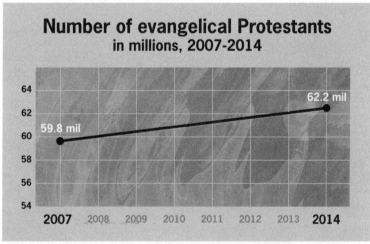

Source: "Number of Protestants Growing," Religion & Public Life, Pew Research Center, May 11, 2015, www.pewforum.org/2015/05/12/americas-changing-religious-landscape/pf_15-05-05_rls2_evangelical200px-2/

Figure 2.5. Number of evangelical Protestants, in millions, 2007–2014

Third, as we can see in figure 2.5, the religiously committed are as religious or more religious than ever. While many are leaving faith, research indicates that those who are religiously committed, Christian or otherwise, are relatively stable or even growing. The decline in Christian identity, then, is the vast middle of the American population, those scholars typically identified as cultural or nominal Christians.

Tracing data from the General Social Survey over the past forty years, Ed Stetzer has argued, "The percentage of convictional Christians has remained relatively steady, with some decline."[34] We are losing the nominal and cultural Christians, those who identify but do not practice or are not devout. As a result, we see that evangelicalism in America is actually *growing*. As figure 2.5 demonstrates, even as religious nones have increased since 2007, evangelicals added 2.4 million to their numbers (not quite keeping up with population growth). Nondenominational churches continue to thrive and are the major success story in terms of rapid growth over the past few decades in America.[35]

[handwritten margin note: Loss is still loss though... they're lost in both states I'd say (identify and not).]

The loss of the culturally and nominally religious Christians is not nearly as alarming and may even have positive implications for Christianity. One of the challenges faced by the advocates of Christian faith is making congregations countercultural enough to be truly vibrant, especially in any culture where those who identify as Christians are in the majority. People choosing to be either genuinely committed to Christian faith or else not identify at all clarifies what Christian faith looks like and forces people to make the choice. The loss in numbers but increase in vitality could be a huge plus for the future of Christian congregations in America.

[handwritten margin note: In some ways, yes; it's not all about numbers. However, we're talking people's souls/salvation here, not a quality vs. quantity business.]

Myth 2: Millennials Are Forsaking the Church, Never to Return

Over the last decade, we have seen a flurry of statistics that supposedly reveal a mass exodus of millennials from the church. Yet when we examine these statistics and the broader narrative closely, it becomes fairly clear that these claims of alarm are exaggerations. One of these statistics, initially shared on a blog before being broadly circulated, reveals how this narrative can catch on quickly:

> There is a well-known statistic that tells us that 80% of youth stop attending church after they graduate high school. As a parent, that's the most horrifying statistic in the world to me! Let me bring that closer to home, that means, in a church youth group with 20 kids, over 15 will no longer go to church after they graduate. In a home, 3 out of 4 of our kids statistically will forsake fellowship by the time they're 18. The cry of all of our hearts should be "why"?![36]

This certainly paints a dire picture, but pushing past the sensationalism, discerning Christians always need to ask where a statistic comes from. The answer in this case: a gathering of some high school youth group leaders who guessed and averaged their guesses.[37] This is hardly a scientific and reliable method. For all of this alarm, what was the central takeaway? Buy a given book on evangelizing youth.

Another study purportedly found that 88 percent of the children in evangelical homes leave church at the age of eighteen, never to return.[38] As it turns out, the only source for this statistic is an annual denominational report recommending radical steps to save families and youth in America. But no actual study was cited, no documentation given. Nevertheless, the stat circulated widely. Various other "studies" and researchers have claimed similar statistics, the worst proposing that 96 percent of American teenagers would leave the faith.[39] Common to each example is its embrace of the Chicken Little Syndrome: fear-inducing arguments designed to sell books, but that also drive problematic or passive behavior.

The problem is that this attitude is addictive, generating a sense of urgency by injecting panic into the discussion rather than thoughtfully considering how the church should respond. In his article "Curing Christians' Stats Abuse," Ed Stetzer helpfully explains how this attitude is counterproductive to Christian mission and outreach. Nothing generates buzz around a book or a conference like statistics that strike fear into the hearts of readers or attendees. Armed with exaggerated or false stats,

> an advertisement for a summit ... declared, "Christianity in America won't survive another decade unless we do something now." The summit organizers claimed that only 4 percent of today's teenagers would be evangelical believers by the time they became adults. "We are on the verge of a catastrophe!" the advertisement screamed.[40]

As Stetzer details, the advertisement then markets the book or summit as the silver bullet that can turn the tide.

It turns out that the source of this distorted statistic was an informal survey of 211 young people conducted in the mid-1990s and spanning only three states.[41] This is clearly not a representative sample. As Stetzer summarizes, we cannot draw such "an unwarranted inference ... from a small, non-representative sample to reach conclusions about the future faith conditions of entire generations!"[42] Especially when the unrepresentative sample is contradicted by a number of much more representative samples, including the sample in our current research project.

The sad truth is that these statistics that provoke Chicken Little Syndrome sell books and conferences. It is largely why they get used, circulated, and become part of the negative narrative. Over time, as they are repeated in publications and from leaders at summits, these questionable statistics become the dominant narrative. In only a few short steps, they move from blog to believable to broadly viral.

What are the actual figures for high school dropouts? A report by Lifeway Research explains that "66 percent of young adults ages 23-30 stopped attending church regularly for at least a year between ages 18-22." The report goes on to say that "among church dropouts who are now ages 23-30, 31 percent, or about a third, currently attend church twice a month or more."[43] So the loss rate is more like 46 percent for Protestant churches. That is alarming enough without putting it on steroids and claiming 96 percent.

More to the point, there is actual evidence to be hopeful for Christians reaching young adults. With the problematic parts of this myth exposed, in the next chapter we can focus on what the true statistics tell us about the receptivity of young adults and how churches are successfully reaching them today.

Myth 3: The Church Is Dwindling in America and Will Disappear in a Generation

This myth has proven especially popular among pastors and missiologists. In fact, in my first book, *Evangelism Outside the Box*, I touch on this idea in trying to exhort Christians to see the unchurched as a harvest ripe for evangelism. At that point, as now, I was hopeful that by changing our approach to evangelism and outreach we might better engage a shifting culture.

Yet where I suggested we had an opportunity, others have been quick to emphasize alarm or pessimism. Two quotes from influential missional books perfectly capture this message: the church as we know it is nearing extinction.

> The church in America is in big trouble. We're on the endangered species list.[44]

> It is our belief that one of the core tasks of missional leadership is to assist the church to find new forms and expressions of church or bear the responsibility of the church's effective extinction in our day.[45]

The second quote comes from an Australian church context but has been widely embraced in the American context as well.

I should also say that current missiologists such as Alan Hirsch, Michael Frost, and Lance Ford are good friends, highly respected colleagues, and profound thinkers about the church. But I want to balance their tendency (and mine) to overstate the crisis and the impending extinction for the church, which at this point in time they might want to balance as well. For instance, Alan Hirsch had a tendency to be critical of nondenominational megachurches from his Australian home but now works with many such congregations. Nevertheless, as a prophetic voice, he often also has to fight disillusionment, as do we all.

So is the American church on its last legs, nearing effective extinction? Not even remotely. Fifty-five percent of Americans attend a church, synagogue or mosque,[46] and 51 percent do so at least once a month.[47] Millennials leave church at high levels during their eighteen- to twenty-four-year-old period,[48] but they return to church at a rate that is consistent with earlier generations between twenty-five and thirty-four.[49]

[handwritten margin notes: umm... Why are synagogues and mosques included in "churched"?]

The church in America in particular and religious institutions in America in general have not disappeared in three hundred years and are not likely to any time soon. And whether the church declines steeply is more dependent on the quality of the church's life and witness than on the shifts in American culture. I will unpack that point more in chapter three.

Myth 4: Trust in the Church Is at an All-Time Low, and Past Experiences Are Largely Negative

One striking characteristic of the unchurched is that many have some significant background with the church, and two-thirds are not interested in returning.

[handwritten margin note: What experience? He defined unchurched as having never regularly attended (38), so]

According to our 2016 "Unchurched Report," only 25 percent of the unchurched were never churched. That 25 percent of all unchurched

[handwritten margin note: What does he mean here?]

translates to 11 percent of all Americans who have never attended church regularly. For 75 percent of the unchurched, we had them once, and we lost them.

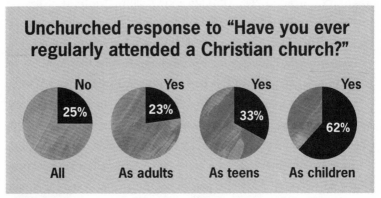

Source: "Unchurched Report," Billy Graham Center Institute and Lifeway Research, April 24, 2019, www.billygrahamcenter.com /youfoundme/research

Figure 2.6. Unchurched response to "Have you ever regularly attended a Christian church?"

Why did they leave? People cite many reasons, but three stand out above the rest.

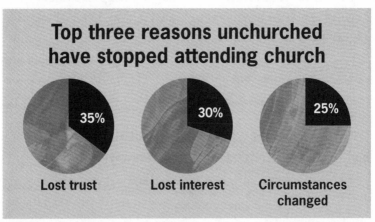

Source: "Unchurched Report," Billy Graham Center Institute and Lifeway Research, April 24, 2019, www.billygrahamcenter.com /youfoundme/research. This percentage was determined from a factor analysis conducted by the Billy Graham Center Institute, which revealed these groupings of reasons.

Figure 2.7. Top three reasons unchurched have stopped attending church

Though the top reason was a loss of trust, notice that only 35 percent of the unchurched cite that reason. About a third of the people who used to attend church and now do not lost trust in God, the church, or Christians. That reality is not to be taken lightly, but it is also not to be amplified and made to sound as if it applies to most Americans. It does not. Sometimes the church gets a bad rap, and sometimes the church deserves it, but the stats are not as adverse and serious as we have often been led to believe by alarmist news articles and spurious stats.

good to admit sometimes

What's more, only 5 percent of unchurched individuals lost trust *in God* because of a negative experience in their lives for which they felt God was somehow responsible.[50] In other words, despite having broken trust with the church, these individuals may still be very open to God and to faith. They just are not as open to Christians and congregations. Most of the 35 percent lost trust in a Christian or a church because of a bad experience. All these people are not necessarily gone for good. Many of the previously unchurched people we talked to had left the church due to broken trust but then returned after trust had been rebuilt. I think of Tina, who went to church as a kid but stopped because she felt judged for becoming pregnant in high school.[51] She visited a different church but felt like the church was always asking for money. At that point in life, she still believed in God, but she had trust issues with church and church people, and she felt she could still have God without needing to attend church.

hope!

Then she met a church member passing out fliers for an event that she thought would be good for her daughter. So she went with her daughter, who liked the experience. Tina went back. She kept going back. The hospitality of the congregants and the level of acceptance of Tina as a single mom rebuilt broken trust and brought a "done" who had left because of trust issues back to church, back to God, and back to optimism about her life and her capacity to contribute. Hospitality and acceptance kept her coming back.

I hope I can be this to someone

Rebuilding broken trust is always the necessary first step for people with broken trust. But broken trust is healable. *Don't forget this!*

What's more, broken trust is not the norm for most of the unchurched. Most who exited left not because they lost trust but because they felt church was irrelevant or their life circumstances changed. One of the major reasons emerging adults, people between the ages of nineteen and twenty-nine, leave church is that they leave their family of origin and don't reengage in church elsewhere. Their life circumstances change. Or, as Rodney Stark puts it, "Having left home, many single young adults choose to sleep in on Sunday mornings."[52] That could become fixable as emerging adults grow older.

Others leave just because they did not find anything compelling enough to stay (30 percent of those who left told us this was their primary reason for leaving). Howard Hendricks used to say, "It is a sin to bore a kid in church."[53] I think it is not just kids who are hurt by being subjected to services that stimulate sleepiness and boredom and feel irrelevant. One reason so many nondenominational churches have grown so rapidly is that their leaders and pastors have focused on how to engage people on issues that are relevant and compelling in their lives. *Be careful not to become too focused on 'relevance'...*

Building a New Narrative

These myths have been central to the narrative that the church is dying in America. While they have caused significant panic and alarm, the data suggests that the picture they generate is either exaggerated or flat-out wrong. Let me quickly recap where these myths fail:

- *Myth 1: America is not becoming non-Christian, "a nation of nones."* In reality, the majority of the people in America still identify as Christian and probably will for about another twenty years. Even among the unchurched, those who identify as Christian are still a majority. While nones are on the rise, this stat lumps together receptive people with those hostile toward Christianity.

- *Myth 2: Millennials are not leaving the church at the high rate that we have heard but rather at a rate of about 45 percent.*[54] Although deeply concerning, this is not as different from past generations at the same age as we might think.[55] Faith remains far more relevant to the emerging generation than we have been led to believe.

- *Myth 3: The church will not be extinct in America in a generation.* Although nominal Christianity may be fairly dead in a generation, the ranks of the committed remain relatively stable.

- *Myth 4: Some of the unchurched in America have serious trust issues with the church (35 percent of those who left), but many more (65 percent of those who left) do not indicate broken trust as the main reason they left.* Most unchurched individuals either never found a compelling reason to stay or else simply had a change in life circumstances that ended their involvement. As we will see in the next chapter, many of the unchurched have a much more positive view of the church than we would expect.

These four myths together have helped reinforce a false narrative about receptivity in American culture. Many of us have embraced this false narrative, and we need to nuance it in some cases and shed it entirely in others. At the end of the day, the main problem with the church reaching new people, developing reproducers who advocate for faith and invite others into congregations, and then influencing communities for good is . . . the church! The biggest challenge congregations need to overcome is our own mindset and not the hostility or apathy of the larger culture. We need a new and better narrative that more accurately reflects the reality of the attitudes of the unchurched toward congregations, Christian faith, and spiritual conversation.

And we need better and more culturally sensitive and effective ways of capitalizing on the receptivity that is there.

What is the new narrative? What are the attitudes of the unchurched to the church and the Christian faith? How can congregations approach the unchurched and irreligious effectively in America today? Let's turn to those questions next and begin constructing a new narrative that can better serve and ignite congregations in their mission.

Questions for Discussion

1. Rick mentions four myths that are widely promoted in the press and among Christians:

    • America is becoming a "nation of nones"

    • Millennials are forsaking the church, never to return

    • The church is dwindling in America and will disappear in a generation

    • Trust in the church is at an all-time low, and experiences are largely negative

    Which of these myths have you heard or believed, and how have they affected you?

2. What did you learn in the chapter to help counteract the negative impact of these myths?

3. What one thing in the chapter most encourages you to have missional imagination?

    — people are more interested than I think;
      why don't I go out and ask/see
      for my self?

Embracing a New Narrative About the Unchurched

My wife, Mary Kay, and I moved from Wheaton, Illinois, to the South Loop in Chicago three years ago. The spiritual and cultural contrasts between Wheaton and the South Loop could not have been more striking.

About an hour outside Chicago, Wheaton is known as home to one of evangelicalism's flagship colleges, at which I am a professor. Wheaton College was founded in the middle of the nineteenth century and produced some of the best-known evangelical leaders, including Billy Graham, whose center for evangelism the college still houses. In our neighborhood in Wheaton, a third of our neighbors were evangelicals attending independent churches such as Wheaton Bible Church or historic Protestant denominational churches such as Anglican or Presbyterian ones. A third of the residents were Catholics who regularly attended a local parish church. The final third were a mix of various other religions, including Parsee Indian neighbors next door who practiced the ancient Zoroastrian faith and religious nones in the house across the street who were turned off by the right-leaning religion and politics common in our neighborhood.

Even as people in the neighborhood were open to spiritual conversations, this rarely translated into actual change. Most were advocates of their own faith perspective, enthusiastic about engaging in spiritual conversation but not terribly effective at influencing one another. In one sense, it was a very open and eclectic mix of spiritual perspectives. In another sense, despite a veneer of politeness and courtesy, people were not often responsive to the message of advocacy for different faith perspectives. We didn't influence each other much, at least from a religious perspective.

Our South Loop neighborhood was, on first impression, the complete opposite. Nones abounded, as did millennials. Diversity was the hallmark of the neighborhood, and tolerance its primary value. Like Wheaton, educational institutions were important, including Columbia, a school focused on arts and communication, along with the School of the Art Institute of Chicago, Robert Morris College, and Roosevelt University, the latter two known for urban diversity and serving underresourced communities. In many contexts artists do not tend to be committed to traditional faiths and dogmatic propositions. What's more, these universities and colleges were not known for any connection to faith, unlike Wheaton College. There were other kinds of diversity as well. On our condo building floor, half the condos were occupied by gay couples. Suburban Wheaton and South Loop urban Chicago seemed worlds apart.

Surprisingly, however, people in the two contexts were equally interested in spiritual issues and conversations, even passionately so. The urban friends we made in the South Loop were, if anything, more open to being influenced by others. They did not have everybody in a box and did not know where you were coming from until you told them. Of course, building trust was still critical. Several of our neighbors had had negative Catholic backgrounds and were somewhat distrustful of the church. What's more, any kind of dogmatism or judgmentalism was not received well. But the urban dwellers were much more receptive than I expected.

I think of our neighbor Barry. He and his gay partner were having relational challenges and came to Mary Kay and me for relational counsel. Both of them had admired the authenticity of our marriage, our commitment, and our honesty about our struggles. One of our conversations had centered on the various stages of serious relationships and why recommitting to already committed relationships is so common and needed, or else these relationships become hollow and barren. We talked about how long-term relationships need seasons of recommitment because the people in those relationships change every five to seven years and no longer necessarily have the same needs and desires with which they started the relationship and which drove them to commit in the first place. All of us were stimulated by the insights we all shared, and it built a bond among Barry, some of Barry's friends, Mary Kay, and me.

We began to meet and talk about relationships and our struggles more. Though Barry's partner traveled often so we didn't get to see him as much, we became close friends with Barry and came to love and respect him deeply. Our conversations about spirituality led to opportunities to pray together, and Mary Kay and I then gave Barry a few books about responding to Jesus and to the presence of God. Today Barry is increasingly close to Christ and is in some ways even more spiritually engaged and active than either Mary Kay or me, as he regularly takes retreat opportunities for a month or more, often carrying along the books we have recommended. Journeying together with Barry has been so meaningful. We have inspired and influenced his faith, and he has influenced and inspired our faith as well.

Barry has not acted according to the script we expected. He and others like him have been profoundly more open to Christian faith and spiritual engagement than we ever thought possible—more open than most of our friends in Wheaton! I have discovered both personally and from the research I have done that the narrative we are telling each other and often embracing about the growing hostility of Americans toward the church and the increasing apathy and disinterest in faith is not accurate. The script we expect often keeps us from reaching out, and this false narrative shuts us down from seeing the many opportunities that are all around us. We need a new and more accurate narrative about the openness of Americans to spiritual conversations, congregations, and Christian faith. This chapter will begin to lay out that new narrative and take a big-picture look at the research that supports it.

I believe that Jesus' words about a plentiful harvest are just as true today as they were in his day. What we need is not naysayers, pessimism, and doom but rather laborers who see the harvest that is there and know how to cultivate it. Our problem starts with a false narrative about a disappearing receptivity coupled with a lack of the skills, attitudes, and abilities needed to cultivate the ripe American harvest and to reach the people who are receptive. The harvest is plentiful to those who have eyes to see it, a heart that is open to how it is expressed, and the skills in watering, nurturing, and cultivating the spiritual interest that is common among people in our culture today.

Facing the Reality of Hostility

How negative or hostile are unchurched people toward the church? Figure 3.1 shows the range of views that unchurched individuals hold toward the Christian faith. Because survey respondents were invited to

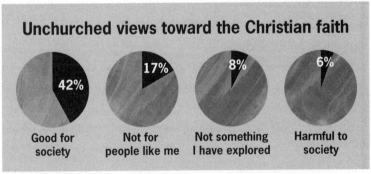

Source: "Unchurched Report," Billy Graham Center Institute and Lifeway Research, April 24, 2019, www.billygrahamcenter.com/youfoundme/research

Figure 3.1. Unchurched views toward the Christian faith

select all responses that applied to them and were offered a number of other possibilities, the percentages don't equal 100 percent. But for our purposes, notice the contrast between the most and least widely held views. The vast majority of unchurched people in our society do *not* think the Christian faith is harmful to society. Only 6 percent think that. By contrast, 42 percent of unchurched individuals think the Christian faith is beneficial to society. That positive perspective is held not only by unchurched individuals but also by those who are religiously unaffiliated. Pew Research Center explains that even most of those who are religiously unaffiliated (the nones) think positively about churches because of the way they create social bonds and serve the poor.[1]

Other answers people gave include that the Christian faith is "not for people like me" (17 percent answered yes) or "not something I have explored" (8 percent answered yes), but no answer was more common than that the Christian faith is "good for society," and no answer was less common than that the Christian faith is "harmful to society."

In light of the research, why have so many people, especially evangelical Christians, come to the conclusion that the larger mainstream American society is so negative toward faith and especially evangelical faith? I believe there are at least three factors:

1. The political polarization in the country between conservative and liberal has been so caustic and cauterizing, and evangelicals have generally been perceived as conservative in their political orientations, that the arguments and denunciations have been a reflection of the *political* polarization in the country but not reflective of a corresponding *religious* polarization, which is not nearly as pervasive, powerful, or profound.

2. Atheists have been in the minority, have felt persecuted and dismissed, and have generally become fairly strident in their denunciation of Christian faith, as it is the dominant faith in America and thus the one at which they aim the most. Atheists

use a megaphone and have given the appearance of being much more influential and numerous than they are.

3. Evangelicals have a fundamentalist past and a tendency to feel marginalized and pushed out, after enjoying a majority and privileged position through much of the nineteenth century. The history of marginalization from the 1920s on was so profound that it still shapes the perceptions of many evangelicals and fundamentalists even today.

Since such a small percentage of unchurched individuals believe that the Christian faith is harmful to society, it is not surprising that the actual hostility factor toward Christian faith and the church is fairly low! As figure 3.2 bears out even more starkly, only a tiny minority (1.5 percent) give their Christian friends a hard time about their faith. Again, respondents were invited to select any responses that applied to them.

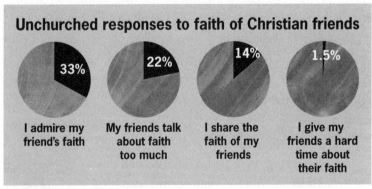

Unchurched responses to faith of Christian friends

| 33% | 22% | 14% | 1.5% |
| I admire my friend's faith | My friends talk about faith too much | I share the faith of my friends | I give my friends a hard time about their faith |

Source: "Unchurched Report," Billy Graham Center Institute and Lifeway Research, April 24, 2019, www.billygrahamcenter.com /youfoundme/research

Figure 3.2. Unchurched responses to faith of Christian friends

There is and will always be a possibility of encountering hostility when we share our faith, but the reality is that it happens far less often than we may expect. This 1.5 percent measure could be seen as the persecution factor for conversational-relational witness, and although it's real, it's negligible when we step back and consider the broader persecution taking place against Christians across the globe. In many countries, people risk their lives when they choose to confess that Jesus is Lord.[2] Imagine explaining to someone who has risked life itself in order to witness about Jesus that we in America merely risk some social awkwardness, and there are one and a half people for every hundred who give us a hard time about our faith. People from persecuted countries might be shocked to hear that stat—not at our persecution level but rather at our silence and passivity levels.

Admittedly, the percentage goes up for the millennial unchurched. Three percent give their friends a hard time about their faith.[3] One could imagine a new, alarming statistic circulating widely: "*Twice* the percentage of millennials express hostility toward the faith of their Christian friends as does the population in general!" But it all amounts to a small percentage either way.

There are other responses people gave as well. Fourteen percent of the unchurched said they share the faith of their friends, and in a separate question, 22 percent said that their friends talk about their faith too much. What stands out the most are the extremes, with the largest percentage saying they admire the faith of their friends and the smallest percentage saying they give their friends a hard time about their faith.

If we fully grasped the implications of these statistics, we would begin to realize that there are many opportunities before us.

Openness to Spiritual Conversations

Julio is another of our gay neighbors who has become a good friend. He attends the University of Chicago, where he is getting his PhD in cultural studies. He focuses his work on queer theory and believes that people in any society need to become much more aware of the ways institutions in society reinforce the power of the privileged and discriminate against the underresourced, the marginalized, and the alternative. For him, the dominant Catholic Church in his home country of Spain, as well as its leaders, like the Pope, have far too often normalized traditional masculinity and marriage and discriminated against "effeminacy" and alternative ways to love one another. He has a suspicion toward conservative institutions, like both the college for which I am a professor and the church that I attend. Such institutions he believes can sometimes "conserve" unjust and discriminatory prejudices and practices. Though I remain deeply rooted in my church and college, and remain quite committed to my evangelical convictions, his challenge to expand my awareness has stretched and helped me to love people who are different than I am with more empathy and understanding. And that challenge and influence has gone both ways.

He recently wrote me that he believes people of faith can better society, that faith as trust in something larger than ourselves is something he deeply respects and is challenged by, and that he values more and more the conversations and connection we have. In his words:

> You are more than authentic. I think you are someone with integrity, someone who has worked and has been curious, and has learned and has taken challenges that have made him better. Someone who has seriously reflected on extremely important things, and who has sound arguments that, I think, can help a lot of people. This is one of the many reasons that I respect you and that I love you as a friend.

There are many encouraging signs about approaches Christians and congregations might adopt to engage people in spiritual conversations and to ultimately engage them in congregations. First and foremost, the conversational-relational approach to witness is still the best approach and continues to have a high receptivity rate almost everywhere.

As figure 3.3 demonstrates, 79 percent of unchurched people are fine with us talking about our faith if we value it. Of course, it is also important to value that other person when we talk about our faith, as in my relationship with Julio. I will never forget my experience with Sam at an Einstein Bros. Bagels, where I wrote my first book.[4]

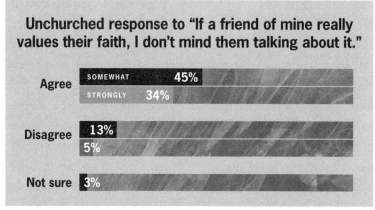

Unchurched response to "If a friend of mine really values their faith, I don't mind them talking about it."

Agree
SOMEWHAT 45%
STRONGLY 34%

Disagree
13%
5%

Not sure 3%

Source: "Unchurched Report," Billy Graham Center Institute and Lifeway Research, April 24, 2019, www.billygrahamcenter.com /youfoundme/research

Figure 3.3. Unchurched response to "If a friend of mine really values their faith, I don't mind them talking about it."

Sam knew I was a Christian and followed me through the coffee urn line, suddenly popping out a question that had been bothering him. "You aren't one of those people who thinks you are right and everybody else is wrong and that you have the only way to God, *are you?*" He got a little louder as the question tumbled out of his mouth. How would you have responded? I do believe Jesus is uniquely the way to the Father, but I certainly strive to not be the kind of person who comes off as if I am right and everybody else is wrong. I hate it when people come off arrogant that way with me. So just to make sure I understood what Sam was really asking, I asked him, "Why do you ask?" He went on to share a story about a cousin who carried a big Bible, told him he was headed to hell for his alcoholism and unbelief, and judged his lifestyle often and severely. Sam's cousin clearly valued his faith, but just as clearly he did not communicate that he valued Sam.

No one that I know wants to hear friends talk about their faith in *that* way. But make no mistake, most unchurched people are fine with us talking in personal-conversational ways about our faith. Even people like Sam who do have trust or hostility issues often would feel fine about sharing why, which is often the first step toward genuine and positive faith conversations. Sam and I went on to have many such conversations and later studied the Gospel accounts of the life of Jesus together. I can also say that after building trust with Sam, I was able to share openly and confidently about the uniqueness of Jesus as the way to God. When people trust that we value and respect them, they will value and respect our beliefs, even those that are challenging and go against the cultural tide of tolerance.

Of the 18 percent who disagree that they are fine with Christian friends talking about their faith, only 5 percent strongly disagree and are *not* fine with people talking about their faith. That is a good measure of a significant inward hostility level for some people, and we fairly quickly find out when it is there. At that point in the conversation, our best approach is not to talk about our own faith but to hear what matters to the other person and then to find out what has turned them off so much. Usually we will discover they have experienced judgmental treatment that has broken trust and turned them off. Until trust is

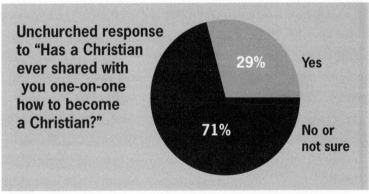

Source: "Unchurched Report," Billy Graham Center Institute and Lifeway Research, April 24, 2019, www.billygrahamcenter.com/youfoundme/research

Figure 3.4. Unchurched response to "Has a Christian ever shared with you one-on-one how to become a Christian?"

rebuilt, faith conversations will not be welcome. But again, only 5 percent of the unchurched feel strongly that way, and those friends become important informants to us about what congregations and Christians have done to hurt others, giving us opportunity for apology and learning.

In relation to faith conversations, many unchurched people would also say they have never had someone explain how to become a Christian.

Less than 30 percent of the unchurched have heard how to become a Christian in the context of a meaningful relationship with another Christian. If 79 percent don't mind their Christian friends talking about their faith, and 71 percent have never had someone explain how to become a Christian, it seems like there is a huge gap between people who would be fine with hearing and people who are actually sharing.

The Power of Personal Invitations

From our survey of two thousand unchurched individuals, half of them told us that they would respond positively to an invitation to

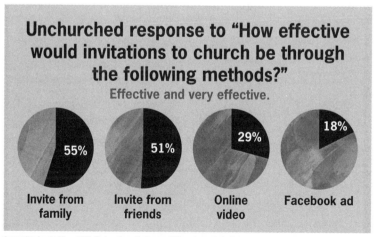

Source: "Unchurched Report," Billy Graham Center Institute and Lifeway Research, April 24, 2019, www.billygrahamcenter.com/youfoundme/research

Figure 3.5. Unchurched response to "How effective would invitations to church be through the following methods?"

attend a church if the invitation came from a friend. That is one out of two. And 55 percent tell us they would respond positively if the invitation came from a family member. These empowering statistics need to make their way to every congregation in America. These are action-catalyzing statistics *and* true, not alarmist and misleading.

Let me unpack what these numbers mean. This statistic is a measure of *receptivity*, not a measure of certainty. Receptivity is much higher than you might think, but to turn receptivity into additional attenders and members of a congregation will take courage, conviction, consistency, and creativity on our parts as congregations and as Christians. The investment of time, energy, courage, and creativity is worth it because there really is a receptive host of people who are unchurched and open. They just need us to care enough to go the extra mile to help them reconnect or perhaps connect for the first time.

I think of my friend Nancy who would identify as a none on surveys. She is a spiritual explorer and adventurer who influences many other people with her thinking. Having dabbled with ideas about mindfulness from Buddhism and psychic phenomena from more New Age kinds of thought, she believes that any spiritual path, as long as it is respectful of others and authentic to oneself, is a good spiritual path to be on. In the midst of that, however, she prays to Jesus several times a day and is wondering what part Jesus is to play in her life. For her, figuring that out is an important part of her next adventure.

I recently extended an invitation to her to visit my church with me. Initially, she was very open and interested and even said yes to my invitation, but when it came down to it, she needed to check the church website out, look over the videos and the tone of the communication, and discern whether my church would be a safe place for her. Growing up in a strict Christian background, she heard often from Christian churches that she was going to hell and does not want to attend a church only to get ambushed by that message again. Some of her hesitation also comes from a fear that others might expect her to be a committed Christian, to know the Bible, and to believe what the church believes right from the beginning. She wants to seek, but she wants to do it in a safe place where she will feel accepted and not judged for her questions. She will never forget how, in response to her honest questions, the pastor of her former church told her she just had to believe and have faith.

Nancy had the two great fears many unchurched people have when they consider attending a church. Nancy wondered whether she would feel judged and whether she would feel like she was expected to be something she wasn't. In our interviews of previously unchurched people, which I focus on in part three, person after person told us the reason they hesitated to visit a church initially was that they were afraid they would be judged for their lifestyle or their ignorance about the Christian faith and lingo, or else that they would be expected to be all in, committed right away. Keep those fears in mind when you invite people, because crossing the threshold of a church is a greater challenge than just wanting to or being open to. The way we invite people and the sensitivity we show to the fears people have could go a long way toward helping people cross that threshold.

In addition, when people say that an invitation to a congregation from a friend or family member would be effective in getting them to attend a congregation, they sometimes have particular congregations or denominations in mind. If they identify as Catholic, and they are from a Catholic family, then their picture of where they would be invited by a friend or family member is probably to a Catholic church. People have varying rates of receptivity in part in relation to what kind of church we invite them to, and they can be more open to invitations to some kinds of churches than others. One of the findings from our recent Billy Graham Center / Lifeway study on the effects of the 2016 election is that more nonevangelical people became more negative toward evangelicals as a result of the association of evangelicals with

Donald Trump.[5] Interestingly though, most of these kinds of bumps toward receptivity or toward antagonism are short lived and situation based. Expect this short-term trend to bounce back the other way if the intense polarization we are in starts to go the other way.

One reason for the success story of nondenominational churches is that they are not categorized easily by unchurched people, and so they do not necessarily carry advance stereotypes or prejudices when unchurched people consider attending one. That lack of category can be an advantage, and churches need to consider that dynamic in how they help their people invite others to visit.

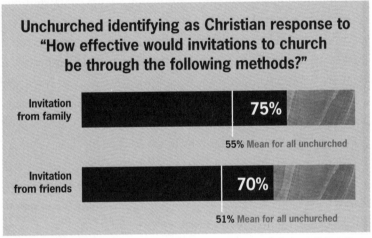

Source: This data comes from additional analysis conducted by the Billy Graham Center Institute on the data from the *Unchurched Survey*.

Figure 3.6. Response to "How effective would invitations to church be through the following methods?" from unchurched who identify as Christian

Figure 3.6 gives us a clue to the most receptive unchurched people we will encounter. Fifty-six percent of all unchurched people identify as Christian, and it turns out that that group is especially, and even overwhelmingly, receptive. Seventy-five percent of unchurched people who identify as Christian say an invite from a family member would be effective, and 70 percent say an invite from a friend would be effective. So if you ask someone whether they have a religious background, and they tell you yes and that it is Christian or Catholic and that they still identify with it, they are highly likely to respond positively to an invitation to accompany you for a visit to a congregation.

Connecting Online

What other ways are there for churches to communicate and connect with unchurched people? Let's look again at the different avenues and the receptivity response rate in figure 3.5. The best nonrelational way to approach the unchurched is through an online video about the church. Such a video could be posted on the church website and provided via email or other social media to people who want to check out the church before attending for the first time. More than one out of four unchurched people would be receptive to this approach.

In our research we found that top-10-percent conversion-community churches had learned to excel at this approach. Often when churches set up a website, they think only about communicating with people already at the church, or else with people who are already Christians and are just looking for a new church to attend. But the most effective churches are hospitable to unchurched and irreligious people *even on their website*! Look at North Point Community Church and its ministries, for instance.[6] Check out one of the top ministries it offers and how it is described.[7] Or look at Saddleback Church.[8] But it is not just large and well-known churches. Consider websites of smaller churches as well.[9] Websites are the new front door or entry point for people who want to visit a congregation. One church I know has videos on its website under the heading "If you are considering visiting our congregation for the first time," featuring people who share about their first visit. They do not talk about some big life change they experienced, but only about how welcomed, nonpressured, nonjudged, and cared for they felt. This small church gets a steady stream of visitors.

Remember Nancy. After being invited, the first place she went to check out whether the church would be a safe and welcoming place to visit was the church website. She found welcoming messages, including a short video testimony from a woman who had experienced feeling judged at a previous church when she got divorced. The woman sharing her testimony went on to explain that she returned to God at my church because my church embraced her, accepted her, and walked with her through her healing process.

That is not to say my church is lax about ethical boundaries. There is a significant difference between accepting people and sliding into a moral and spiritual "anything goes" attitude. As a matter of fact, good, moral, and theological boundaries characterize churches that are reaching and retaining people and growing over the long term. I explore that dynamic more in the last chapter. But these churches also know how to accept people where they are when they first come in and how to help them belong before they believe. That attitude came across in the video on my church's website, which proved to be quite compelling for Nancy.

Looking at figure 3.5 again, it is interesting to note that 18 percent of unchurched people would be receptive to an advertisement on Facebook, leaving that approach in last place. Facebook does better with millennials, though younger millennials are turning more to other forms of social media these days.[10] For the population in general, Facebook ads are straggling behind things such as door hangers, billboards, and visits from church leaders to neighborhood homes. Facebook, aware of research like ours, has been changing the way it advertises, and it is probably improving how people would assess its effectiveness. What's more, a vehicle such as Facebook or Instagram may have a lower effectiveness rating but can probably be circulated to many more people.

Engaging the Unchurched Through Events

We have seen that how we invite unchurched individuals has a significant impact on their level of receptivity. Building on that, *what* we invite people to first can also make a difference, as figures 3.7 and 3.8 illustrate.

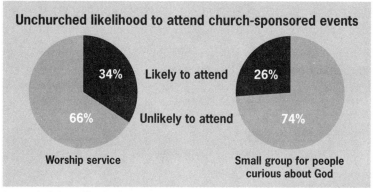

Unchurched likelihood to attend church-sponsored events

34% Likely to attend   26%

66% Unlikely to attend   74%

Worship service   **Small group for people curious about God**

Source: "Unchurched Report," Billy Graham Center Institute and Lifeway Research, April 24, 2019, www.billygrahamcenter.com /youfoundme/research

Figure 3.7. Unchurched likelihood to attend church-sponsored events

It is significant that the weekly worship service of a church is *still* the most likely entry point into the life of the church for unchurched people, as we can see in figure 3.7. You will get help in this book on how to become more hospitable toward unchurched people in your worship service. It is not that you should make your worship services primarily *for* unchurched people, though many churches, including some of America's largest, have done just that (e.g., Willow Creek in Chicago, Lifechurch.tv in Oklahoma and now other states, and North Point in Atlanta). But the key for most churches is to become hospitable to unchurched people in your worship services. How you greet them, whether you have adequate direction about what they are to do, how you address them in worship and sermons and applications— all are key means of welcoming unchurched people so that they know you expect them and want them and are including them in your life as a congregation. Why will they want to come if they are not wanted, welcomed, expected, addressed, and prepared for?

Small groups could also be a key first step for some, as one in four unchurched individuals indicated likelihood to attend one. Neighborhood groups, missional communities, moms groups, Starting Point, Alpha, and Christianity Explored programs have all become key ways that unchurched people visit and see whether a church might be helpful for them.[11] These are the entry points that create belonging for unchurched people right from the get-go.

Unchurched individuals communicated some openness to attending spiritually oriented events, including small groups and worship services, but they are far more open to attending events hosted by churches that are focused outward into the community, as figure 3.8 demonstrates.

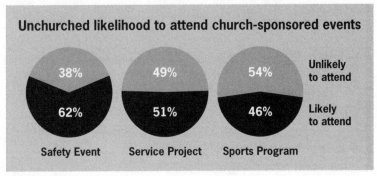

Unchurched likelihood to attend church-sponsored events

Safety Event	Service Project	Sports Program	
38%	49%	54%	Unlikely to attend
62%	51%	46%	Likely to attend

Source: "Unchurched Report," Billy Graham Center Institute and Lifeway Research, April 24, 2019, www.billygrahamcenter.com/youfoundme/research

Figure 3.8. Unchurched likelihood to attend church-sponsored events

Sixty-two percent of the unchurched say they would attend an event sponsored by a local church focused on making the neighborhood safer. Security is a concern for everyone, and churches that serve the community by fostering conversations about safety get points and people. Of course, we don't just sponsor such events to get points and bring unchurched people to the church. We sponsor events on safety because we care about neighbors and we care about safety. Having unchurched people step onto church ground or into space used by a church community is a side benefit, and a good one given our desire to serve and connect with people all around us. People will often visit a church first to explore an issue that everybody cares about, whether churched or unchurched.

Future Expectations

In addition to our exploration of what kinds of events unchurched individuals would be open to attending, we asked unchurched people how likely they were to attend church regularly sometime in the future. The results, reflected in figure 3.9, are encouraging.

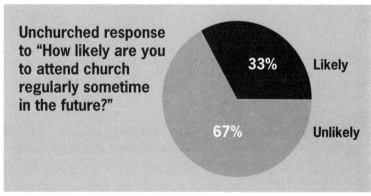

Unchurched response to "How likely are you to attend church regularly sometime in the future?"

33% Likely

67% Unlikely

Source: "Unchurched Report," Billy Graham Center Institute and Lifeway Research, April 24, 2019, www.billygrahamcenter.com/youfoundme/research

Figure 3.9. Unchurched response to "How likely are you to attend church regularly sometime in the future?"

One-third of unchurched Americans expect to return to church *regularly* sometime in the future. That is 47.6 million adults and children who are *expecting* to return to regular church attendance in the future.[12] If all 350,000 churches in the United States reached out effectively to those who expect to return, every church in America would grow by 136 people.[13] Some churches would fold in 136 people easily. For others, it would be earth shaking to experience such an influx. Are we ready for that? If it happened, we could be on the verge of a revival of church life in the United States, and it's possible. It represents a massive number of people who are open to being invited, welcomed, and connected to a local congregation.

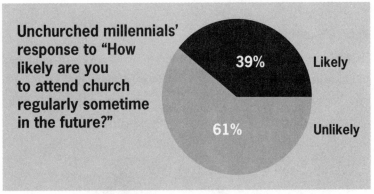

Source: This data comes from additional analysis conducted by the Billy Graham Center Institute on the data from the *Unchurched Survey*.

Figure 3.10. Unchurched millennials' response to "How likely are you to attend church regularly sometime in the future?"

Surprisingly, millennials are at the head of the line. As figure 3.10 demonstrates, 39 percent of all unchurched millennials, or twenty-five million, expect to regularly attend church in the future. A higher percentage of millennials expect to return or begin attending church than any other age group. I bet you did not see that one coming. But others have found support for this reality as well. Though 66 percent of millennials stop attending at some point during their early emerging adult years (ages eighteen to twenty-two), nearly a third of those millennials return to regular church attendance between the ages of twenty-three and thirty. This makes the actual loss of regular church attenders 46 percent, at least among Protestants. There are even more emerging adults who return to some level of congregational involvement.[14]

In the midst of this fairly encouraging data, it's important to acknowledge that a majority of the unchurched, nearly one hundred million people, don't expect to be attending church regularly in the future. Although some people may be disheartened by that level of disinterest, to me that is not so surprising. They are not attending now and don't expect to, but that does not mean that they won't. It just means engaging some of them will take more effort, commitment, and wisdom.

Despite the reality that two-thirds of unchurched individuals do not expect to return to church, it is more striking to me that one out of three unchurched people do expect to become connected to congregations. Why isn't this reality part of the dominant narrative we tell? It is immensely empowering to realize that one out of every three people we engage who does not now go to church expects to. They are the receptive.

Embracing the New Narrative

Despite some alarming signs of the state and direction of the church in America, there is a remaining part of the story that fills out a much truer narrative. Receptivity to church is *much* higher than we have often thought or been led to expect. One out of two people say they would accept an invitation from a friend or family member to attend a church, and nearly four out of five are fine with hearing about the faith of their friends if it matters to their friends. Remember that nearly fifty million Americans (47.6 million, to be more precise), one out of every three unchurched people, expect to be regularly attending church in the future. For millennials the percentage goes up to nearly 40 percent.

Yet for all the encouraging numbers, congregations and pastors and people are discouraged rather than optimistic about the receptivity of the people around us. We are not as encouraged, energized, and excited as we have reason to be, but that can turn around based on real re-search and real stories of what is going on in America with the un-churched, who are much more receptive than we realize. Let's adopt a new, or at least revised, narrative, and let's be emboldened, wise, and engaging. It turns out many churches have adopted this much more positive narrative and are finding that their results bear out their more positive narrative.

Susan had a long, slow journey to my church. She had been abused when she was younger and entered a marriage because she became pregnant. In her marriage she experienced physical abuse for several years, began to drink and then take drugs, and tried to take her life. In the hospital she connected to a lay pastor visiting someone in his small group who shared a room with Susan. The pastor was accepting and encouraging and told her he would love to see her find faith and have her life be turned around.

After getting out of the hospital, she met a guy who invited her to his church—my church. As she began to attend, she cried every week for several months in response to the message of hope she heard and the acceptance she felt. She became part of a small group and then began to serve others in the group through hospitality and meeting concrete needs for food and encouragement when she could. Slowly, she began to feel better about herself, and she eventually came to faith. Within a couple of years, she had invited many other friends, was leading a small group, and had married the man who had initially invited her. Her life was turned upside down, and her kids were being loved and brought up in faith.

She ended up at a church that truly believes in the new narrative that tells us congregants that people are much more receptive than we think and that is constantly telling stories of the unlikely people that have come back to God. If we will care, welcome, extend invita-tions, enfold people, and help them contribute, they will come to faith, join congregations, reach their friends, and influence others. As we will see throughout this book, the new narrative is embraced by many of the churches that are most effective at outreach in the country. It is part of what we can do to become more effective in evangelism and outreach at our own churches: adopt a new narrative that embraces the perspective of Jesus. The harvest *is* plentiful, and the workers *are* few, and congregations that raise up such hopeful, optimistic, bold, and inviting laborers *will* grow, reach people, and improve communities.

That is the invitation of this chapter and this book to you and your church. Will you embrace a new narrative and the invitation of Jesus? Will you see the receptive harvest and learn to cultivate people, relationships, spiritual interest, and influence?

Questions for Discussion

1. What was the most surprising finding from this chapter for you? Why?

2. Out of all the good news for congregations in this chapter, what do you think would most motivate people in your congregation to reach out with greater hope and expectation, and why?

3. What steps could your congregation and leaders take to communicate the good news from this chapter to your congregants, and what help will they need to use this information effectively as they seek to care for and reach out to friends, neighbors, and colleagues?

4

Engaging the Receptive Millennials, Nones, and Nominals in Your Life

R obert grew up in an evangelical denomination and felt that he was loved but not helped that much in his life by church. When he took up smoking marijuana, he felt a lot of judgment and rejection. Robert felt that there wasn't much power or relevance in his church, and he is now lukewarm or even a little hostile to organized religion. But it turns out that Robert, as an unchurched none, deeply desires to be spiritual, prays often to Jesus, is considered very loving by many of his friends in his extended community, and is very open to connecting to a congregation.

Elli is a millennial. She considers herself spiritual but not religious. When I first met her, she wore sparkly clothes and had put glitter on her face, and when asked she fairly quickly made it clear that she didn't really believe in God or a higher power. She felt very disconnected from her past experience in an evangelical church. Elli felt that many people in that tradition were more into control and security than they were into creativity and making the world a better place. She thought they were good people, but she related that if she could find a congregation that really cared about the world, could accept her as she is right now, and really understood and appreciated nature and the environment, she would love to connect with it.

Both Elli and Robert are unchurched, very spiritually open, believe that they will attend a congregation regularly in the future, and would be interested in having friends and people to talk to about spirituality and faith. Yet for a variety of reasons, they don't feel like they can talk to their Christian friends. As a result, these conversations are rare, and when they do occur, Elli and Robert perceive them as agenda driven rather than a mutual dialogue. They don't feel understood or respected. While they would describe themselves as people who value spirituality and religion, they are not being reached or renewed through relationships with committed Christians. In addition, they are hesitant about attending a congregation for fear that they will be judged rather than accepted and that they will be expected to be something that they aren't yet able to be.

A biblical character who fits their profile is a man Jesus encountered named Zacchaeus. You can find his story in Luke 19.

Zacchaeus in modern terms could easily fit the category of "none" or "nominal." He was a tax collector, one who was despised and judged in his culture. People would have assumed he could not possibly be receptive to God or to the local synagogue. He collected money from the Jews to give to the Romans. He not only collected taxes but also supervised others who did. And he was very short. Not attractive. Not valued. Despised. Probably not someone you would want in your church.

It turned out that appearances were deceiving. Zacchaeus was far more receptive than people in his time realized. He wanted to see Jesus but knew that because he was short he would not be able to when the crowds gathered. So Zacchaeus scoped out the parade route Jesus would follow when he came to Jericho, and Zacchaeus found a way to see Jesus. He discovered a tree along the road that he could climb. He knew Jesus would walk right by. He ended up being able to see Jesus—but he got far more than he bargained for.

As Jesus and his very large coterie passed by, Jesus noticed Zacchaeus. He looked up and called out his name. And then he did something scandalous: he told Zacchaeus that he wanted to eat at his house. Zacchaeus was *not* religious in the minds of all the synagogue people. He was not someone they desired to convert or to connect with in their congregation. The religious people of Jesus' day had no interest in having Zacchaeus as part of their congregation. But Jesus saw what others did not. He saw receptivity. He saw desire to follow Jesus. He had missional imagination for what Zacchaeus could be and do.

So Jesus went to his house to eat. He saw, understood, and affirmed the spiritual interest Zacchaeus had. As a result Jesus reached Zacchaeus, and he reached all of Zacchaeus's friends.

Zacchaeus is a story and paradigm of the change that this book is designed to bring about. People we think are not receptive are. If we can capture missional imagination for these people, it could bring about a renewal of the church in American culture. And here is the other key thing to capture from the story of Zacchaeus. In his culture, Zacchaeus is why Jesus walked the earth. Jesus says it this way in Luke 19:10: "The Son of Man came to seek and to save the lost." Zacchaeus was the very image of what it meant to be lost. He was who Jesus came to seek and to save and to welcome.

This chapter applies the heart and mission of Jesus to millennials, nones, and nominals. It is a hinge point of the book because it suggests the receptivity of many in our culture who have been written off by many people in the church, and especially because it lays out a different approach to the many receptive people in our culture who we are not reaching and retaining in congregations. These are a large percentage of the unchurched: those who are spiritually open yet wary of organized religious services. While we may dispute how accurate their perceptions are, the perceptions are ingrained in a sizable and growing portion of the population. As a result, congregants are losing many opportunities to reach receptive people open to conversation, open to invitation, open to church connection.

Some of you might at this point be feeling a sense of dissonance. I have argued that research suggests that more people in the United States are receptive to the Christian faith than popularly believed. The writers and researchers who argue for a closing of American culture to the Christian faith and a corollary rise of secularism and pluralism are vastly overstating the case. Yet for many Christian readers, this idea is too good to be true. You hope that people are still receptive, but due to either your experience of their indifference toward your faith or your baseline skepticism, you are unsure.

In order to preemptively address this concern, this chapter will delve further into the state of the unchurched in America today. Who are they? What do they think of Christianity? What are some clues to their spiritual questions and concerns? How can Christians overcome negative perceptions and engage these communities of unchurched in ways that are both constructive and fruitful? This chapter seeks to answer these questions in regard to three groups of unchurched who frequently present challenges for church outreach: millennials, the religiously unaffiliated (nones), and the religiously nominal.

To facilitate this discussion, I will explore each group in two respects. First, I will overview other research and our research indicating receptivity to spiritual conversations and congregational invitations. Then I will explore a model of engaging unchurched people who are nones, millennials, and nominals that could have a significant impact in how people today respond to congregants and Christians.

Often the reason people do not seem receptive to our faith is that we do not capitalize on their receptivity but instead raise their resistance. It is not a lack of receptivity on the part of others but rather our approach that needs to be changed.

The recent Barna report, *Reviving Evangelism*, confirms what I am suggesting here. In their surveys of one thousand practicing Christians and then one thousand lapsed or non-Christians, they found that lapsed and non-Christians are very open to spiritual conversations with people of faith, but don't tend to look to the practicing Christians they know for those conversations. Why? Lapsed and non-Christians feel like practicing Christians don't have the same conversational values. Sixty-two percent of lapsed and non-Christians would be interested in talking with a person of faith who listens without judgment and 50 percent said they would want to talk with a person of faith who does not force a conclusion. But sadly, the majority of lapsed and non-Christians don't think practicing Christians have those qualities.[1]

In this chapter I will suggest an approach toward spiritual conversations and invitations and apply it to nones, millennials, and the nominally religious. This approach gets us a little closer to cracking the cultural code of persuasive conversation for the unchurched, and does so without giving up passion and conviction for the truth and power of the gospel and the uniqueness of Jesus.

Millennials

One of the major issues affecting congregations today is the increasing alienation and exodus of emerging adults from the church and from any Christian identification. According to Pew's religious landscape study, younger millennials (born 1990–1996) identify as nones at a 36 percent rate, higher than the 23 percent that represents the American population as a whole.[2]

At present, millennials represent a very substantial but somewhat misunderstood age group for the church, and they are possibly the most strategic age cohort for the church's future, though the generational cohort coming after (Gen Z, born after 1996) is also increasingly important for the church.[3]

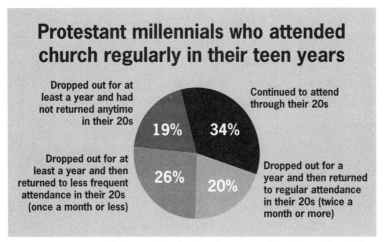

Protestant millennials who attended church regularly in their teen years

Dropped out for at least a year and had not returned anytime in their 20s — 19%

Continued to attend through their 20s — 34%

Dropped out for at least a year and then returned to less frequent attendance in their 20s (once a month or less) — 26%

Dropped out for a year and then returned to regular attendance in their 20s (twice a month or more) — 20%

Source: "Most Teenagers Drop Out of Church as Young Adults," Lifeway Research, January 15, 2019, https://lifewayresearch.com/2019/01/15/most-teenagers-drop-out-of-church-as-young-adults/

Figure 4.1. Protestant millennials who attended church regularly in their teen years

Fifty-four percent then stay or return to being regular attenders. And only 19 percent leave and don't return. That is a far cry from the grim picture we often get in the statistics that circulate about millennials. What's more, when nearly 40 percent of unchurched millennials tell us that they expect to return to regular church attendance in the future, this data gives a lot of support to say that they will.

I am also very interested in knowing what happens to Catholic regular attenders after the age of eighteen, but I don't have that data. Judging from the work of Christian Smith in his book on Catholic emerging adults, though, the percentages that leave and don't return are likely higher.[4] While there is an abundance of competing theories, significant questions remain as to why 19 percent of Protestant emerging adults are leaving the church and not returning and why another 26 percent are leaving the church and then returning to less frequent attendance. Of course, there are also many millennials who did not attend church regularly in high school.

We still need to feel urgency about answering what might help them be retained or choose to return, but we also need to revise our analysis of the magnitude of the problem and what it signifies. If only 19 percent leave never to return, 81 percent return at some level. We are not fighting a vast disillusionment and desertion of millennials but rather a more nuanced issue that combines many factors. I will be exploring a number of those factors from my research in parts 2 and 3.

Building on previous research by Christian Smith, Patricia Snell Herzog, and Kara Powell, our survey of the unchurched found indications that emerging adults are generally open to Christian faith and congregational involvement. Thirty-nine percent of unchurched emerging adults expect to be attending church regularly in the future, as compared to 33 percent of Americans in general.[5] Millennials are more positive and less negative toward the church than we might expect.

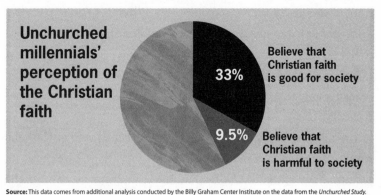

Source: This data comes from additional analysis conducted by the Billy Graham Center Institute on the data from the *Unchurched Study.*

Figure 4.2. Unchurched millennials' perception of the Christian faith

As figure 4.2 reflects, one-third of unchurched millennials think the Christian faith is good for society, and less than 10 percent think the

Christian faith is harmful. They are very receptive to invitations to church from friends and family members (55 percent say such invitations would be effective in getting them to attend) and to events sponsored by churches, especially community service events and sports program opportunities (nearly 60 percent say they would be likely to attend these kinds of events sponsored by local churches). So there are indicators of significant receptivity to conversations and invitations.

One millennial's journey toward Christ and a congregation. Brady is a millennial. He grew up in a more evangelical background but would now say he is a none. He smoked pot in high school, felt judged, and developed friendships outside church that became much more important than the ones in church. After graduating high school, he drifted away from all involvement in church and began to develop community in the Portland area with people who would say they are spiritual but not religious. Brady would say that about himself too.

Ron, a devout member of local congregation, built a friendship with Brady. They both loved hiking, met out on a trail, and began a conversation. After talking about various hiking trails, Ron discovered Brady liked disc golf too. He invited Brady to join him at Pier Park for a hike and a round with the disc. Brady decided to give it a try. After a successful outing and over a local microbrewery beer, Ron began asking Brady about his spiritual background. Brady shared his experience of feeling judged growing up in a church and how he walked away. Ron showed empathy and mentioned how he too had had an experience of feeling judged when he was having difficulty in his marriage. So he could understand how Brady felt.

Then Brady started sharing about his belief in God, using language for God that was quite vague. In particular, Brady shared how he prayed often to "God, or the universe, or science, or whatever you want to call the universal consciousness." Ron had not heard that language before but jumped in to affirm Brady that he prayed daily, then asked him why and what prayer did for him. Brady talked about how he felt he was on the earth for a purpose and that he prayed to stay in line with that purpose and to fulfill what he was on earth to do. He felt the world needed to be changed and that the answer was "everyone connecting to that God or universal consciousness or whatever and loving one another as we sense our connectedness." Ron agreed the world needed to change and loved hearing Brady's heart for prayer, for connecting to God, and for bringing people together. Ron then shared he found that sense of connection through Jesus. He prayed every day many times to Jesus, and he wanted to see people brought together in the ways Jesus brought people together and changed the world when he walked the earth. Brady affirmed Ron's relationship with Jesus and admitted he often prayed to "Jesus and the Father."

Ron asked Brady whether marijuana helped him spiritually. Brady at first said it did. But he also had been realizing that marijuana, though it gave him a sense of profound connection with others, did not strengthen his will or discipline to reach his goals, and he said he had been thinking about that a lot lately. Ron challenged Brady to consider taking a break from smoking pot and see the impact. Brady decided to do what he called a cleanse, a time of getting rid of all the toxicity in his body by staying sober from all drugs and alcohol for a month. In response, Ron told Brady Jesus could help him if Brady would ask. Then he asked Brady whether he could pray for him. Brady wanted that. So Ron prayed for the strength of Jesus to fill Brady and help him reach his goals and to get marijuana into the right place in his life (which from Ron's perspective was to not smoke it, but he didn't tell Brady that right then).

After the prayer time, which moved Brady (he mentioned that it had been powerful and even shed a few tears), Ron invited him to a small group that he was part of. Brady ended up attending and has been going now for several months. Right from the beginning, Ron and the other small group members welcomed Brady and prayed for him, and Ron began asking Brady to help greet people and to bring snacks each time. Brady got involved, began to contribute, and is coming close to a positive response to an invitation to fully trust and follow Jesus. One important step in that spiritual process for Brady was watching *The Passion of the Christ*. That movie captured Brady's attention, and Ron and Brady have started talking about the death and rising of Jesus and why it was important.

Brady is one of the nearly 40 percent of unchurched millennials who expect to attend church regularly in the future and are very receptive to invitations into the lives—and down the road into the congregations—of friends and family members.

Religiously Unaffiliated (Nones)

One of the major features of present-day American religious culture is the rise of the nones. Pew tells us the fastest-growing religious category in the country is what many have designated "nones."[6] What are nones? They are people who tell us on surveys that they have no affiliation with any organized religious group. So they could equally well be called "the unaffiliated," as Pew often does.[7]

The unaffiliated or nones are made up of three primary groups when surveys are given. When asked about their religious affiliation, they answer that they are either atheist, agnostic, or "nothing in particular." Here is what I want to most emphasize in this section. Many "nothing in particulars" value religion or at least spirituality, believe in God, and pray, and many are quite open to faith conversations and congregations as well as to being influenced by others in their spiritual convictions. It turns out that nothing in particulars have nothing in particular in common with atheists and agnostics, except that none of these groups identify with religious institutions. But when it comes to spirituality, belief in God, prayer, and receptivity to spiritual conversations and invitations, nothing in particulars are far more receptive than most atheists and agnostics.

So why has this term caught on in the culture? It has given language to people who did not have a category before and who tend to not even like labels and categories. In addition, the size and growth of nones has given a sense of significance, validation, and even political and spiritual voice to people who have not had those in the past.

Here are some statistics that help illustrate the diversity among nones. Close to one-third of all nones, including 43 percent of nothing in particulars, tell us religion is either important or very important to them.[8] A little over twenty percent pray daily. A majority think religious institutions benefit society because they build social bonds and care about the poor.[9] As of 2012, 5 percent of all nones attended a worship service weekly, and more than half of all nones described themselves as either religious (18 percent) or spiritual but not religious (37 percent), though given trends, these percentages are likely to fall over time. Eighty-one percent believe in a force or higher power that can be accessed through prayer of some sort.

In our survey, 20 percent of nothing in particulars expect to be attending a church regularly in the future (five million people in the United States), compared to only 4 percent of atheists and agnostics who expect to be attending church regularly in the future.[10] Seventy-five percent are fine with their Christian friends talking about their faith, and 44 percent feel that an invite from a friend would be effective in getting them to visit a congregation.[11] Unchurched atheists and agnostics express much lower rates of receptivity (e.g., only 25 percent of atheists and agnostics think an invite from a friend would be effective in getting them to attend a congregation).

One way to see the difference between the receptivity of atheists, agnostics, and "nothing in particulars" that came out of our research is pictured in figure 4.3.

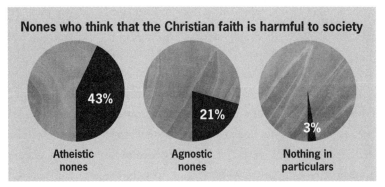

Nones who think that the Christian faith is harmful to society

43%

21%

3%

Atheistic
nones

Agnostic
nones

Nothing in
particulars

Source: This data comes from additional analysis conducted by the Billy Graham Center Institute on the data from the *Unchurched Study*

Figure 4.3. Unchurched nones who think that the Christian faith is harmful to society

As figure 4.3 reflects, 43 percent of atheists think the Christian faith is harmful to society, 21 percent of agnostics do, and only 3 percent of "nothing in particulars" do. The stark contrast in that one attitude is echoed in many other measures of spiritual receptivity and openness to Christian faith.

So although it is true that nones are moving in a secular direction over time, rates of receptivity are still fairly high, and rates of openness to spiritual conversations (78 percent) and invitations (44 percent) are still quite encouraging.[12] As I have reiterated several times, I believe the greatest challenge to congregations is not the shifting or secularizing culture but a discouraged, pessimistic, secularizing, or silent church.

One none's journey toward Christ and a congregation. Lisa is in her fifties, teaches at a downtown urban university in Manhattan, and lives with her lesbian partner, Leslie, in a condo in the Greenwich Village area. She grew up Catholic and also attended a parochial school. She felt fine about her Catholic background, but it had lost its relevance to her. She also knew that the Catholic churches she had attended would not accept her as gay, and so she steered clear of the church for many years. She describes herself as a none.

Cheri and William lived next door to Lisa and Leslie. They started conversations on the elevator about the condo building they lived in and agreed that there were problems that needed to be addressed. The bond started there. Lisa mentioned she loved hosting people and also enjoyed talking late and drinking wine with friends. The next week, Cheri picked up a bottle of good wine and texted Lisa when she got back to the condo, inviting her to share a quick glass of good wine if she had a few minutes. Lisa and Leslie came over, and the four spent an hour talking. It turned out Leslie liked good wine even more than Lisa did. Lisa and Leslie invited Cheri and William to stop by over the following weekend. Conversations during the weekend time drifted into how hard it is to maintain relationships with one's partner. All four shared some common struggles of communication in their relationship.

Later Lisa talked about those conversations being a meaningful time, and she wondered whether Cheri and William could give her some relationship advice. They met a couple of weeks later, and Lisa talked about her struggles with Leslie and how hurt she often felt in the relationship. Cheri and William asked about her spiritual background and whether that ever helped her. She said that she often prayed and meditated and that it helped. Cheri and William affirmed her spiritual desires and practices and asked whether they could pray for her. They prayed about the struggles with Leslie and the hurt she felt, and about finding healing and direction.

After the prayer, William challenged Lisa about her dependence on Leslie, noting that Leslie seemed to be using Lisa a bit. Lisa agreed and said she would think about it. As she got up to leave she mentioned she needed a retreat time and had a trip planned to a desert area in California, where she planned to take extensive time to pray and think about things. Cheri suggested Lisa take Henri Nouwen's book on desert spirituality, called *The Way of the Heart*, because it had profoundly helped Cheri during a challenging and lonely time in her life. Lisa took it, went on the trip, and read it. The next time she got together with Cheri and William, Lisa could not stop talking about the book, the experiences she had in prayer, and the ways she had taken steps toward Jesus.

The three of them started to talk about forming a book club small group and reading other works of Nouwen. Lisa loved the idea, so the group formed and has discussed one book all the way through and now has started a second. They meet for the club every month on a Sunday afternoon. Each time Cheri and William get to share about their experience in church that Sunday morning. Lisa is now at a point where she has responded positively to an invitation to attend a local Anglican church that "gets" urban people, which is where Cheri and William attend. Lisa is increasingly positive toward Cheri and William, toward Jesus, and toward reconnecting to a congregation. They regularly have prayer times together and talk about how to grow their spiritual lives. Lisa is seeking God, taking retreats, growing spiritually, and thinking a great deal about Jesus, even while her relationship with Leslie has been deteriorating. God is powerfully at work. A person Cheri and William had not expected to be receptive was deeply receptive and is making the journey toward Christian faith and Christian community. She has also begun the process of separating from Leslie, a very painful process but one that is driving her toward God and healing and away from obsession with her partner.

Lisa is a none who feels somewhat alienated from the church because of her sexual choices and sense of identity but who is far more open to spirituality, Christian faith, and even a congregation than most of us would expect. Like many nones, she is spiritual but not religious, prays often, believes the Christian faith is a good thing for society and now even for herself, and is profoundly receptive to the right approach and to the process of moving toward Christ and a congregation. She has now moved many steps in that direction.

Lisa shows us one other critical dimension of how to connect today with nones. Lisa joined a small group long before she was ready to visit an established congregation. These kinds of small groups that are open to the unconventional spiritual journeys of today's spiritual seekers will be a crucial step in the process of establishing connections with congregations for many nones. Churches need to think in terms of planting many microchurches, small groups of two to ten, that can become the entry point into significant conversation for many nones and could even ultimately become new congregations.

Nominally Religious

The largest percentage of unchurched in America is still the nominally religious, those who identify as either Protestant or Catholic. Though many nominals are becoming nones, nominals still loom large in the religious landscape of America and will for some years to come. Fifty-six percent of the unchurched in America identify as either Protestant (31 percent) or Catholic (25 percent). Less than 1 percent of the unchurched identify as Orthodox.[13]

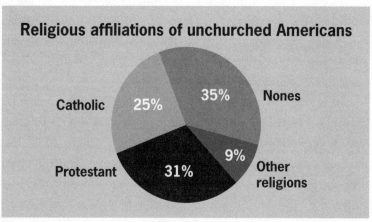

Religious affiliations of unchurched Americans

Catholic 25%
35% Nones
Protestant 31%
9%
Other religions

Source: This data comes from additional analysis conducted by the Billy Graham Center Institute on the data from the *Unchurched Study*

Figure 4.4. Religious affiliations of unchurched Americans

Among the population as a whole, including churched and un-churched, 70.6 percent still identify as Christian.[14] So the mission field of America is still majority nominal Christian.

Not surprisingly, these unchurched nominal Christian are the most receptive people to spiritual conversations and invitations of any group in America. A few statistics make that clear quickly. Forty-nine percent of unchurched Protestants and 44 percent of unchurched Catholics expect to be going to church regularly in the future. These stats add up to a total of thirty-nine million people in the United States who are not only receptive but who actually expect to return. What's more, 75 percent say an invitation from a friend or family member would be effective at getting them to visit a congregation.[15]

One person's journey toward Christ and a congregation. For years Richard had attended a Presbyterian church, and then he switched to a Unitarian church when his wife wanted to try that out. At an earlier point in his life, he had prayed for his sister-in-law and seen her cancer move into remission, taking that experience as a sign of God at work. As Richard has gotten older and read the works of various skeptics who question basic tenets of faith, claiming that science and faith are in opposition and that basic beliefs about Christ are nonsensical (that of his resurrection and others), he has gone through a crisis time of faith and of seeking. He has been reading books on nones, on faith, on doubt, and on the impossibility of believing basic Christian teachings. Rick grew up with Richard who was an older relative. In their conversations about faith, Richard admitted he wanted to be a person of faith but was not sure whether he could. Along the way, he was helped by an early Unitarian who still had some faith but had jettisoned many traditional Christian teachings.

Rick and Richard began to have conversations about basic beliefs. One conversation was about Scripture and the "errors" in Scripture. Rick was able to share his struggles with those questions and a time in his life when he came close to walking away from faith. Then Rick shared what had helped him during that time and a model of biblical authority that made sense to Richard. At another point, Rick and Richard had a long discussion about the viability of faith in the modern world. Rick gave Richard a book by N. T. Wright and Marcus Borg called *The Meaning of Jesus*. Richard came back a month later and said, "My search is over. I am a person of faith in Christ. That book was so helpful. Rick, you have helped me find my faith more than all the priests and pastors I have known, and I plan on spending the rest of my life becoming more like Christ in my life and in my family relationships." Richard has been renewed. He had entered a time of deep questioning and searching. But his questions and doubts were a sign of his interest and passion and search for conviction. He is following Christ in a renewed way and has committed his life to living that out.

Richard is now part of a congregation that is helping him connect and grow. He was open and responsive to congregational invitations and involvement. He has found a strong faith unexpectedly through the process of friendship, spiritual conversations, seeking, reading a thoughtful book, and searching for an authentic path to be a person of faith.

I should also mention that the "Rick" in the story is me, and the "Richard" in this story is my dad!

Nominal Christians Among People of Color

Some of the most receptive people toward Christian faith in the country are people of color, including those who have recently emigrated from other lands. The church is growing fastest among such groups, and many are experiencing passion for God, spiritual renewal, and tremendous impact in planting churches and seeing churches explode with growth.[16] In addition, the Pew religious landscape study notes that the African American Protestant churches are not in decline, one of the few historic churches that can say that.[17]

Figure 4.5 shows the future church attendance expectation for different racial groups.

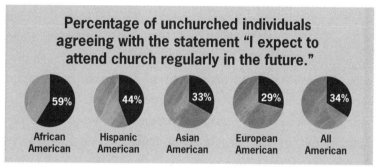

Source: This data comes from additional analysis conducted by the Billy Graham Center Institute on the data from the *Unchurched Study*

Figure 4.5. Percentage of unchurched individuals agreeing with the statement "I expect to attend church regularly in the future"

Let's briefly look at each of the groups of color.

Unchurched African Americans are the most religiously receptive and spiritually committed people of any ethnicity. Sixty-one percent of all unchurched African Americans identify as Christian, with the vast majority (50 percent) being Protestant.

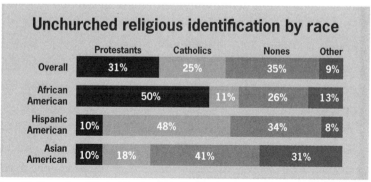

Source: This data comes from additional analysis conducted by the Billy Graham Center Institute on the data from the *Unchurched Study*

Figure 4.6. Unchurched religious identification, by race

One out of every four unchurched African Americans self-describes as a person who is devout with a strong faith. Eighty-eight percent of unchurched African Americans said on our survey that if a friend values their faith, they don't mind their friend talking about their faith. Nearly 60 percent told us on the survey that they would consider an invitation from a friend or family member to attend a congregation to be an effective way of getting them there. Finally, 59 percent of unchurched African Americans *expect* to attend church regularly in the future, compared to 34 percent of unchurched Americans in general.[18] There is a huge level of receptivity among unchurched African Americans.

Hispanic unchurched people of course identify predominantly as Catholic (48 percent), though 10 percent identify as Protestant. Thus Hispanic and African American groups have relatively similar percentages of their total population who identify as Christian. But their rates of receptivity are quite different. Only one out of ten unchurched Hispanic people self-describes as devout and having a strong faith, contrasted with one out of four African Americans. In general, Hispanic people fit the patterns found also among white or Caucasian unchurched people, except that Hispanic people expect to be attending church regularly in the future at a higher rate: 44 percent compared to 29 percent for Caucasian people.[19] Hispanic people also are less likely to think the Christian faith is good for society, possibly based on attitudes toward some of the challenges the Catholic Church has faced recently, though historical factors related to the Catholic church's identification with the conquest of native peoples and cultures might also play a role.[20]

Asian American unchurched people have the lowest percentage of those who identify as Christian (29 percent compared to 56 percent generally). Yet 33 percent of unchurched Asian Americans still *expect* to be attending church regularly in the future, matching the general unchurched population of 34 percent who expect to attend regularly.

Furthermore, 45 percent of unchurched Asian Americans say that invitations from family and friends would be effective at getting them to visit a congregation. Overall, unchurched nominally Christian people, whatever their ethnic background, are a harvest waiting to happen.[21]

An unchurched nominally religious African American renews her faith. Destiny is an unchurched African American. She grew up in a Missionary Baptist church, and every once in a while on a holiday she might return. She was raped when she was young and never found the healing or the acceptance that she longed for in her church. But she didn't expect to, so she didn't really blame the church. She also felt that the pastor had lived for himself and been a philanderer who was committed to building his own kingdom. Still, she loves the church she grew up in, thinks it was a force for good in her life, and would be willing to return. Even though she no longer attends, she does not feel as though she ever really left. She wants to talk about faith and sometimes longs to reconnect to God. If she could find a congregation that accepted her, invested in her life, and displayed integrity to her, she would embrace the opportunity to be part of that congregation and to renew her "religion," as she put it.

Danita is a strong Christian attending a Progressive Baptist church. One day while she was shopping for clothes for a niece, she met Destiny, who worked at the store. They clicked. Destiny was preparing to run a marathon and so was working out all the time. Danita loved working out too. They decided to do a run together to cheer each other on. It ended up being fun and good for both of them. So they got together afterward for coffee.

Danita began to ask Destiny about her spiritual background, and she could affirm much of what Destiny believed. But she could also see that Destiny had a very eclectic moral life. Danita was a little blown away when she heard about some of Destiny's sexual adventures, but she wanted to see Destiny come to know Christ and find a church that would help her work that out over time. Destiny also had shared she was turned off by the faith of her holiness church friend, who never "smoked or drank or wore suggestive clothing" like Destiny often did, and was constantly criticizing Destiny.[22]

Once Danita had built trust with Destiny, she started to challenge Destiny's way of putting together a very eclectic moral life alongside believing in God and still feeling loyalty toward her church. Danita knew that in their shared African American context, lots of people believed in God and were open to congregations but did not have a commitment to Christ as first in their lives and thus needed to be challenged to commit to Christ as Lord. Danita also knew that Destiny did not need to hear about the holiness practices and rules her friend at work was always promoting. So Danita challenged her to find out what Christ was really all about and see whether Destiny might want a relationship of commitment to God. She then invited Destiny to her progressive Baptist church. Destiny was blown away by the stories she heard of changed lives. After a number of visits to the church and then involvement in some of its service opportunities, Destiny finally gave her life to Christ and is gradually changing in her moral convictions and practices.

Many millennials, nones, and nominally religious are more receptive than we realize, especially when we approach people with acceptance and respect, and bring the "heat" later on when we have earned the right to influence.

Approaching the Unchurched

Clearly there are signs of receptivity among unchurched people in American culture. Yet the potential will remain dormant unless committed Christians can successfully adapt their outreach models and attitudes in a way that capitalizes on the spiritual needs and questions of these unchurched individuals. How do we make the most of the receptivity of those around us and connect with them in such a way that we could actually influence their spiritual journey?

In approaching many conversations with millennials, nones, and nominals, I have become convinced that if we change our approach, we will find people generally receptive to our spiritual influence. Of course, they also expect our openness to their ideas and insights as well. Through conversations with people such as Brady, Lisa, Richard, and Destiny, I have seen and heard how our approach makes a difference and that we can learn to capitalize on receptivity and catalyze spiritual movement.[23]

The first key to activating the receptivity of unchurched individuals is trust. In their book *I Once Was Lost*, Don Everts and Doug Schaupp name trusting a Christian as the first step unchurched individuals need to take in their journey toward Jesus.[24] We have found this to be consistently true in the research and interviews we conducted as well. As Christians, we must reach out in friendship to unchurched individuals around us and find ways to build trust in all arenas of life. It is important to also ask about and connect with the spiritual part of their lives, intentionally affirming what we can along the way. Paul models this "build trust first and then discover and affirm the spiritual story of the other" model beautifully in a city called Athens. He went into a Greek pagan world, not all that dissimilar from our postmodern, spiritually and morally eclectic world, and he discovered receptivity and exerted spiritual influence. Here's the gist of what Paul did when he entered Athens to speak to people not dissimilar from the people in our day. His experience is recorded in Acts 17.[25]

First, Paul connects to and affirms the Athenians' culture, and he uses their language and methods of communication where he can. He spoke in the Areopagus, as did others who wanted to discuss new ideas. He used ancient rhetorical patterns of communication and incorporated examples from their own context.

[Handwritten margin note: Finding these can be hard, but I must!]

Here is that first step toward spiritual influence in the lives of others—building <u>trust based on common interests, convictions, and values.</u>

Second, Paul discerns and affirms their spiritual interest and search. He chooses to like them and share that he likes them. He <u>affirms what</u> he <u>can</u> and builds on common ground. He proposes to answer a question that they have already been asking: Who is the unknown god to whom they have dedicated an altar and who is above and beyond all the other gods?

[Handwritten margin note: not everything but what is good there but what does paul point out and celebrate]

This second step is huge for most millennials, nones, and nominals today. <u>Until you "get them" and accept where they start spiritually, you will never become an influencer.</u> The two top qualities they're looking for in us as spiritual conversation partners are that we "<u>listen without judgment</u>" and that we "do <u>not force the conversation to a conclusion.</u>" That is where we need to begin with people in order to build trust and deepen interaction into influence.[26]

Here is where we start to wade into the deeper waters of the particular challenges we face in our American context. People in the United States "choose our religion" to echo the title of Elizabeth Drescher's book about nones. One might even say that we go further than choosing our religion. We create it, picking and choosing among the various ideas we encounter, and the feelings and experiences we have. Morality comes from our own inner sense of right and wrong. And God can certainly be a convenient and enriching addition to life, but only one factor among many. Underlying this approach to creating our own religion is an assumption in American culture that is as unquestioned as it is problematic. The <u>self is sovereign.</u> <u>We all have a god complex.</u>[27]

At the heart of biblical Christian faith is the recognition that <u>God is God and that we are not.</u> This transition in what we worship, from self at the center to God at the center, is the critical transition each of us must make . . . <u>again and again.</u>

[Handwritten note at bottom: True, so true ✓]

Of course, how we make the conversational and relational transition from accepting people and communicating that we "get them" into providing a pointed challenge to the way we all tend to have a god complex is not easy. I would suggest we make the transition through confession rather than through pronouncement. As we share our struggles with ways we replace God with other people, things, and ultimately ourselves, we can raise the question about whether they can relate. Most people will. And particularly in times of crisis and dissonance when whatever people have put at the center disappoints and fails, people become more open to change, reorientation, and conversion.

So in this passage, Paul challenges the idols of wood and stone the Athenians had put in the place of God. We in twenty-first century America need to be challenged on the idol of autonomous and sovereign self with which we have replaced God. Elsewhere Paul makes it clear that this transition in allegiance and worship is at the heart of Christian conversion and is the source of Christian transformation: "If you confess with your mouth that Jesus is Lord and believe in your heart that God raised him from the dead, you will be saved" (Romans 10:9 NLT).

When this posture of accepting and "getting" people that are very different than we are spiritually is also very difficult for most practicing Christians, who find it hard to affirm the spiritual convictions of many people in our diverse subcultures today. Of course, it does not stop at blanket affirmation, as Paul's next step demonstrates.

yes!

Third, Paul challenges their misguided way of fulfilling their search and satisfying the hunger of their souls. He does so by quoting their own authorities and reasoning in a way that will make sense to his hearers. He at first aligns with their understanding of truth to the degree he can. They look to their own poets as authority figures, so Paul quotes their poets. They think logically and philosophically, so Paul reasons logically and philosophically. He gets them to admit what they already believe, and then, after confronting their inadequate

What truths are in modern culture that can point people to Christ?

answers, begins to share his own ideas. Paul deconstructs what they put their trust in using their own arguments, logic, and authority.

After building trust and communicating affirmation, this step is the key one toward spiritually influencing them to become open to change. Everts and Schaupp suggest this step of openness to change is the hardest, especially in a relativistic "whatever floats your boat" world. This step of deconstruction before reconstruction is one that Tim Keller talks about a lot in his work on reaching urban secular people today.[28] When we have successfully challenged people about whatever they have replaced God with, the fourth and final step of influence gets so much easier.

Last, Paul gives them some surprising evidence that supports his message and points to an unexpected way to fulfill their spiritual search—through Jesus. We know in the end it is always all about helping people we care about take their next step toward Jesus. But how do people who think they know what Jesus is about get a fresh start and take a next step? How do receptive people who would respond have the opportunity to do so? Here are the four steps we've identified:

1. Build trust based on common interests and values.

2. Affirm what you can of their spiritual beliefs and practices. People will not let you influence them until they feel like you "get" them and accept them.

3. Challenge whatever it is that has replaced God in their lives (also being quick to share about how often you have done the same).

4. Talk about what Jesus has done to heal and rescue and reorient you toward God, inviting them to take a next step toward Jesus.

The best way to begin in each of these steps is to first listen and affirm, and then engage through your authentic story of experiencing something similar. Paul does that all the time when he shares his initial resistance to Jesus and his unexpected turn, as recorded in Acts 9, for instance.

These steps can even help us with the most challenging issues we face in conversations and in cultivating receptivity. Three of the most difficult conversational challenges committed Christians can face today in relationships and spiritual conversations are:

1. How can we influence tolerant and relativistic people who distrust and reject any exclusive and absolute understanding of truth and morality?

2. How can we influence people committed to acceptance and affirmation of sexual and gender identities who distrust, dismiss, and feel rejected if we claim—as will many readers of this book—monogamy and heterosexual practice in the context of marriage as biblical norms?

3. How can we influence politically liberal people who value pro-choice, justice, and diversity politics far more than pro-life and religious freedom politics?

Undoubtedly, sometimes trust will break down and receptivity will diminish in conversations around fundamental disagreements such as these. These are not just superficial differences but fundamental questions about identity and who has the right to influence our sense of identity. In a polarized society such as ours, disagreements are sometimes unavoidable. But we can maximize our relational connection and influence by focusing on a conversational process that helps other people work through these kinds of issues at their pace and in ways that God leads them. In each case, we consider how we can build trust around common concerns, affirm everything we possibly can, challenge on the issue of what people replace God with, and then invite people to consider the person, ways, and truth of Jesus and take the next step toward Jesus.

I think of Sam, who pointedly asked me whether I am one of those people who thinks I am right and everyone else is wrong and that I have the only way to God. I responded, "I hate that kind of arrogance and self-righteousness, Sam. But I do think that the only way to God is through the grace and mercy and help of God. I can't do it on my own. Jesus is the God who climbs down the ladder to get me and bring me up, not a God who shows me the ladder I have to climb to get to God. That wouldn't help me. I needed Jesus. What would help you?"

I think of my gay friend Cliff, who asked me what I believe about gays and lesbians. I responded, "I love you, Cliff! And my question to you is always the same, 'Will you let Jesus be the voice to tell you who you are?'"

And I think of my friend Beatrice, who asked me how I can identify with a group like American evangelicals, who seem to reject immigrants, express racist attitudes, and oppose the leadership and giftedness of women. I responded, "You know me, Bea. And you know my mom, who helped form my profound valuation of women. You know the family I grew up in and that I hate racism, long for women to flourish in leadership and in their giftedness, and feel that hospitality to the stranger and immigrant is a deeply biblical value. I also love life, including the life of the unborn, and believe in the importance of religious freedom. Personally, I doubt seriously that Jesus, were he living on earth today, would find it easy to be an elephant or a donkey. They are both partly right and partly misguided. We need a third way beyond the polarizing anger that is dividing our nation. I deeply believe Jesus is helpful in finding that third way."

Trust. Affirmation. Challenge. Invitation. These are four simple steps you can take to become a spiritual influencer and discover the receptivity of others all around you. These steps will also help you avoid the conversation mines that lie close to the surface in our nation today, ready to blow up relationships and spiritual communication and progress. It doesn't mean the mines will not go off sometimes, but at least not as often and not unnecessarily. Many receptive people will respond to a simple, respectful, open-hearted conversational approach. What's more, so will many people who are initially unreceptive. God is at work in the hearts of all, and he loves to work through us in the process, as we can see in Rajiv's story.

Rajiv was of Hindu background, but nominally and not devoutly so. He met my son in the emergency room. Both struggle with mental health issues. My son Steve had found Christ through a great entry-point ministry for seekers called Alpha. Steve had a heart for Rajiv, even in the midst of the struggles that had led him and Rajiv to meet first in the emergency room and then on a hospital ward that they occupied together for a week to stabilize and recover. Rajiv would have said he was not receptive to Christian faith at that point in his life. Though Hindu in background, he was an atheist. But Steve cared for Rajiv, asked him how he was doing, and offered to pray for him. In Rajiv's time of need, he accepted. Steve prayed a number of times for him during their stay, and he always communicated care and interest in Rajiv.

I ran into Rajiv a year later at a Christian conference. When he got out of the hospital, he had become receptive to faith, partly through the prayers of Steve. Then another friend began to engage Rajiv in spiritual conversations, affirmed him, challenged him, and then invited him to a congregation. Rajiv responded to those conversations, has committed his life to Christ, and has become a very winsome and thoughtful advocate for Christ and his own congregation. As he listened to me talk at this conference about all the receptive people in our culture, he raised his hand and said quite boldly, "Don't forget, God is at work and can reach the unreceptive too!" And then he came and told me his story. Paul's process had worked with Rajiv, an initially very unreceptive person.

People who are unreceptive can become receptive as we build trust and affirm their journey. Investing in trust on the front end will help cultivate influence with many unreceptive people, who can often become receptive, embrace faith, commit to Christ and to a congregation, and become advocates to others. After all, the Christian movement has always grown in these ways, whether the culture seemed receptive or unreceptive. What was key is that the church had missional imagination to see a harvest and took the steps to build trust, affirm what they could in the spiritual search of others, challenge them on what they had replaced God with in their lives, and pointe to Jesus to bring restoration, healing, and direction. As we live our faith, share our lives, love the people around us, and keep on the lookout for opportunities to help people take the next step toward Jesus, we can make a difference and have an influence.

Questions for Discussion

1. Millennials are people born between 1981 and 1996. What challenges have you faced as a millennial, or as you have tried to understand and connect to millennials about Christian faith? What thoughts did you have as you read this chapter that might help you take those relationships and conversations the next step?

2. Nones are people with no religious affiliation. They include atheists, agnostics, and "nothing in particulars." Many might say they are "spiritual but not religious." What challenges have you faced as you have engaged nones in conversations about spirituality and faith? What is a next step you could take that might help you move forward in those relationships and conversations?

3. Rick gives a four-step conversational model taken from Acts that includes building trust with people based on common ground, asking about and affirming everything spiritually you can about them, beginning to challenge whatever it is that they have replaced God with in their lives, and then sharing the healing and reorienting experiences you have had with Jesus. Which of the four steps comes easiest to you, and where do you most need to grow?

4. How do you respond to people who have some of the concerns Rick mentions in his list of three key conversational challenges today?

5

Exploring the Conversion
Community Equation

During the 1990s I was an outreach and discipleship pastor for an Anglican church that was approaching one thousand members. A number of us went to a large conference hosted by a church that had become successful at reaching irreligious people. We sat in a large auditorium, watched outstanding dramas and world-class videos that moved us and set us up to relate to the message that would be preached. We also enjoyed the inspirational worship band, led by very charismatic, cool leaders who wore color-coordinated clothing. Then we listened to messages that motivated us to move heaven and earth to reach the irreligious, people far from God, and we would help them become fully devoted followers of Jesus. Who wouldn't want to do that? Heading home, I was inspired with countless ways to change our ministry. I started using videos in my outreach and Sunday worship service opportunities. I developed a drama team and recruited a director. In no time we were off to the races.

Not long after that I ran into some problems. For one, I was already too overloaded with the rest of my job to actually give the time needed to develop the new initiatives. Even as I was inspired with new and innovative opportunities for our church to explore, inspiring ideas of new things to do didn't magically eliminate all the responsibilities and relationships I already had. Second, our Anglican-style church just wasn't ready for the videos and dramas. For a congregation whose worship had only just entered the twentieth century, the marvels of the twenty-first were far too alien. Third, orienting our service for seekers and skeptics proved to be no silver bullet. Not only were our resources for these practices already overstretched, but the motivation necessary to achieve and sustain success in the long term was far more difficult to draw out than advertised. It was a mini disaster. Not only did many of the initiatives flounder, but the failure made us feel inadequate or insufficient in contrast to those at the conference.

Yet the truth is that we were not alone. Many churches like ours, without adequate skills, ethos, and resources, tried to adopt this model and failed. More than simply not being a silver bullet, the process was not one size fits all. We needed a process that fit our church, culture, and philosophy. We did not need research that proscribed tailor-made practices but rather research that helped us understand the unchurched and how our specific community could respond. Needless to say, I had a good heart and good intentions but took some wrong turns on the way to good goals.

Many of us face similar struggles when it comes to adopting an approach to mission and evangelism. We don't have the bandwidth to add anything new, certainly not something that takes considerable energy, time, and people to accomplish. We are already in ministry overload. I think of my friend Ron, an effective evangelist and the teaching pastor at a large church. Ron leads his team in generating a culture of mission and evangelism while also navigating the challenges of a multisite ministry at his church. He could not be more motivated than he already is to reach irreligious Americans and to help them stick and become disciples. But the number of priorities he has, and the demands of his church and his congregation to attend meetings and to care for the people already there, are overwhelming. He is in ministry overload. To tell him that he needs to add ten more hours of things to his week so his church can become a community experiencing more growth through reaching unchurched people will go nowhere. He has the heart but not the margin.

Most concerningly, as a result of our lack of margin many of us risk falling victim to mission drift in our ministry. With the term *mission drift*, I'm building on the research by missiologists Steve Beirn and George Murray in *Well Sent: Reimagining the Church's Missionary-Sending Process*. Beirn and Murray argue that mission drift involves "wandering from the original purpose [of the ministry] and eventually replacing the purpose." In essence, it is letting some other goal or objective become the mission.[1]

I saw this problem explained most clearly by one of the pastors in our cohorts. Harry, an African American pastor in an urban multiethnic context, has always wanted to reach unchurched and irreligious people. Always. It has been a passion for him and was a big part of the reason he went into ministry. At the first meeting of the pastor cohort I was leading, Pastor Harry realized his church activities and demands had swallowed him whole. Spread too thin, Pastor Harry had lost passion and practice for what was originally his primary mission: reaching the people all around him who didn't know Jesus yet. How many of us could say the same thing? We didn't mean to, but we slipped or were sucked into mission drift. His story has a happy ending, but will ours?

As we are carried along, we often realize something crucial is missing. Originally so confident in our mission, we reach the point where that clarity and direction are obscured. The easy questions about what we and the church are supposed to be doing are buried under a weight of responsibilities and busywork. The mission has become about us and not about the world and people in need. So we look for a solution. But, like I did, we look to the latest success story, the newest model, the latest book by a successful pastor. In all of these we dream about what we wish our church could look like, and we latch on to the simplicity of a silver bullet—a single, magical, mythical method that can turn it all around and lead us to the promised land of success, impact, and conversion growth.

Guess what? It doesn't exist. Not only will you not find it in this book, you won't find it in any book, in any one church, or in any pastor. But we still try. Every year some churches succeed wildly, and they publish and purvey new models, methods, and "movements." Or a particularly gifted communicator arises and makes it all sound so easy and obvious. The end result is that we jump on the bandwagon for a while but in the end are left empty and far short of our goal, looking for the next silver bullet. Gradually, cynicism can set in, and we also lose our ability to get our people to believe that what we promise and envision will ever actually happen.

My latest experience with this "fad and then fade" phenomenon is the recent focus on missional communities. I was working with a large megachurch in another part of the country that sold out to the missional-community strategy. Every leader in the church had to be in a missional community. These missional communities, often led by people who formerly had led small groups, all had to have an outreach strategy. They had to focus on connecting with one another for community in order to help everyone be missionaries where they lived, worked, studied, and played.

I loved the vision and the values, but the church had oversold missional communities as some fix-all for everything wrong with the church. Its leaders promised that if they just did *this*, all the other problems would be solved. Unsurprisingly, as the leaders tired themselves out trying to maintain the momentum and hype, the effort stalled, and people reverted back to type. Soon groups were being led by pastoral-type people more than outreach-type people, and inevitably the whole thing ran out of gas. Leaders went back to the small groups they used to have and mostly never really left, but they now had fewer small groups because of the fallout. The people who had jumped into the missional-community vision were now a little burned out and not particularly interested in acting on the next great idea that might come along.

To sum up, we are so busy, we have so many priorities, we are overwhelmed by our options, and we are steeped in a culture that markets the latest fad as a silver bullet for all our problems. All this, and yet we often remain unsuccessful at reaching out to the unchurched. This often leaves us at a loss. Where do we even begin? What if we could pursue a more fundamental and principled approach, an approach that worked across all different sizes and types of churches and that was reproducible by the average pastor and everyday leaders in a church?

Our research has *not* given us a silver bullet but rather a simple equation to pursue for the long haul. Our research shows that churches successfully pursuing this simple equation or process are getting better at growing through reaching unchurched people and are having a greater impact on their community.

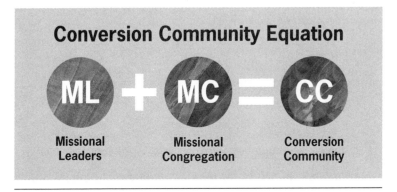

Figure 5.1. Conversion community equation

Missional leaders plus a missional congregation leads to becoming a conversion community.

Missional leaders are leaders in the church who model personal outreach. They build friendships, initiate spiritual conversations, share their faith when they have opportunity, and invite people into Christian community when the time is right. But missional leaders not only model personal evangelism; they also model integrating an evangelistic concern into the ministries they lead. They do this by encouraging their leaders to personally reach out but also by helping the ministries they lead to become more hospitable to irreligious people, which leads us to the second part of the equation.

A missional congregation is a congregation that cares about irreligious and unchurched people by building relationships outside the four walls of the church and by being invitational and hospitable, very intentionally, to irreligious and unchurched people whenever they connect to the congregation. A missional congregation does not just have a few leaders who are reaching out but many leaders and participants who together create an entire congregational culture that engages with people outside the church, brings people into the church, and extends spectacular hospitality when they visit. Such congregations have a DNA of extension, invitation, and hospitality. Whether you visit the weekly worship service, a regular ministry of the church such as the ministry for high school students or kids, or a compassion outreach of the church into the community, this engaged, invitational, and hospitable culture characterizes the congregation as a whole.

How do I define a conversion community?[2] A conversion community is a congregation that demonstrates three main qualities:

1. The congregation is growing (at least 5 percent per year).

2. Unchurched people are coming to the church, committing to Christ, and staying (at least 10 percent of the attendance

each year consists of people who committed to Christ that year and stayed).

3. Outreach and witness are integrated into every ministry and priority the church has.

The end result is that these churches attract people whose lives change and who become winsome witnesses and advocates for Christ and their congregations.

That equation and these terms sum up the findings of our national research with forty-five hundred churches.

That equation sums up our interviews of fifty-seven pastors at top-10-percent conversion-growth churches and what those pastors are doing that is resulting in growth through the conversion and retention of unchurched and irreligious people.

That equation sums up our interviews with forty-one previously unchurched people who had been nones (nothing in particular), dones (had regularly attended a church in the past but were done with it), and drifters (people who had just drifted away from a congregation because of life changes or life circumstances).

That equation also sums up our approach in our cohorts with pastors. We have seen it work in churches that have adopted the equation and pursued the process: small and large churches, denominational and nondenominational churches, urban and suburban and rural churches, churches with pastors who are powerful preachers and charismatic leaders and churches with pastors who aren't.

So this definition comes from our research across the country and characterizes what the top-10-percent conversion-growth churches in the country are doing right. This approach does not prioritize some silver bullet. Rather, it values a process of moving toward a way of congregational life that becomes the norm over time and through change.

One of our research projects in particular was helpful in the formation of this equation. In our surveys of the senior pastors of fifteen hundred churches, we were able to identify the top ten factors that _predicted_ conversion growth. Notice I say _predicted_. These patterns were not just present; they were predictive of conversion growth. It is pure gold in research when you find causes and not just correlations. Correlations give you things that are present at the same time that the results you want are present. But they may or may not be causing the results. Predictive factors are _causes_. When you find those, you are hot on the trail of what can actually bring the change you are looking for. You find predictive factors through a statistical methodology called regression analysis. Through regression analysis, our team was able to look at the impact of each individual factor below in changing the outcomes related to conversion growth.

Here then are the top ten predictive factors of conversion growth:

1. Church invites, includes, and involves the unchurched
2. Leader regularly teaches a next-steps class
3. Leader regularly attends evangelism training (e.g., missional pastor cohorts)
4. Leader regularly personally invites people to Christ
5. Church puts its money where its mouth is, into outreach
6. People (not just the pastors or professionals) are reaching out
7. Leader translates the regular message to unchurched people and their lives
8. Church ministry engages the community
9. Church culture attracts transfers as well as unchurched people
10. Leader blocks out time in the calendar to personally reach out

That's a lot to take in in one read! But notice what happens when you break that down into our equation.

In terms of developing missional leaders (ML),

- The leader blocks out time in the schedule to reach out intentionally every week outside church activities and the church office. The leader is living it, so the leader can lead it (number 10).

- People are reaching out. The pastor is hearing stories of people building relationships and sharing their faith. This factor is more predictive than that the pastor reaches out. But people won't reach out unless the pastor does so first (number 6).

- The lead pastor regularly invites people personally to commit to Christ. The pastor does not just accept people where they are but also demonstrates a heart to see people commit fully to Christ (number 4).

- The lead pastor receives outreach training and inspiration through a conference or event at least annually. The pastor stays fresh and fired up and passes that on (number 3).

In terms of developing a missional congregation (MC),

- The church grows through transfer *and* conversion growth. Churches that are engaged, invitational, hospitable, and welcoming grow, period (number 9).

- Churches engage their communities in compassion and ministry, and they share their faith through those experiences (number 8).

- The lead communicator translates the regular weekly message for unchurched visitors. The service does not need to be aimed at unchurched and irreligious people. But irreligious people need to feel like they are included and addressed (number 7).

- The church puts its money where its mouth is, including into local evangelism. In a major case study we did, we found that culture change that was significant, consistent, and sustainable only began when the organization generated a funded, strategic plan for conversion growth and pursued it over a ten-year period (number 5).

- The leader regularly teaches a next-steps class so that visitors have an easy, quick way into the next stage of involvement and commitment (number 2).

- The unchurched show up and stick much more often. Why? Both our quantitative-survey research and our qualitative-interview research showed that these churches really know how to invite, include, and connect unchurched people to the congregation (number 1).

Note that, ultimately, the missional community (MC) part of this equation is even more important than the missional leader part of this equation. Six of the factors, including the top two, are missional community factors, and four are missional leader factors. In the end, it is the culture of the congregation that trumps everything. Culture eats strategy for breakfast, as one of my favorite leadership gurus is credited with saying.[3] This means that you can adopt whatever method or strategy you want, but at the end of the day you have to change your culture into a culture of outreach, invitation, and hospitality if you want to grow through reaching unchurched and irreligious people and so become a conversion community. That is why we work in our pastor cohorts on a culture-change process and not just a program-addition process. And it is why we tell our pastors that it will take three to five years to get to the DNA we are pursuing. Though the missional community part of the equation is more telling, to get there through successful culture change means you need leaders who can be the change you are seeking. That is why we begin with the missional leader part of the equation.

Where does missional imagination, our focus of part one, fit into this equation? Missional imagination is the environment in which missional leaders and a missional congregation grow into becoming conversion communities. As we keep being reenchanted by the mission of Jesus and see the ripeness and receptivity of the harvest, we will have a new narrative that will drive us forward with faith, optimism, and hope. As we hope, so we act. As we act, the truth of the new narrative will be backed up by results as God blesses. Conversion communities pick up momentum as they move forward, guided by hope and seeing conversions. They prove the new narrative.

So a good final picture of the conversion community equation might look like this:

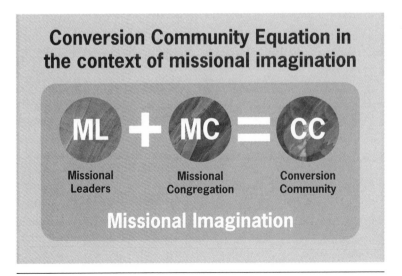

Figure 5.2. Conversion community equation in the context of missional imagination

Our top-10-percent conversion-growth churches model this equation and have become conversion communities, such as Centro Cristiano Emanuel.[4] Located in an urban Hispanic community in a larger metropolis in Massachusetts, Centro Cristiano Emanuel has both Spanish-speaking and English-speaking congregations. The church was founded in 1997 by the father of the present pastor, Pastor Chacon, and had grown to a multisite church with a mix of ethnic groups in several parts of urban Boston.

The church cares about the unique social and emotional needs of both of the congregations. It is also a conversion community. In 2016, with twelve hundred total attenders, the church grew significantly and saw 250 people make first-time commitments to Christ.

This culture of outreach is part of the DNA of the church. Pastor Chacon reaches out personally to neighbors and friends wherever he can. He invites people to commit to Christ every weekend, but not just in church services. What is more striking is that his people reach out and invite friends to check the church out. They are excited. To them evangelism is not primarily a program. It is a way of life and of being the people of God in Boston. They follow up with every person who commits. So they not only reach people but they also retain those new believers and help them become excited advocates for the church and the gospel.

The church is their family, but it is not an ingrown family. The people in the congregation are warm, welcoming, and friendly to every outsider who visits. This congregation typifies the engaged, invitational, and a little over-the-top hospitable culture that top-10-percent conversion-growth churches across the country demonstrate. Of course, engagement, invitation, and hospitality need to fit the cultural context. We are not all called to be warmly and expressively Hispanic. But whatever it looks like in our context, this church has it.

The pastor preaches for the Christians in the church, and his sermons are biblical and challenging and substantive, but he knows how to make sure to include applications and comments for unchurched and irreligious people who visit. He practices hospitality in his preaching to the outsider.

Pastor Chacon remembers a couple, Hector and Eliza, who started to inch their way into the church. Their son had taken his own life, and depression had settled around the couple like a blanket. Eliza was invited by one of her friends to a service focused on learning to handle the losses in our lives. She went and kept going. Hector dropped her off every week but never came in. He had experienced a judgmental congregation growing up and felt alienated from church. But his wife began to change, to grow more at peace with her life and her losses. Finally, he got up the courage and curiosity to cross the threshold and visit the church with his wife.

People welcomed him, loved that he was there, and told him how much they appreciated his wife. He started to feel at home. Later, when he gave his life to Christ, he joined a cell group and began to grow. Today Hector leads seven cell groups, and many people have come to Christ and the church through his ministry.

No wonder this church has grown to twelve hundred attendees and every year about 15 percent of them come to Christ and stick. The church has now planted seven campuses and is even starting to become a conversion movement. A conversion movement is when conversion growth spreads beyond the initial church to other churches, so that conversion communities are starting to multiply. I will explore the dynamics of becoming a conversion movement in chapter twelve.

Of course this church, like any church, has problems, weaknesses, and challenges. But you can bet the people who are there love the energy, the vibrancy, the joy of being part of a conversion community where freshly redeemed people are constantly contributing and growing, then turning around and reproducing, engaging, and serving unchurched people and the needs of their local community. As a result, they are inviting their friends in large numbers.

Pursue that over the next several years, and your church too will begin to be a conversion community like Centro Cristiano Emanuel. When churches embrace the new narrative about the unchurched that I shared in the last two chapters, and when they then reach out in effective and vibrant ways to connect to unchurched people and to serve their communities, their churches experience conversion growth at a higher rate. The primary problem we face is not the shifting culture or unreceptive people. The primary obstacle is the quality and focus of our life together as the church. Your church could become a conversion community too as God blesses!

For those of you who hear this story and notice that Emanuel had evangelistic DNA right from the start, and you then think your church doesn't, have no fear. We will also explore all along the way how to lead change in your church culture, develop new DNA, and revitalize your congregation through mission. Developing missional leaders and then a missional congregation will be the focus of the following chapters, with a constant refrain in the forefront: when the church is the church, the gates of hell, shifting cultures, and apathetic people cannot hold it back!

Questions for Discussion

1. Has your congregation ever tried to reach out and felt like you failed? What happened, and what was the impact on your willingness to try other ideas?

2. Of the top ten predictive characteristics listed for conversion communities, where are you strong, and where could you grow?

Part 2

Developing Missional
Leaders

6

Modeling Outreach
Others Can Imitate

Many churches have people to fill the ministry roles needed but don't have reproducing leaders who are reaching people, who then get excited about their new faith and their new congregation and turn around and reach others. Our leaders are not leading people to faith, and when they bring new people into congregations, it seems to be the exception rather than the norm. Instead of looking outward, we often spend our energy and attention on those of us who are already in church. This was certainly the case at Colby's church.

Colby is pastor of outreach and missions at his five-hundred-member church in a small city in northern Illinois. When he started, he wanted to know whether his church was influencing his community. He wanted to know whether his leaders were missional where they live, work, play, and in this case eat. So he started visiting the different restaurants right around where the church was located, and the breakfast-and-lunch restaurant right across the street from the church was his first stop. Many of the pastors and people at the church often met at this neighborhood diner. When Colby had lunch there during his first week at the church, he engaged a waitress and the manager in conversation, asking them how long they had been working there. The waitress had been there five years, and the manager had been there ten. As the conversation continued, Colby asked whether they had ever heard of Heartland Church or met anybody from that church. "Don't think so," they both responded. Colby politely pressed a little further, asking them whether any Christians had been kind to them, or shared an encouraging faith story with them, or prayed for them. "Not that I recall" was again the identical response.

Colby then pointed out the church, which could be seen through the front window of the restaurant. The waitress commented, "Oh, that's a church? I wondered." The manager was a little more enterprising. He handed Colby his card and encouraged Colby to let people over there know about their fine restaurant and their great lunch specials. He even told Colby about his passion for the restaurant and his desire to serve people well. Basically, Colby left thinking that he had heard more "good news" (about the restaurant) than any person in the restaurant had ever heard about the faith or the church from the church people right across the street.

Colby discovered that people and pastors from the church had met there hundreds of times but had not effectively reached out in that context. Colby longed to see his church come alive and develop reproducers. But as he looked around at the leaders with whom he was starting to work, few had shared their faith story or served their local community. He needed to develop missional leaders who could become reproducers where they live, work, study, and play.

Contrast that with my friend Lon, who is a pastor of a Bible church in a western suburb of Chicago. Lon takes every opportunity he can to meet people at the restaurant across from his church. He has prayed for a number of the waitresses and invited several to visit his church.

Whenever he shows up at the restaurant, he is always greeted with big smiles, partially because he tips very well!

I was with him recently, and one waitress immediately responded to his offer for prayer. She was having surgery in a couple of weeks and said she would deeply appreciate our prayers for her and for her family. I was inspired as I watched this interaction, as were the couple of church leaders who were with me at this lunch meeting. Not only did we pray right then for her, but we also thought about our own opportunities and the ways we could extend simple kindness and courtesy in conversation to the people in our lives who served us in various ways. We could see ourselves asking the same question Lon asked. Lon and his church are very well known at this restaurant, and people have often heard good news about the congregation and about the faith.

Leading by Example

How then can we restore a missional and evangelistic edge to people and churches that are inwardly oriented? A lot is riding on the answer to that question, but it can feel overwhelming and beyond our ability to bring about this kind of fundamental change. Is there anything we can really do?

The good news is that many churches are living out that outward orientation and expressing missional and outreach edge. We can learn from their best practices. So let's turn to the research to see how we can either grow more outreach oriented and missional or increase our focus on mission if we already are effectively reaching out.

Figure 6.1 shows us that pastors of top-10-percent conversion-growth churches are engaged in personal relationships and spiritual conversations. The first step in helping your congregation develop missional leaders is to *be* one yourself. It is very hard to lead what you are not living. The first step in becoming an evangelistic and missional church is to have a missional senior leader.

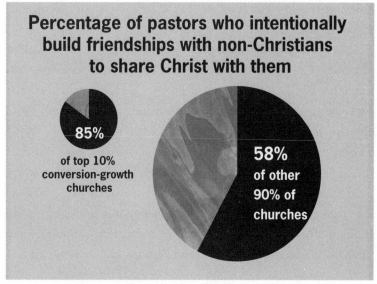

Percentage of pastors who intentionally build friendships with non-Christians to share Christ with them

85%

of top 10%
conversion-growth
churches

58%
of other
90% of
churches

Source: Billy Graham Center Institute and Lifeway Research, Evangelism Survey of three thousand Protestant Churches. For more information on this study, refer to appendix 2, part C.

Figure 6.1. Percentage of pastors who intentionally build friendships with non-Christians to share Christ with them: top-10-percent conversion-growth churches compared to the other 90 percent of all Protestant churches

But here is where we face the first significant barrier. It is harder to be a reproducing missional senior leader of a congregation than it looks. Here is one reason why. Pastors can be hard for their people to imitate when it comes to outreach. Pastors tend to pursue a lot of outreach opportunities that their people could never reproduce. Pastors baptize babies or adults, depending on the tradition. Many unchurched friends and family members show up, and pastors get to share their faith story and perspective, but the people in their congregations don't have that same opportunity. Pastors get to preach at the regular worship services to the unchurched people their people bring along. Pastors get asked to pray at family gatherings and sometimes even at secular events in the community. The bottom line is that pastors often practice types of outreach that their people could never imitate. However, many pastors in our interviews of top-10-percent conversion-growth churches went beyond these pastor-only opportunities and showed us a very different pattern. They practiced outreach that their people could imitate—and it made a huge impact. Their people caught their enthusiasm and then could reproduce their actions.

Harvey became the pastor of a small, struggling church and decided to lead his congregation to focus outward by focusing outward himself first.[1] So instead of asking his church members to reach out and invite people, Harvey simply began reaching out and inviting people himself. Then he began to take a few others along. One night Harvey went with a few men from his church to Starbucks, and over the course of the evening, he struck up conversations with Starbucks patrons. Several of the conversations went in a spiritual direction. Harvey even had someone end up committing his life to Christ. This experience left a lasting mark on the men who had come along, and they were so inspired that they started reaching out more and inviting people themselves. Harvey explained, "It wasn't something that I had to teach them or preach [to] them. It was something that I showed them is normal, that this is what we should be doing." Though it may be unusual to see a one-time conversation turn into a person who commits their life to God on the spot, just modeling good relationships and good spiritual conversations in everyday contexts can have a big impact on the people who are with you or those you share the story with later.

Harvey, a bivocational pastor, also works at an insurance agency with many atheists and other unchurched coworkers. During the summers his coworkers all do triathlons, and for the past three summers Harvey has joined them in training for the triathlons and has invested in these relationships. His faith and his love are evident to his coworkers, so much so that this past year his boss introduced him as the agency chaplain and even had him pray for different needs that were expressed. Because of Harvey's example, many of his church members have followed suit and have begun reaching out in their own spheres of influence.

The Impact of Church Size

Harvey is the pastor of a small congregation who prioritized making time to connect relationally with unchurched people. Our study of fifteen hundred small churches clearly demonstrates the importance of personal evangelism by the lead pastor. You will notice from here on that whenever I graph the results of the small church study with fifteen hundred churches, I use top 20 percent versus bottom 50 percent because of the sample size needed to picture statistically significant results. Figure 6.2 illustrates the difference between top-20-percent churches, which are growing, and bottom-50-percent churches, which are declining.

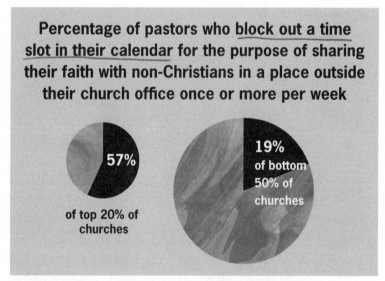

Source: Billy Graham Center Institute and Lifeway Research, Small Church Evangelism Study. We used top 22 percent and bottom 50 percent in this research study because of sample size. For more information on this study, refer to appendix 2, part E.

Figure 6.2. Percentage of pastors who block out a time slot in their calendar for the purpose of sharing their faith with non-Christians in a place outside their church office once or more per week: top-20-percent churches compared to bottom 50 percent

The difference is striking. Three times as many top-20-percent church pastors set aside time weekly for reaching out beyond the church and sharing their faith. Committing to intentional personal weekly outreach is a marker of pastors leading churches that are growing through conversion. They model outreach their people can imitate, and then their people do. Leaders in the church catch it from the pastor and then model it for the people they lead, cascading outreach passion and practice throughout the church.

We have seen how this commitment to integrate outreach into the normal rhythms of life is important for pastors of small churches, and the same is true for those leading larger churches. In our study of the top-10-percent conversion-growth churches, we realized that this priority of personal evangelism actually increased for pastors as church size increased.

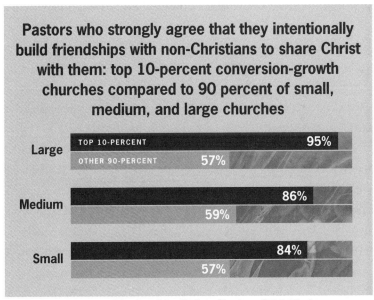

Pastors who strongly agree that they intentionally build friendships with non-Christians to share Christ with them: top 10-percent conversion-growth churches compared to 90 percent of small, medium, and large churches

	TOP 10-PERCENT	OTHER 90-PERCENT
Large	95%	57%
Medium	86%	59%
Small	84%	57%

Source: Billy Graham Center Institute and Lifeway Research, Evangelism Survey of three thousand Protestant Churches

Figure 6.3. Pastors who strongly agree that they intentionally build friendships with non-Christians to share Christ with them: top-10-percent conversion-growth churches compared to other 90 percent of small, medium, and large churches

In the top 10 percent of churches we studied in terms of conversion growth, the larger the church, the more time the pastor spends intentionally building friendships with irreligious people to share faith. One would think that larger churches would place even more institutional and internal demands on their top leader, but it turns out that senior pastors of larger churches can specialize more in a few things they do well, and they often have more power over how they use their time. Effective missional pastors and leaders <u>find a way to carve out the time</u> and <u>set the priority</u> to reach out to the unchurched <u>personally</u>. Thus they tend to model this personal intentional witness even more, which then has a very significant impact on the culture of the church and the lifestyle of the other leaders.

Someone who models this well is Dave Ferguson, who is the lead pastor of Community Christian Church in Naperville, Illinois. In addition to sharing his obsession with reproducing churches, Dave can also speak quite personally and authentically about being a missional and reproducing leader. He will often tell stories about a neighbor he is reaching out to or about how someone in the congregation who used to be irreligious has changed over time to become an apprentice leader in the church.

For years I have taken students to Community Christian Church to learn from Dave's example. As Dave shares these stories with my students, he sometimes waves his prayer diary in the air when he talks about it. One of my students asked whether he could read part of the diary, so Dave handed it to him, and the student was blown away by what he read. In the pages of the prayer diary, my student found a story about a young woman from Dave's neighborhood who had been irreligious but joined Dave's small group and was changed over time in profound ways. As influential as it was to read about this story of transformation, what was particularly powerful was seeing how many times Dave had prayed for this young woman along the way. It was amazing to see that Dave was actually living what he was leading. No wonder so many people have found their way back to God in the multisite church that Dave leads.

As a pastor of a large multisite church, his advice to other pastors of larger churches is that they pay the most attention to two opposite levels of their leadership. Invest in the top level of leadership: the people right around them who most influence the whole church or the multiple churches they oversee. And then invest at the most grassroots level of the church, reaching out personally to unchurched people, leading some kind of neighborhood group, and apprenticing people who are coming to Christ or who could multiply the group. These two levels are the most strategic investment senior leaders and leaders of the various ministries of larger churches can make.[2]

Moving Past Our Excuses

In light of the research, it is undeniable that the senior and ministry leaders' example in modeling witness for the broader congregation is crucial. Having worked with many pastors and leaders, though, I have often heard them say, "Yes, but."

"Yes, but I don't have time."

"Yes, but I am very tired after a long day with people from my church, and the last thing I want to do is talk to my neighbors. I need alone time, family time, and time to recharge."

"Yes, but I don't have natural ways to build friendships with people who don't know Christ. So I reach the ones my people bring me or the ones I get to reach when I do baptisms or funerals."

"Yes, but I need to mainly focus on my family when I am not doing my job."

"Yes, but my time is better spent strategically in other ways."

"Yes, but I am not gifted in evangelism. I am a teacher, pastor, or discipler. Not an evangelist!"

Kerry was a pastor in one of our cohorts who finally got honest enough to say he had a lot of "yes, but" statements going through his mind that were holding him back. He had six kids, who wanted his time. His wife also wanted his time and was very direct about his kids needing to be a priority for him. He had leadership responsibilities for a growing congregation of over one thousand people as well as regional responsibilities for supervising pastors of six or seven church plants. In addition to all this, he had a leadership role on the national leadership team for his denomination. He just could not squeeze in another commitment or priority.

In one of our cohort meetings, another senior leader of a church challenged Kerry. "If you can't reach out and reproduce, your people never will either. All your people have their own 'yes, buts'! If you can't solve yours, they will never solve theirs." We then spent about forty-five minutes talking about the challenge Kerry faced and making some simple suggestions about what he might do. Here are a few ideas we suggested to Kerry that you might find helpful as well:

- Maximize your two-fers, which are things you already need to do that could double up as an opportunity for outreach. These things could give you a two-for-one return on your investment of time because unchurched and irreligious people are involved already. For example, one way to do this could be to do your office work out in the community once a week. Janet decided to give it a try and started working once a week at a local coffee shop that had some character. It didn't take long before she began meeting people and having conversations. After a few months, she saw one of her new friends give her life to Christ. Now you will almost never find Janet in her office on that day of the week. She is hooked on the really good coffee, but even more on the opportunities to build relationships and have spiritual conversations with unchurched people.

- Do something you love with people who aren't connected to Christ or a congregation yet. You can either join something already happening, such as a golf league, or start something that isn't yet happening, such as a book club. Colby, from our first story in this chapter, joined a golf league and started another one in his neighborhood. He loves to golf, and he loves to share his faith story. He has had ample opportunity to do both, and the leaders in his congregation are catching on, starting and joining golf leagues, book clubs, and workout groups more and more often.

- Use painful experiences in your life to connect to other people who are not connected to Christ or a congregation to get their support and also to share your faith perspective. I have a son with mental health challenges and have joined support groups in the community a couple of times now. I was helped by hearing others share similar struggles and had the opportunity to explain how my faith had been a help to me in the process. I also shared how my son had come to Christ during his initial diagnosis, and as a result several of the people in the support group began to consider how they might connect their struggling children to a good church and to faith. Suffering becomes redemptive when it helps us connect with others, share in our mutual pain, receive encouragement from them, and encourage others in our turn.

- Look for opportunities both to serve others and to ask for help from people in your neighborhood. Although people typically tend toward the first option, sometimes the second option is even better. Several years ago Mary Kay and I asked our neighbors, a married couple we had met, to watch our pets while we were on vacation. They did a fantastic job and ended up going above and beyond. What I mean is that they gave our diabetic cat complicated medication every day for ten days. We had found out the cat was diabetic just before leaving for vacation and offered to let them decline the opportunity, but they took it anyway. To thank them, we took them out to a really nice restaurant and were delighted to discover that the spiritual conversation that began at that meal eventually resulted in our neighbors committing to Christ. They had helped us, which put them in the power position and built trust in a deeper way than if we had found a way to serve them first.

After exploring these suggestions, Kerry found a way to more intentionally integrate outreach into his life. He already attended soccer games once a week for one of his kids, so he decided to volunteer to help the coach during the games. In doing so he became more aware of and intentional about praying for opportunities to serve others and to share his faith. Over time he developed a friendship with the head coach, and Kerry saw him become open spiritually. Six months later, when Kerry invited the coach along to visit the church for a Christmas service, the coach gladly accepted the invitation. Meanwhile, the whole church had heard from Kerry about the coach and were praying. Several church members met him by the door to welcome him. He felt accepted and expected. Kerry had become a reproducer, and his people had caught the vision for outreach.

Few victories are more sweet or more influential in turning a church outward. The good news is that it does not take lots of extra time or a radical change in priorities to grow in being a missional leader. The main things it requires are an increased awareness of the opportunities that already exist in the normal rhythms of your life and a renewed commitment to intentionally make the most of those opportunities. Depending on your current habits, it may also require a willingness to put yourself into new contexts in the broader community, where relationships with unchurched people can develop naturally. However, no matter where you're starting from, none of these adjustments is insurmountable. It is possible to integrate outreach into our lives, no matter how busy they are, and as we reach out to people in the community, we pave the way for others in our church to do so as well.

Prioritizing Evangelism

Some people understand the importance of modeling but get overwhelmed by the need to model everything. Pastors and leaders often tell me, "Every person or book that recommends changing my church culture in some way tells me it starts with the senior leader and other leaders prioritizing it in their own life. I just can't do that with everything."

In the midst of all the things vying for our time and attention, it's important to focus on the mission Jesus articulated. In a wonderful passage in Matthew, Jesus sums up the whole reason he came, his main growth strategy, and the kind of person he wants to develop as his follower: "'Come, follow me,' Jesus said, 'and I will send you out to fish for people.' At once they left their nets and followed him" (Mt 4:19-20).

Jesus makes disciples. The word *disciple* means learner, but not primarily in the sense of learning head knowledge. Instead the emphasis here is on learning a lifestyle. Perhaps a better word for *disciple* would be *apprentice*. All apprentices of Jesus are witnesses to him and to what he has done in their lives. It is hugely important for every leader to become an apprentice of Jesus who is a witness and then to make others into apprentices of Jesus who are also witnesses. In fact, Jesus does not make any other kind of disciple, and if it is that much of a priority for Jesus, it must be that much of a priority for our churches, our leaders, and ultimately each of us. Although we may not be evangelists, each one of us is a disciple and therefore also a witness.

Ministry leaders are first and foremost disciples themselves, and in light of that they are called by God to integrate witness into their lives. Brad is a great example of a pastor who struggled to prioritize evangelism but then discovered how powerful it is when leaders model outreach in a way that is accessible to everyone. Brad leads one of the campuses of a fairly effective and well-known outreach-oriented church. Over time the church had lost its missional edge, and most of the leaders were helping run a large and demanding organization and focusing on the needs of the people already there. Brad joined the cohort to make his church recover a lost fire and the vibrancy for outreach that had characterized it in its earlier days.

One of the key practices in the cohorts we facilitate through the Billy Graham Center is that we keep each other accountable. Every thirty days we get together and encourage each other, inspire each other, equip each other for witness, help solve the outreach problems and challenges our churches face, and share stories with each other of how we are modeling outreach that our people can imitate. Brad knew what we were after, but for seven months he consistently came with stories of doing outreach his people could never imitate. One month he talked about meeting somebody at the service and then having a great conversation in his office, ultimately leading that person to Christ. At a Christmas service he was really excited about a family one of his people had brought to the service with whom he got to speak afterward. In story after story, Brad just kept telling tales of his wonderful experiences that only pastors get to have.

With gentleness but clarity, all of us in the cohort kept encouraging Brad to take risks in his neighborhood and to join something where he would rub shoulders regularly with unchurched and irreligious people. Despite our encouragement, for seven months his only story of outreach that others could imitate was of a disaster he related to us at one cohort meeting. Without strong relationship building, Brad went over to his neighbors' house and invited them to the Christmas service. Without trust built, his neighbor was not too warm to the invitation. So a several-month period of awkwardness set in. The neighbors were as chilly as the weather. That was Brad's one story of practicing outreach that his people could imitate—but he realized he didn't actually want them to.

Finally Brad found a way to hang out with unchurched and irreligious people. He joined a health club and began to build trust, share about life, and sweat and detox together with others in the health-club community. Soon he had some stories to tell. He began sharing stories about building trust with people. When you sweat and suffer together, you can't help but feel connected!

Brad gradually got to know the other people in a class he was taking at his health club. Pretty soon he was sharing his faith story with others, and he ended up having a couple of significant spiritual conversations. Then he invited a few people to a church service, and one couple came. All of a sudden, Brad had stories to tell. He was now a witness his people could imitate, and he was so excited about it that he was electric. As a result, many people on his staff team followed his example, joined a health club, and started taking classes. Soon they were all sharing their stories and influencing people where they lived, worked, studied, and worked out.

Marcy, who was part of Brad's staff team, especially jumped in. She had been leading Alpha, an outreach program, but the only people who attended the events were people from her church who were already Christians and congregants. In response to Brad's stories, Marcy started building relationships with her neighbors, eating together with them, hanging out, and sharing life's ups and downs. Over time several of Marcy's neighbors began coming to Alpha. The feeling at that meeting was one of excitement and anticipation, and the Holy Spirit was very real to people. Marcy was now a missional leader, having caught the vision from her pastor. Suddenly programs could actually reach people, because there were missional leaders building relationships who could invite unchurched people to these programs, which had been intended for unchurched people but never worked before. Faith in that church community for reaching irreligious people began to rise.

As Brad began to build the priority of outreach into his life, he started to see the emergence and reproduction of missional leaders. This shift made a huge difference in the leadership culture of his church, and it began to affect the number of people coming to faith and coming to the congregation. His church was reclaiming lost ground and becoming a conversion community again. That shift toward becoming a conversion community is possible for every church, and it begins when the leaders model outreach that others can imitate.

Questions for Discussion

1. What are the biggest barriers to your own growth in practicing outreach others could imitate?

2. As you consider the ideas that cohort members gave Kerry to grow in practicing outreach others could imitate, including maximizing two-fers, doing things you love with people not yet connected to Christ or a congregation, using painful experiences you have had to connect with others not yet connected to Christ or a congregation, and looking for opportunities to help others and to get their help, what steps could you take to grow as a witness?

3. Who in your life could keep you accountable in the challenging area of growing in outreach? How might that work for you?

4. Consider using the resource titled "Developing a Prayer List" to develop a list of people you are praying for and want to reach out to in your life. See the Billy Graham Resources in appendix one for information on how to access this online resource.

Multiplying Missional Leaders

J ake is senior pastor of a wonderful biblical church and loves to reach out. He is always charging his people up to do the same. He leads people to Christ regularly. He is modeling outreach that other people can imitate. How do his people respond? For a long time, they cheered. They applauded him. They affirmed him for his evangelistic heart. Then almost none of them ever put their toe in the water of being a witness for Jesus themselves. Jake wanted missional leaders and missional people, but most of his people were the audience and not the actors. More on Jake's story to come.

Many church people can be like Jake's were. After all, people may think, we pay the pastor to do that sort of thing. That is one of the many responsibilities that comes with the role, one of the many hats the pastor needs to wear. Why else do we pay the pastor to be the professional?

But when we as the people in our churches make somebody else responsible for the outreach mission of the church, whether the senior pastor or other professionals, or the outreach committee, or a traveling evangelist, then the people in our lives who do not know Christ and are not connected to a congregation never will be. It is that simple.

Although church culture change must begin with the life of the senior leader, it cannot stop there. It has to go much further, into the lives of the other leaders and congregants in the church. That handoff is the critical one if any church is actually going to develop missional leaders and become a conversion community.

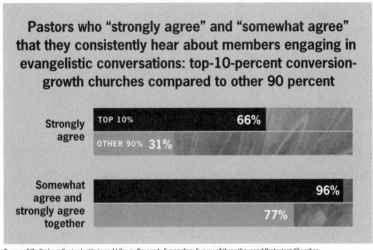

Pastors who "strongly agree" and "somewhat agree" that they consistently hear about members engaging in evangelistic conversations: top-10-percent conversion-growth churches compared to other 90 percent

Strongly agree
TOP 10%   66%
OTHER 90%   31%

Somewhat agree and strongly agree together
96%
77%

Source: Billy Graham Center Institute and Lifeway Research, Evangelism Survey of three thousand Protestant Churches

Figure 7.1. Pastors who "strongly agree" and "somewhat agree" that they consistently hear about members engaging in evangelistic conversations: top-10-percent conversion-growth churches compared to other 90 percent

As figure 7.1 shows, pastors of top-10-percent conversion-growth churches are more consistently hearing reports of their members engaging in evangelistic conversations. In fact, these pastors are twice as likely to strongly agree that they hear stories of other people in their church actively sharing their faith than the remaining 90 percent of churches. Churches that are effectively growing through conversion growth have found ways to activate their people to be witnesses wherever they live, work, play, or study.

We found this statistic in our survey of three thousand churches of every size, and we also found it in our survey of fifteen hundred churches with attendance of 250 or smaller. Both surveys highlighted this statistic as *predictive*, meaning that if the people of your church are sharing their faith and faith story regularly, your church is far more likely to become a conversion community. What's more, having multiple people in your church who are reaching out and sharing their faith is significantly more predictive than having an exceptionally evangelistic leader. In other words, senior leaders need to be modeling outreach if their people are ever going to be missional leaders and followers of Christ. However, our research shows that getting all our leaders and people throughout the church to become missional is the gold standard. That is when things really start to move forward, when people are reached and communities are influenced for good.

So how can you catalyze your people into vibrant and effective witness? By returning to Jake's story and taking a closer look at how he began to activate others toward outreach, we will discover key tools to help us multiply missional leaders in our own contexts.

Jake had been effectively reaching out to unchurched individuals in his life for years. He'd also been consistently sharing outreach stories with the members of his church, but despite his best efforts, his church members didn't seem to be mobilized toward outreach at all. In our cohort conversations about the research and stories from other pastors, Jake began to see his situation differently. He realized that his people saw him as an extrovert who was a great salesman for whatever he was excited about and therefore someone who was really good at evangelism. As a result, many of his people couldn't relate to him or imitate him.

Jake knew that he needed to change his approach, so he chose Colby to help champion evangelism in his church. Colby was a business-oriented, down-to-earth guy and the people in his church could identify with him. Colby already carried a passion for evangelism and loved using meals and celebrations to reach out. He gradually built relationships by hosting people in his backyard for burgers or barbecued pork or by inviting people to meals at local restaurants. He also loved playing golf, so he joined a golf league and began regularly connecting with other men in the community. He naturally shared his faith story as he cared for people, ate with them, and played golf with them.

Not long after that, Colby began sharing stories with the church about how he was reaching out to the community and the ups and downs he was experiencing along the way. The stories were told in a way that made everyone want to take somebody out to eat as well. Colby communicated so much enjoyment when he shared about his golf league that everybody wanted to join one, even people who hardly played golf. Reaching out to others with God's love sounded so fun and natural, and people began to believe that they could do it too. Colby was someone people felt like they could imitate, and they wanted to. Jake began to share some of the ways he struggled with outreach, and as he communicated his stories differently, people began to identify more with him as well.

Excitement began to grow as more and more people in the congregation started becoming missional and outreach oriented. Over time, many leaders and people in the church started sharing their faith stories with their unchurched friends, eating with them, and bringing them along to church. Along the way Colby practiced an informal but very intentional form of accountability as well. He asked his key leaders every time he met with them how their personal outreach was going, and he would share as well how it was going in his life. The culture of the church was shifting and had reached a tipping point. The biggest factor was that people now were taking risks, sharing faith, expressing love and excitement. They wanted to be like Colby, and as a result, they also became more like Jake. As witness became an increasingly integral part of their overall congregational life, the congregation started to look more like Jesus. The conversion-growth rate at the church began to go up and has done so for several years now.

The Impact of Imitation

As demonstrated in the research and in Jake's story, imitation is the key way people become more effective and engaged witnesses to what God has done in their lives. People need to see others with whom they can identify and then watch them live it out or hear stories that they can reproduce. Gradually, as they take steps to imitate the example put before them, they will begin to experience the power of practicing witness in their own lives. Pretty soon, you won't be able stop them. They will have caught the vision and are going to give it to others. Multiplication has begun.

This principle of imitation, reflected in our research, is also based on the science of mimetics.[1] *Mimetics* means imitative, as in mimicking others.[2] It is the science of how words, phrases, and behaviors get passed from one person to another or one group to another. Think about phrases or behaviors and how they spread. Those phrases, words, or actions we want to see spread to others are called *memes* in the science of mimetics. Like genes that pass on physical characteristics, memes pass on ideas and actions.[3]

Take a simple meme such as "Where's the beef?" a famous phrase on Wendy's commercials years ago.[4] What made it so memorable and spread it so widely? The commercial featured an unforgettable image of a tiny ninety-year-old woman driving away from a fast-food restaurant that had served up a little dollop of beef on a big bun. She was outraged from paying so much money for no beef, which left her asking, "Where's the beef?" The succinct phrase "Where's the beef?" combined with the actions and emotions reflected in the commercial lodged these words in the memories of watchers and led to the action of trying out Wendy's, as well as to the retelling of the commercial and phrase all across the culture.[5] This phrase went viral long before we even had the internet to spread things quickly and cheaply. When we combine word, action, emotion, and image, creating a story, and they all line up and reinforce one another, we lodge memories in the minds of the people who watch and listen, and those people act on the memory and retell it to others.

Many less trivial examples abound.

Martin Luther King Jr. created an enduring meme with his "I Have a Dream . . ." speech. His dream of an America where people are judged not by the color of their skin but by the content of their character helped change thinking and behavior around what it means to be a good human being and a moral human community in our country. The words about his dream, the actions he had done to make it a reality, the image he portrayed as an unbroken and unbowed and immensely dignified black man in America, even the timbre of his voice, all combined to tell a story of the promise of the defeat of segregation and racism in America, and that dream still resonates and rings true years later.

We need a new meme for what it looks like to be a good disciple, a good follower and imitator of Jesus. To echo Martin Luther King Jr. just a bit, I have a dream for missional leaders and missional congregations that are growing by reaching new people instead of shuffling the already convinced. I am captivated by a vision of people and congregations that care about the world, serve people in need, and long for people to have hope and find a home with God. They apprentice their people to love others, reach out, and multiply kindness and morality and God in the world—and it all goes viral.

Missional leaders love it when outsiders who have wandered far and long enter into a congregation, are genuinely welcomed, and hear the good word about God's love. Every outsider who begins to enter into a congregation is worth a celebration. We need new memes that people adopt and reproduce in others. The defining meme at our church and the vision we work toward is "helping people find their way back to God." We celebrate it, baptize people who do it, model it, and say it endlessly. It is a meme that shapes everything we think and do. We say it five times in every worship service, we've put it on all of our walls in big letters, and it is the banner over all we do.

The most powerful vehicle for transmission of new memes is imitation. People see a thought or behavior pattern. We say it, dream it, do it, story it, and symbolize it. It gets their attention, lodges in their memory, finds expression in their speech and action, and then gets passed on to others through the repetition of this imitation process. This is reproduction and multiplication in your church that can change your culture and turn your congregation into a conversion community that reaches new people and changes your local community for good. That imitation process is the heart of the culture change most churches in America desperately need, and it is much more within reach than most of us realize.

What does this process of imitation look like in real life and in real churches? It looks a lot like my friend Chad, who is a pastor of a Bible church in a small community in northern Michigan. Chad takes every opportunity he can to meet people at the café where he does office work. He has had opportunities to get to know the owners and the people who stop by or who hang out at the café, to pray for them, to care for them in small ways, to talk about life's troubles, and he has led some of them to Christ and to his congregation. He has had meetings with some of his church leaders there as well. They get to see the quality of relationships Chad has built. As a result, his leaders start to dream of the ways they could reach out and care for people in their lives. Chad models a new behavior pattern, and it has caught on. He is a mimetic reproducer.

Spreading the Stories

But we can't take everybody with us everywhere, can we? As a result, memes—new behavior and thought patterns—can spread often through speech and especially through <u>story</u>.

Sherry is a fitness coach (and cross trainer) who was turned off by the church long ago. She had felt judged because her church had told her she was going to hell a number of times. As a result, she had an allergic reaction to churches and to religious people. Sherry and I began building a friendship. I got her input on some of my questions regarding my personal fitness and referred some of my other friends to her as well. Sherry warmed up to me and my friends, and she began to grow in her relationship with Jesus, even though she was not yet ready to grow in her relationship with a church.

I began to tell other people in my congregation, as well as some of my students, stories of Sherry's journey and bad experiences with Christians and churches. I also shared how she had turned the painful parts of her journey into a commitment to help others through her coaching practice, and how she had experienced increased openness to Jesus. After hearing about the opportunities I had to share God's love with Sherry, my students and friends began to wonder what opportunities they might have in their own lives, and they started to reach out themselves as well.

Then I invited Sherry to my church to tell her stories in person. She talked about what turned her off about the church, how she turned her hurt into healing for others, but she also talked about the way she prays to Jesus now every time before she coaches people in fitness and health. Sherry is encouraged by the love and appreciation she is feeling each time she shares with Christians about her past, her coaching practice, her love for people, and her attraction to Jesus. My church and the members in my small group have also been blown away. They are experiencing the dream and the reality of what it looks like when we welcome and engage the outsider, even the mistrustful and the alienated, and just tell our stories. Their picture of witness and of what it means to be a disciple is changing, and so is Sherry's picture of Christ and of congregations.

Sherry's life was changed by the stories I shared with her of my own life, and the stories she shared have deeply affected me and my church. Stories carry transformational power, and we need stories to be told by lots of people in lots of places, including Christians practicing witness, unchurched individuals responding to witness, and new believers who talk about how they were reached. Steve Carter has written a book in which he shares about how he now gets people to tell their story of conversion and new commitment to faith.[6] He always asks them who first engaged them in spiritual conversation, who first talked to them about Jesus, how they were approached, how they were nudged toward faith and toward a congregation. He wants to create new heroes of the ordinary people who practice kindness, conversation, and spiritual witness in their everyday lives. He also wants the people listening to the story to realize they can have a part in influencing others toward faith and toward congregations.

As a congregation, it is also helpful to use every means of communication a church has: the church website, Facebook, sermons, bulletins, three-minute testimonies, video testimonies, every possible way to tell these kinds of stories—stories of people who have been a witness to their friends, stories of friends who have responded and moved toward Jesus. Every story is golden, including failure stories, because they help people realize that unless they are willing to fail, they will never succeed. I have been encouraged just by listening to some of the video stories on the website of Granger Community Church, a Methodist church in Indiana that has collected and recorded lots of inspiring and authentic stories.[7]

Stories are powerful ways to affect change. Jerry Root, director of the Evangelism Initiative at the Billy Graham Center, is a master storyteller and notes that according to Aristotle's *Rhetoric*, effective communication needs three components: logos (the content of the message), ethos (the credibility of the speaker and an awareness of the audience), and pathos (the emotion of the speech). Root says, "If I do not have pathos, I cannot move people to action, to doing something. So if you want to move people to act, you have to have the kind of communication that reaches the heart, and it's almost always [through] story and the imagination."[8] In fact, Jesus used stories to bring about change in people's lives, as he spent a great deal of time telling parables to his disciples. Stories are disarming and inspiring, and as we share stories of changed lives, many will be moved to transformation themselves.

Activated Through Accountability

Yet there is something else that is more critical and catalytic than telling stories. The most powerful driver of change is providing accountability for the new actions you want people to take. This is not control but accountability in the form of opportunities to share how things are going, how much progress people are making, and what next steps they want to take. It is accountability aimed at supporting and nurturing people into the missional leadership shift we want to see.

This is a timeless principle. When we look through history, we see that the Methodists understood it, and it was what set them apart in terms of their expansion and effectiveness. Their class system provided unparalleled accountability for how people's souls were doing and how their witness was going. Classes were the entry point and focus of Methodist life. Classes were small groups that people joined and in which they found assurance of salvation and accountability for spiritual progress. In contemporary society, the book *The Four Disciplines of*

Execution makes the same point.[9] Discipline four in the book is providing accountability, and the authors tell us that until you implement that discipline, you have not even begun to play the game. Implementation is more dependent on accountability than any other single factor.

The sad reality is that most churches have absolutely no built-in accountability structure related to witness or outreach. Most senior pastors I talk to are never asked by their board how their personal evangelism life is going. Most church leaders I talk to never bring the issue up with any of the people they lead, except now and again in introductions to what basic discipleship looks like. In other words, we believe that apprentices of Jesus are witnesses and that they are created and called to reach out, but we have no ongoing system of accountability to bring that about in our people or our churches. So outreach passion and practice come and go but are rarely a deep, enduring, and vibrant part of the life of our congregation or of our people. That must change if we are to reach people and influence communities around us.

Let me tell you how we have solved the accountability challenge in our cohorts, because you can do exactly the same thing in your congregation and with your leaders. Our cohort meetings happen once a month, so every thirty days we have instituted a particular accountability practice. The exercise itself is called the One Degree Rule, which I got from my friend Kevin Harney.[10]

We ask each pastor to pick a number between one and ten to describe the level of their passion and pursuit of witness over the past month. Were they a missional leader over the last month, and to what degree? One means they are stone cold, apathetic, nonpracticing. The fire is out. They aren't even praying for anybody who is unchurched or irreligious, much less doing or sharing anything. Ten, however, is red-hot. At that level on the scale, they are praying for people, looking for opportunities, having conversations about faith, inviting people to a congregation or opportunity for Christian community, seeing progress, and longing to see people around them come to know Jesus and find faith. So each leader gives a rating between one and ten.

Then we have them each tell a story of a spiritual conversation or experience with unchurched and irreligious people in the last month. Did they build a relationship, or share a faith story, or find out about another's spiritual journey? Did they invite a person to faith or to the congregation? As we share our stories, we are encouraged, even when the story feels like a failure story. We can imitate each other and take risks. We get fired up, and the flame grows a little higher and hotter. Sometimes we have to be honest and admit that we just didn't do very well this last month. But then we lovingly kick each other in the backside a little, and the stories of people who did see progress give us faith that we can see progress too.

And that leads us to the third part of the One Degree Rule exercise. We talk about how we could raise our evangelism temperature one more degree in the next month. Who do we want to talk to? Who are we praying for? What opportunities do we have to care for others or to ask for their care? This is encouraging and inspiring accountability, and it is the most powerful tool I have found for seeing leaders implement what we all say we need to. To date we have worked with 182 pastors of 182 churches. We just administered the year-end survey, which we ask pastors to complete after their first year in a cohort, and over the last year 100 percent of our pastors say they are now more engaged in witness. They're having more impact, and many of them have seen people come to faith or come to their congregation, primarily because of this one practice. How often do you get 100 percent change in improved engagement? Storytelling and accountability combined are incredibly powerful. Together those practices can lead to a changed culture in which your leaders and people's outreach is regular and effective, wherever they live, work, play, and study. That can change your church. That can reach new people. That can influence your community.

Multiplying Missional Leaders

I think of the cohort we did in Austin, Texas. Last time we met, we had some good stories. Tim shared he was only four out of ten in his outreach temperature but that he had experienced a great conversation with a neighbor who had been closed off before. Chris shared he was a two and had had a setback this last month because he had become consumed with an internal church crisis, but he recommitted to reaching out personally over the next month. Next, Chuck shared he was an eight. He had led a friend to Christ with whom he had been meeting for the last six months. The friend was struggling in his marriage and had become very open to faith. But not only had Chuck had a great month; so had the people he was leading. He had been praying for five of the people under his leadership to each lead one person to Christ this year. We are just halfway through the cohort this year, and he reported that seven of the people he leads have each led someone to Christ over the past couple of months. In the year prior, none of them had. You could feel the faith in the room rising, and the dream for what might happen if all our leaders were practicing this kind of storytelling and accountability. We would be well on the way toward becoming a conversion community.

Our research shows that having missional leaders predicts conversion growth for congregations. It starts with the senior leaders and moves forward through imitation, storytelling, and accountability. It's not magic, and it's not impossible. It's doable for every one of us. We could have more missional leaders. We could have more conversion growth as God blesses. God takes our little efforts and turns them into fruitfulness. We could also have more influence for good in our local communities.

Maybe the most critical step we could take is to commit ourselves to becoming better witnesses by talking about witness, giving our temperature, sharing our stories, and checking in with each other every thirty days to talk about next steps we can take. We can hold each other accountable in this critical area of our life with Christ. Could you do that? Could you institute a fifteen- to twenty-minute sharing time once a month in every leader and ministry meeting you have regularly? If you do, you will see your church grow in your momentum toward outreach, and you will see your most valuable resource, your people, become better missional leaders—just like Jesus dreamed.

Questions for Discussion

1. As you think about leaders in your life, who has most helped and inspired you to become a better witness? What was it about what they did and who they were that inspired you to imitate them?

2. Practice the One Degree Rule with your group.

  - Give your outreach temperature by picking a number between one and ten, with one being stone cold and ten being red hot. Why is your temperature what it is? See the Billy Graham Center Resources in appendix one for information on how to access the online resource for this exercise.

  - Share a story of a recent spiritual conversation you had that encouraged you and could encourage others. Why was that an encouraging conversation?

  - What could you do to increase your outreach temperature by one degree over the next month?

3. What would it take to provide regular accountability and story-telling in outreach for your group?

Part 3

Cultivating a Missional Congregation

8

Belonging to the Broader Community

As we begin to develop missional leaders, we generate enthusiasm within our congregation. Yet research indicates that churches that truly grow through conversion and reaching new people are those that move beyond just individuals enacting these practices and toward generating a *culture* that values and prioritizes these practices. Among top-10-percent conversion-growth churches, it is not just individuals but the congregational community as a whole that is characterized by missional engagement.

In this chapter, I want to focus on how to develop this kind of missional congregation, how leaders can generate and sustain a culture where outreach is built into the DNA of their people rather than allocated to certain individuals. Again, our entry point into this discussion is the equation we saw in earlier chapters, which is depicted in figure 8.1.

There is a tendency among Christian leaders intent on cultivating a conversion community to place their emphasis on training and deploying leaders. Yet, as I noted earlier, our research indicates that developing a missional community is actually a far more predictive element of the equation. Thus, far from a secondary concern for pastors thinking through evangelism and mission, developing a

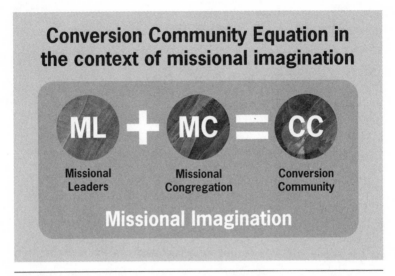

Figure 8.1. Conversion Community Equation in the context of missional imagination

missional community—the focus of part three of this book—lies at the heart of a conversion community. Through focusing their efforts and thought on how to establish this kind of congregation, leaders will be far more effective in producing and sustaining a community intent on and effective in outreach. This is not to say that developing missional leaders is unimportant. As we have seen, the two work in a cyclical fashion. In congregations where missional leaders have been identified and equipped, cultivating a missional congregation will be *much* easier. Where leaders have vision and experience in outreach, congregations have the resources necessary to implement a missional culture. Likewise, as you develop a missional congregation, attracting and equipping leaders who contribute to an established culture becomes easier.

In this chapter I will first broadly survey the four-step process that defines missional congregation. With this entire process in mind, we will then dig into the first step: what it means for missional congregations to belong in their communities.

The Process of Developing a Missional Congregation

The first step in developing a missional congregation is understanding what this congregation looks like. What are all the various pieces required? How do they fit together in a way that makes the whole exceed the sum of its parts? In our research of the top-10-percent conversion-growth churches, a consistent theme emerged among those who were able to cultivate a culture of outreach and conversion: *the church clearly understood it belonged to a specific community, which it blessed through service and outreach with the ultimate aim of bringing those in their community into their congregation as beloved children of God.*

Unpacking this statement, we can see three discernible steps to this process. First, the congregation has a distinct sense of *belonging* to its community, the place where its people live, work, study, and play. Second, those in the congregation BLESS their community, an acronym we will look at below, understanding and ministering to its specific needs. Finally, the church builds on the relationships it has developed as a means of bridging the gap between the church and its community in bringing people to church. Looking at figure 8.2, we can see that this process begins from situating God's people within the world, where they can then be used by God to draw their neighbors, friends, and coworkers into fellowship with the church. A missional community begins by sending out so that in time and through service it might bring back in.

In other words, missional congregations begin where missional leaders begin. What missional leaders do as individuals wherever they live, work, study, and play, missional congregations also do in their local communities and cities. They belong and bless, and they bring people into relationship with their congregation as they seek to serve their community. As we drill down into the details of these steps, we will uncover nuance, such as how to welcome visitors into community and equip emerging leaders. Yet it is crucial to grasp the totality of the process: Churches generate an identity by which they belong to their

Figure 8.2. The process of developing a missional congregation

community. Within these communities they BLESS those outside the church. Over time they bring those in the community into the church fellowship, where they find a new sense of belonging as a beloved child of God. Then these new congregants join in the pursuit of belonging out there and blessing and bringing others.

Missional Churches Belong in Community

Among many Christians, even the language of *belonging* can raise suspicions or provoke eye-rolls. Invariably, when I present this research, I receive a consistent response along the lines of, "Hold on, Rick. We are to be *in* but not *of* the world. We don't *belong* to this world." While it is correct that Christians need to be on their guard against becoming too attached to this world, this criticism loses sight of what Jesus means in John 17:16. He is not asking us to distance ourselves from the communities where we live, work, study, and play. Rather, Jesus reminds us that we must keep our Christian identity, one of being citizens of heaven (Phil 3:20-21), intact as we engage our neighborhoods, workplaces, and local communities. How else could we reach people? We will never build trust and relationships with people in our workplaces, recreation spaces, and neighborhoods unless we truly belong to those places and spaces and people. Relationships are always built initially by what we have in common with others. We can't build trust and relational connection from the sidelines.

My colleague and fellow missiologist Beth Seversen argues for belonging in communities through developing genuine relationships as a way of thinking about Christian mission. She noticed that many Christians concerned about outreach today emphasize creating entry points in congregations for unchurched people to belong before they believe. And that is very important. But she also noticed that before people will visit, they need to trust us. They will never trust us if all we practice is drive-by conversations about converting or coming to a congregation, or even just drive-by service opportunities. We need to belong to our neighborhood or workplace or community before we can influence. I believe that is what Jesus means when he directs his disciples to go two by two into towns and to find a person of peace and stay there. Belong there and influence people through relational networks. That was the pattern Jesus practiced and then mandated for his apprentices. I believe Jesus still mandates that pattern.

So belonging "out there" will be the focus of this chapter, specifically belonging in places where congregations serve and in neighborhoods where people gather.

After we belong, we bless (chapter eight) and we bring (chapter nine). Too much has been made of the dichotomy between being attractional and being extensional or missional. We *must* be both. People mainly find their way home to God through congregations and not just on their own or through individual conversations out there. They will rarely visit a congregation that does not attract them, and even more rarely will they return to an unattractive congregation or experience.

If we are to reach and disciple people today, we have to face how much of the conversion process happens *after* people attend a church initially. Once people visit a congregation, there is a further process of conversion that happens in Christian community. They belong before they believe, they begin to become a Christian, and then they are sent into the world to bless and belong and bring others. The process spirals upward and outward, renewing itself again and again as new waves of people belong out there, then bless and bring along other new people, who belong, become, and are sent all over again.

This in brief was the pattern we saw in top-10-percent conversion-growth congregations. Each of the following chapters will unpack a part of this pattern so that by the end of this next section you will have a good picture and a good plan for becoming a missional congregation. Let's start with that first step in the outer ring, belonging out there in the world, where we engage people from our community.

Before we can serve well, we need to *belong*. Otherwise, as Steve Corbett puts it, helping hurts.[1] As we have been taught by John Perkins, Wayne Gordon, and the Christian Community Development Association, if we are to bless underresourced communities, we need to belong first.[2] We need to relocate, then reconcile with people in the community, and then together create initiatives and find resources (what Perkins calls redistribution). If we can't serve by relocating, we at least need to partner well with congregations that have.

Three Strategies for Belonging

In our research and throughout the cohort leader labs, three consistent strategies emerged for how members of congregations can develop a sense of belonging to their surrounding community. Invariably, conversion communities relied on a mixture of these strategies not only to reinforce a missional culture within their church but to be effective in how they were engaging their broader communities.

Strategy 1: Members of the congregations build relationships with people in the community/neighborhood. A missional congregation belongs through its entire congregation collectively seeking to build relationships within the community where they are seeking to reach people with the gospel. While seemingly obvious, this was a recurring point church leaders cited as evidence of their success in outreach. Choose what you focus on out of your strengths, your network connections, and your passion. It is better to have one compassion ministry that goes deep than five that stay superficial and programmatic. That focus is the key to making this dimension of becoming a missional congregation simple, if not always easy. Do *not* have lots of compassion initiatives until you have one or two that go deep in relationship and impact. Then meet needs out of mutual relationships.

Stories from our research abounded for every type of community. Pastors and leaders got involved in community organizations such as United Way or housing for the homeless. Many churches built relationships with local schools. Several churches offered daycare for the kids in the area. In each case, though, the emphasis was not programmatic but natural and relational. People didn't try to merely come up with projects to help people. Church leaders and laypeople met community people, built relationships, and asked what they could do that would really help and be received and embraced.

This grassroots bridge building within a congregation is embodied in City United and Mile High Vineyard Church, a congregation led by Dave Runyon in Arvada, Colorado.[3] In an attempt to build relationships with the local government, Pastor Runyon and his church invited the mayor of Arvada to speak to their local gathering of pastors. Afterward, when the church leaders asked the mayor how they could better engage the community and serve the broader city, they were stunned by his answer. Cutting right to the point, the mayor asked the church to contribute through creating and empowering a sense of community: being good neighbors, connecting with those in various neighborhoods, and generating a sense of goodwill through their service. In essence, the mayor asked them to love their neighbors. For Christians, this encouragement should sound somewhat familiar. In Luke 10:25-37, Jesus focuses on the centrality to the Christian faith of loving one's neighbor; that loving of one's neighbor is inseparable from loving God. Indeed, this story serves as a practical demonstration of what it means to live out the two greatest commandments: "'Love the Lord your God with all your heart and with all your soul and with all your strength and with all your mind'; and 'Love your neighbor as yourself'" (Lk 10:27).

Too often the idea of loving our neighbors is merely an abstraction. We pay lip service to its importance in Scripture and to our faith, yet the real test is turning this idea into reality for the people with whom we live and work. Worse yet, we can reduce loving our neighbor to some general sense of kindness or civility, thus hollowing out the radical and intimate kind of love that Jesus is envisioning in Luke. We lose sight of what it means to *be* a neighbor. Dave realized that the mayor and Jesus were asking people to love their actual neighbors in concrete and even sacrificial ways, not just to be vaguely kind to people they might generally encounter. That challenge led to a journey that has now affected many cities and at least one thousand churches around the country as pastors and leaders have sought at a new level to do as Jesus directed.

Strategy 2: Churches need a bridge between the congregation and community, a person who simultaneously belongs to the church and belongs to the community. More than just emphasizing broad relationship building, conversion communities rely on leaders who can straddle the line between church and community. Even as they are committed members of the congregation, they are also well-respected members of the community and neighborhood. They have lived in and served the community in various aspects for years. In essence this leader is a core member of the community and therefore has trust and is able to influence.

Consider Emmanuel Faith Community, a midsize church in a small town. At one time it had plateaued and was even shrinking. A new pastor took over and began to model reaching out and getting his people to do so as well. The church started adopting the local high school. They encouraged parents to attend the PTA meetings and to find out how they could serve the school. At that point a broker or bridge person emerged. One of the staff at the church, Jordan, became the high school football chaplain. He hung out at the football games. He spent time with the kids. He got to know the parents. He belonged, and then he blessed them through counseling, a listening ear, and his presence. They came to trust Jordan and seek him out when they had problems. Jordan was always there for them. One struggling young man, Shawn, experienced the presence and commitment of Jordan. He also experienced a persistent stream of invitations to visit the youth group that Jordan also led. Finally Shawn gave in, partly just to make Jordan happy and shut him up.[4] Shawn went on to not only attend youth group but also to become a deeply committed Christian and then to lead many of his other friends on the football team and at the school to Christ and to the congregation.

At their core, bridge people broker relationships, drawing people together from different contexts into shared relationships.[5] They bridge social and cultural distance. In our research of conversion communities, four discernable qualities of bridge people emerged.

First, they have a deep and abiding faith and love for Jesus. This faith and love permeate their actions and conversations with those in the community and the church. There is no doubt whether they are Christian believers or *why* they care in such practical ways for those in the community: it is because of Jesus. Thus, even as they have passion for the emotional and physical needs of the community, they are also always ready to witness about what God has done in their lives and what God could do for people in the community.

Second, just as evident as their love for Christ is their love for their church. Bridge people clearly and enduringly love God's church, want to be a part of it, and want to draw others into it as well. They grasp how each ministry not only can care for the needs of the church but can be an entry point for some in the community, and they take pains to ensure that the church is welcoming. At their core, bridge people are compelled to counteract misconceptions about the church in the community while simultaneously working to ensure that the church is open, warm, and nonjudgmental toward visitors.

Third, bridge people model belonging through investing in the community and its people. They may be a principal or a teacher in the local school, or a volunteer chaplain or PTA member. While they may or may not go to school or play on the football team, they are present by attending every game or meeting and volunteering as mentors or chaplains or supporters as opportunities allow. They get to know the families of the community at major events, keeping up to date on their needs, health, and concerns as they arise. Through years of investment, they prove themselves to be trustworthy. Members in the community know these people are not driven by a self-serving agenda but genuinely care about others' well-being and the well-being of the community as a whole.

Fourth, bridge people are not only intent on influencing their community but display a clear willingness to be influenced by others.

They are known for their openness as a means of showing respect and appreciation to those in the community they are trying to win. In essence, bridge people have proved to the community that they are two-way streets: able to speak into the community only because they have proved to take to heart what they have first heard.

Developing bridge people who display these four qualities is a crucial piece in missional congregations.[6] These people give you the relationship and social capital necessary for compassion ministries as well as clear verbal witness and invitation. Jesus called his disciples to pray that the Lord would "send out workers into his harvest field" (Mt 9:38). I believe that these types of people—those who build bridges and broker relationships between church and community— are central to what these laborers look like in today's society. Thus missional congregations pray for and seek out these bridge people in any ministry to serve well and verbally witness. This is one key way to make a decision about which social ministry to prioritize: Where do you have a broker already in place who can help you serve and help you offer a verbal witness, bringing community and congregation to-gether? Such brokers are pure gold. They belong to and "get" the people they are trying to reach, and so they have influence.

Strategy 3: Focus on the unique needs and cares of the community. Unsurprisingly, every community is not the same. Each community or neighborhood has its own set of needs, challenges, and concerns. In other words, no one size fits all in reaching out to a community and developing relationships. No single method or ministry will appeal to every demographic, region, or culture. At the end of the day, people will attend events only if they speak to *their* needs and cares. While some communities might respond enthusiastically to worship nights or small groups, others are more concerned with issues such as neigh-borhood safety or may be more inclined to attend social gatherings before any explicitly spiritual event. Just as with the first two strategies, building bridges serves as an entry point for the church into relationship with people of the community. Over and over again in our research, churches that were conversion communities were obsessed with building bridges whenever and wherever they could. They were constantly thinking about new and innovative ways to engage their surrounding community, finding entry points to begin or grow relationships. These bridges were intentionally and consistently made with the ultimate aim of helping those in the community to continue their journey into congregations and into becoming people of faith. So when you first invite people to the space where your congregation gathers, consider inviting them to a "neutral" and mutually beneficial event. Some encouraging stats along this line are below:

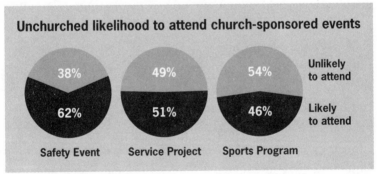

Source: "Unchurched Report," Billy Graham Center Institute and Lifeway Research, April 24, 2019, www.billygrahamcenter.com/youfoundme/research

Figure 8.3. Likelihood to attend church-sponsored events

Our "Unchurched Report" indicates that an event to make the neighborhood safer would likely be attended by over 60 percent of the unchurched, and an event to serve the practical needs of the community would likely be attended by over 50 percent of unchurched people. The three top ways to attract people to attend something your church sponsors are not religious events but ways to improve your community. People are attracted to a faith (and a church) that serves.

Pastor Craig Watson illustrates how these types of community events can be on-ramps into a church.[7] He shared how the leadership team of his church reevaluated the ministries and vision of the church and "really felt we needed to make our church all about reaching outside these four walls. Rather than try to bring people to us, we needed to go to where the people are and really begin to focus more on that." So the church started doing service projects on Sunday mornings a few times a year. Through these and other efforts, they now have initiatives aimed at reroofing widows' homes, reflooring low-income homes, passing out clothing, offering prayer, organizing activities for kids in the neighborhood, and visiting the elderly. Some church members have partnered with a downtown gospel mission and a jail ministry that were already up and running in their community, and others have found ways to regularly and intentionally be present in the community.

Note that these ministries are above all relationally driven more than programmatically driven. For instance, church members have visited the local laundromat to make friends, share concerns, and influence people spiritually. Pastor Watson emphasizes what is key: "We serve with the purpose of introducing people to Christ." Of course the church serves people whether or not they respond spiritually, but the church has that goal of witness and is intentional about reaching it. Churches today are so sensitive to not turning people into projects that they draw back from being intentional about personal witness. But conversion growth ministries like Pastor Watson's church have no such dichotomy.

During one of the service Sundays, Pastor Craig Watson invited a young woman to join them in that day's community service project. She had grown up in a Christian home but had become an atheist because of the hypocrisy she saw in her family. At the time she was strongly against both the church and Christians in general, but she opened up through friendship with the pastor and was willing to attend a service day hosted by the church. According to the pastor, "She was impressed with the people who were serving as part of the church. They weren't fitting the picture of Christians that she had grown to have, so some of those barriers started to come down." Since then she has become increasingly open to conversations about faith and God and has even begun visiting church about every other month.

Creating Space to Belong

At their heart, each of these three strategies is aimed at engaging the community on *its* terms: the unique needs, concerns, and desires of a community in its personality and complexity. In doing this, missional congregations are concerned with creating space for unchurched people to connect with them. This is a crucial first step, the entry point out of which all other steps flow. That may sound obvious, but many churches are not practicing it.

Moreover, in the process of creating this space, missional congregations not only better understand their communities but also counteract the distorted stereotypes of Christians that so pervade our modern post-Christian world. This is key. These strategies are not merely for missional congregations to generate a sense of belonging to their community but also to generate a sense within the community that the church belongs and cares and can contribute—which is equally as important.

When done in concert, these strategies offer multiple bridges for people to engage the church in a space where lasting relationships can be built, sustained, and deepened. Under the direction of Pastor Carter, Calvary Baptist Church illustrates these dynamics of space creation through its sports events and programs.[8] Understanding the draw that sports and other recreational opportunities have for millennials and younger children in the community, Calvary Baptist has hosted the Upwards Basketball Program in its gym over the past seven years.

Every Saturday between December and March, it runs three different sessions of basketball, and the gym fills up with about four hundred people. While the program garnered no new church members in the first two years, Calvary Baptist was satisfied with attracting so many people and building trust within the broader community.

gradual, not instant

Having established this space where the church and community could meet, Calvary Baptist then started to shift its focus to a more intentional outreach. As Pastor Carter recounted, the church wanted to begin moving people "from the gymnasium to the sanctuary to the world."[9] Pastor Carter and his team worked to build relationships, to identify and empower coaches who could serve as brokers with kids and parents (and Pastor Carter himself became such a broker). They also instituted a halftime devotional presentation and welcomed people when they made the challenging leap from the gym to the sanctuary. In doing so the church built on the initial bridge of the program to then build additional bridges through individuals and the congregation as a whole. That initial space created by a basketball program was a launch pad and soon expanded due to the efforts of the entire congregation to engage the community. The following year, twelve people gave their lives to Christ, and three families joined the church. Now that number has grown to fifteen to twenty people who connect to church each year through the basketball program. Through halftime devotionals and simply reaching out relationally, Pastor Carter has found sports events to be a powerful and natural bridge into the community. Too often churches offer programs but not a full-orbed process that leads people through all the steps toward Christ and a congregation.

ministry changes/morphs over time

Carrie is one person who has come to faith and been transformed through the Upwards Basketball Program. She was a drug addict for over twenty years. She brought her children to Upwards and was given a full scholarship for all three of her children. Pastor Carter gave the devotion over halftime the first week Carrie attended Upwards Basketball, and she followed up with a visit to his office on that next Monday morning. She told him, "My life is a wreck. I am miserable. I need a change."

Carrie was raised in the Catholic Church. She said she went through a confirmation and First Communion process but that she had never come to trust Jesus. She continued, "When you talked about Jesus loving me for who I am, I knew I wanted to know about that." So she attended church that following Sunday and returned to the pastor's office the following Monday, where she gave her life to Christ.

At the time she was going through custody battles around her three kids and looking for a lifeline. After giving her life to Jesus, and with the help of the church and others, she was able give up drugs and four years later is still clean and sober. At the time of the interview Carrie had become one of the leaders of the church's grow team, going into the neighborhood to share her faith. She was also one of the leaders of the church's discipleship training and was helping others to find Christ, grow in Christ, and become reproducers by reaching others. Carrie became an apprentice, a learner of the Christian way of reaching out and loving others. Then she became a broker for people from the community. Now she is an advocate and inviter for the church, and her life has been caught and reproduced in and through others. Carrie illustrates and embodies how Calvary became a conversion community. It all came through a community basketball program that became a bridge to faith and a bridge to the church.

How does your church get there? Start with what you already do and build on the natural connections you already have. This can be through sports, concerts and music, art, urban renewal, nursing homes, foster care / adoption centers, juvenile detention centers, book clubs or gardening groups, a daycare center, or so many other things. It starts with belonging out there so that we truly bless and are blessed by genuine relationships. Then we learn the felt needs of the people—from the community or workplace or health club or service site—and prioritize those needs. Together with the people we seek to serve, we meet the needs. If this sounds like too much, remember that focus can make a huge difference. If we focus on one initiative that we can do best and where we most likely will have brokers, we really can get there.

Questions for Discussion

1. Does your congregation belong to a community out there, or is your congregation more of a community all unto itself?

2. Of the three strategies for belonging out there (building genuine relationships with community people, having great bridge people, and focusing on the felt needs and cares of people), what is your best next step as a congregation?

3. How could you identify, equip, and empower the bridge people in your congregation to effectively connect your church to the community in meaningful service and witness? If you can't identify any bridge people in your congregation, how could you find them and partner with them?

9

Blessing the World
to Reach the World

Having laid a foundation for becoming a missional congregation—belonging to the congregation's community—it is imperative that we press on to the next step in the process. Churches that are satisfied with simply belonging to their communities wind up no different from the local YMCA, participating in a community but not influencing its spiritual transformation. Or else people practice pseudobelonging, where they drop in to serve in a program but never develop deep enough relationships to spiritually influence the people with whom they are connecting. In contrast, missional communities build relationships and generate space for engaging those outside the church as an entry point for outreach rather than its culmination. They build on their sense of belonging and the bridges they have constructed to then bless communities. Notice that our belonging puts us into a place where we can bless and influence the community. We belong *to* bless.

As we explore how missional congregations serve their communities, one thing quickly becomes evident. Top-10-percent conversion-growth churches know how to serve people and also know how to verbally share their faith as they serve. In our research with three thousand churches across the country, we found a correlation between

Figure 9.1. The process of developing a missional congregation

serving and evangelism. Churches where compassion and justice ministries were a priority were also some of the best at reaching new people and growing through new professions of faith in Christ. In other words, those that cared about the physical, mental, and social needs of the community were the most likely to be the most effective at bringing people to Christ and to a congregation.

People are not interested in churches that show no desire to make a positive impact on the community. But here is one of our findings that is also quite interesting. Churches that *only* engage in compassion ministry and never verbally proclaim their faith in Christ are the worst at reaching new people and growing their congregations as a result. In essence, both sides of this dichotomy between words and deeds, proclamation and demonstration, proved deficient in the actual task of influencing people toward faith. However, it was churches where *both* were emphasized that saw the most significant impact, churches where service and verbal witness were intertwined and valued. In these cases, there was no dichotomy between social engagement and proclaiming the good news about Jesus, and as a result they proved much more effective in both.

In this chapter I want to explore how missional congregations move from the initial step of belonging to actually engaging and serving in the community. In this respect I will outline two central obstacles churches need to overcome in order to be missional congregations. They need to counteract stereotypes of evangelism both in and outside the church, which have actually hurt outreach, and they need to reject the dichotomy between compassion and communication of the faith. With this in mind, I want to offer a new paradigm that effective missional congregations can use to influence their community. The objective is not simply to proclaim the gospel or to provide ministries but rather to be intentional about *blessing* the community *as* representatives of Jesus.

Obstacle 1: Stereotypes of Evangelism

Often when Christians speak of outreach and serving a community, the conversation revolves around the term *evangelism*. In many respects this is correct. *Evangelism* is an important term with warrant in both Scripture and the history of the church. It means to communicate the good news of Jesus Christ to the world: that God entered human history in Jesus and by way of his life, death, and resurrection offers the forgiveness of sin, reconciliation with himself, and new life.

Yet while evangelism is an important and biblical term, there is little doubt that it carries significant baggage in our modern, post-Christian world. To most people—both Christian and non-Christian alike—the concept of evangelism is scary and unwelcome. It connotes "converting" people, speaking *at* people instead of with people, setting

ultimatums around certain beliefs with the threat of eternal damnation
if they disagree or step out of line. Others' impression of evangelism
is that it is like talking to a salesman. They are being *sold* something
they do not want, with a constant sense that there is a hidden or
underlying *agenda*. While resources for evangelism have played a significant role in helping inexperienced Christians evangelize effectively
for generations, they can also have the adverse effect of making engagement appear scripted. Thus evangelism can lack authenticity and
the dynamism of genuine conversation.

　　All of this leads us to a cultural moment where the idea of evangelism—
literally communicating good news—is suffering from a serious problem
of bad press among non-Christians and even among many Christians
and churches, where evangelism has faded not only in practice but even
in theory. For instance, in a recent Barna study, 47 percent of millennial
practicing Christians, those who attend church regularly and feel their
faith is very important to them, feel it is wrong to share one's beliefs with
a person of another faith in the hopes that they will someday share one's
faith. Or put succinctly in the Barna report, nearly half of millennial
practicing Christians think evangelism is wrong. This attitude is symp-
tomatic of a larger cultural problem we face.[1]

　　While Christians still respect leading evangelists, past and present,
such as Billy Graham, for their ability to lead others to faith in Christ,
such people are depicted as elite or particularly gifted for the task. In
contrast, everyday Christians think that because they don't have a gift
of evangelism, they should withdraw from the attempt. Evangelists
are the Green Berets of Christians: unique and specially trained people
able to perform in contexts no normal person would dare consider. So
we will cheer on the Billy Grahams of the world and celebrate them
when they pass away but never think we can be like them. Or else
evangelists are those people on the street corner who preach hell and
damnation. Who wants to be like them?

In other words, we face a paradox of sorts. In the eyes of the world, *evangelism* is an outdated word that conjures images of salesmanship, inauthenticity, and triumphalism. Yet for Christians, it is a *higher* gift for the select few who have a taste or aptitude for engaging, or else a destructive ego trip for marginalized and unhappy wannabe preachers. It is simultaneously bad in the eyes of mainstream culture and either too good or too bad for contemporary Christians to identify with or practice.

In this climate of cultural tolerance, churches that emphasize traditional language and methods of evangelism often pay a steep price in both their church and their community for evangelism's tarnished reputation. Many are categorized as fundamentalist, fanatical, or a relic of a bygone era or of a backwater region. At present, even among many regular churchgoers rhetoric around evangelism, whether positive or negative, is not helping most leaders and people in congregations engage in witness. When words have become co-opted by negative and nonbiblical stereotypes, we can adopt different language to help people have a different paradigm and set of responses to embracing God's mission, reaching people who are unchurched or irreligious and thus influencing our communities for good.

Obstacle 2: Dichotomizing Compassion and Gospel Communication

One the biggest obstacles facing churches seeking to become conversion communities is that they too often dichotomize blessing people physically and blessing people spiritually. They have two separate ministries: one that cares for the needs of the community and another that witnesses to the community. They mistakenly reduce belonging to service only, and proclamation of the gospel to events and church services only. Inevitably this produces two anemic ministries, as the former is merely programmed service that lacks any mutual relationship and witness, while the latter is an evangelism of words with no relational or empathetic depth and authenticity.

Among conversion communities in our study, the overwhelming majority emphasized both. In his early days at Lawndale Community Church in the underresourced Lawndale neighborhood in Chicago, Pastor Wayne Gordon asked people in the church who had grown up in the neighborhood what they needed. He was expecting grandiose plans, a list of dreams or initiatives: work programs, new homes, all the hot-button and sexy issues that form the basis of stump speeches of politicians trying to win votes come election season or of nonprofit organizations trying to gain massive donations. Yet what the people asked for was far more practical and strikes at the nerve of what it means to bless communities.

Recounting the story today, Pastor Gordon, who is known by many as "Coach," notes that the community simply said, "We need a safe place to do our laundry." Coach was not excited about the "laundry vision." But as the people explained it, the neighborhood laundromat was under gang control and often a place where drug deals went down. The laundromat was not safe. So Coach went along with the laundry vision. Without advertising the need, he received from a rich couple in Barrington, Illinois, an upscale community, a donation of an almost-new avocado-colored washer and dryer, which no longer matched the decor of their home.

Today Lawndale Community Church has a world-changing ministry that has led many people to commit their lives to Christ and is influencing five thousand underresourced people a week through five community health centers, a halfway house for ex-convicts, a leadership-development ministry, a job-placement ministry, a housing-development corporation, a legal-aid service for young black men, and so much more. But it got its start serving in a closet with an avocado-colored washer and dryer, because Coach belonged to the community and served according to the needs the people from the community prioritized. Then he and the people in the community shared faith while serving people and building a congregation. *That* is what belonging and blessing look like. And it can happen at Boeing Corporation and at Barrington Health Club just as much as in Lawndale, though of course with very different needs to meet and different ways to communicate faith.

The first step is recognizing and embracing that a whole and integrated ministry involving relational social engagement and relevant communication of the good news with an invitation to faith and community was the ministry pattern of our founder, Jesus. He may have captured his personal mission statement best in Luke 4:18-19: "The Spirit of the Lord is on me, because he has anointed me to proclaim good news to the poor. He has sent me to proclaim freedom for the prisoners and recovery of sight for the blind, to set the oppressed free, to proclaim the year of the Lord's favor." It is all there: good news for the poor, recovery of sight to the blind, release of the oppressed. For Jesus, proclaiming good news and releasing the oppressed were inseparable.

But knowing that Jesus seamlessly modeled ministries of compassion and proclamation does not mean it is easy. I have lots of experience with *not* seeing it happen.

I experienced this dynamic years ago at Clark Church. We had a number of justice and compassion ministries in the nearby Cabrini Green housing project, which in the 1960s through the 1990s was the second-poorest neighborhood in Chicago. My church cared a lot about that neighborhood. We had a legal-aid clinic, a ministry to the elderly and homebound, a housing development that brought together rich and poor in the same community, an urban Young Life ministry to high school students, and ministry that focused on leadership development, job placement, and tutoring, for which my wife worked. For many years our congregation was quite middle class and upper-middle class, while our primary ministries were among the underresourced.

Yet this was the same church at which a friend of mine named Suzy spent six months trying to find the way to come to know Jesus. She had been attracted by the authentic relationships in the congregation and by the wonderful social ministries in Cabrini Green, but week after week she came and never heard how to commit her life to Christ. Finally, after asking several people and not getting a clear answer, she got up the courage to ask the pastor if she could meet with him for lunch. At lunch she asked him how to have a real relationship with God, and he was happy to tell her. It had just never come up in the other dimensions of the church's life and ministry. We were a world-class church in terms of ministry, service, justice, and influencing our community for good, but we were not good at helping people come to know Christ. What's more, very few of the people we served ever showed up in a Sunday service. We were amazing at living the good news in a struggling community but terrible at communicating the good news and inviting people we served into genuine relationship and faith. Many churches across the country are in the same boat. Fortunately, at Clark we faced our shortfalls and began to change, becoming much more relational and organic in our approach. But for many years we adopted the programmatic more than relational model of meeting people's needs, and we left verbal witness in the background.

Why do churches dichotomize? Why did we? Why do we tend to be good at compassion but resist also becoming good at verbal witness? One reason is that compassion and service feel so good to everybody, in the church and in our culture. Evangelism, however, often feels invasive and lacking in love to our church people.

Churches also dichotomize because of how hard it is to move from serving the underresourced to true relationship and partnership. For a long time, none of the hurting or underresourced people around us joined the church. They were our "project," our "ministry," but not our friends and coworkers. Sometimes that transition is quite challenging for churches, yet if we want to become a conversion community and not just a social agency, that transition is critical. If we don't make that transition, the community is left without the powerful combination of salt and light, at least from our congregation. Fortunately in the case of Clark Church, God was of course still amazingly at work in Cabrini Green through other congregations, and in time we also developed deeper and more mutual relationships, adding people into the congregation and then to the leadership team of our church. We had a lot to learn, but we began to take the necessary steps to do it.

Moving to a New Paradigm:
God's Blessing Through Abraham

Like any new paradigm for spiritual practices or outreach, we must begin with Scripture. We must ensure that both our objective and our motivation are aligned with God's Word. As such, I suggest that for reimagining evangelism an important place to begin is with the story of Abraham in Genesis 12.

Few figures tower over Scripture like Abraham. Along with David and Moses, he is one of the most frequently referenced figures in the Old Testament. Abraham was the one to whom God promised to make his descendants *God's* people and to give them the land of Canaan. In this respect, in Scripture Abraham is considered to be the father of Israel. Yet when we are introduced to Abraham in Genesis, he is not even *in* Israel but in a country far to the north. He is not even called Abraham but Abram.

God's appearance to Abraham in Genesis 12 is truly the *beginning* of the story of Israel. God is going to use Abraham and his descendants to deliver his message to the world. Yet notice that in Genesis 12:1-3, God begins this process by calling Abraham to leave his homeland and to go into the land God had promised. It was in this new land that God will show first his love to Abraham and, more importantly, his love for the world.

The LORD had said to Abram, "Go from your country, your people and your father's household to the land I will show you.

"I will make you into a great nation,
   and I will bless you;
I will make your name great,
   and you will be a blessing.

I will bless those who bless you,
   and whoever curses you I will curse;

and all peoples on earth
   will be blessed through you." (Gen 12:1-3)

Central to this passage is not only God's love for and favor on Abraham but also the notion that through this love God promises to bless the entire world. This concept of God's blessing appears five times in three verses. God is getting the mission of God back on track after it has gone off the rails in the first eleven chapters of Genesis, the first book of the Bible. God's way of reaching and restoring the world has always been through blessing. Since the time of Abraham, God has blessed the people of God so that they might bless those who do not know God. Imagine if we thought of evangelism in our relationship with others as fundamentally the practice of blessing others deeply and truly, in the way God intended from the beginning.

If Abraham is the beginning of a "bless others" paradigm of witness, Jesus is the fulfillment of this paradigm. In John 3:16, perhaps the most famous verse in the Bible, Jesus tells us, "For God so loved the world that he gave his one and only Son, that whoever believes in him shall not perish but have eternal life." And what is eternal life? In

John 17:3, Jesus says, "Now this is eternal life: that they know you, the only true God, and Jesus Christ, whom you have sent." The goal of God's mission is that we all know God in a deep relationship and have God's loving destiny for us and our world fulfilled through that relationship. God fulfills God's mission through blessing us with a love relationship that transforms us and everyone around us, which is the church's mission too. Jesus caps his ministry on earth with just this sentiment, "As the Father has sent me, I am sending you" (Jn 20:21)—to love the world, to bless the world, to reach people and influence communities for good.

Missional Congregations as Blessers

This paradigm for evangelism as blessing is the focus of Mark Russell in his book *The Missional Entrepreneur*.[2] My friend Dave Ferguson told me about this book. Studying twelve business groups in Thailand as they developed and implemented a "business as mission" philosophy, Russell explores the ways business leaders can influence communities using both traditional and nontraditional evangelistic methods. The first six businesses focused on conversion as their primary objective as a company, whereas developing a successful business was considered a byproduct. In a real sense they used business as a means to get into the country and as a way to build an initial presence and trust with Thais. These businesses were much more concerned for the spiritual destiny of the Thai people than for their economic improvement. Russell called these six businesses the "converters."

In contrast, the second set of six businesses that Russell studied were primarily focused on developing businesses that succeeded, hiring local people, and enhancing the Thai economy. Influencing Thai people toward faith in Christ was seen as an *important* and *necessary* byproduct of these businesses. But conversion was not the main or explicit focus. Russell called these businesses the "blessers." Not surprisingly, the blessers did much more social good, employed more Thai people, and generated more income. However, perhaps much more surprisingly, the blessers also converted more people. In fact, the blessers experienced significantly higher rates of conversion—at *a ratio of forty-eight to one* over the converters. Ninety-six people gave their lives to Christ through the blessers over a several-year period, while converters saw only two new commitments to faith.

Why was there such disparity between the two? Here are some factors: The blessers built more deeply genuine relationships, hired people for the longer term, created greater income and capital in the economy, and built deeper trust. Thai people listened when the founders and leaders of blesser companies talked about their faith in Jesus. The Thais were genuinely interested and influenced profoundly by the blessers' natural and timely sharing of their faith. In other words, the blesser businesses belonged more and blessed others more, and so they had far more spiritual influence. key

However, the converters never really became a part of the Thai community, partly because their agenda overshadowed their relationships. That is often how the process of spiritually influencing others works, not just in Thai culture but in American culture too. People do not care for our agendas unless they know we understand them and that we care and are committed to their well-being. People want authentic relationships, and they want to know we are for real and for them. They want to feel blessed before they respond to our influence. So the blesser approach is both profoundly biblical *and* it works, both in Abraham's time and in ours.

Our research also discovered this pattern of churches blessing their local communities on lots of levels as a key predictive factor in being in the top tier of conversion-growth churches.

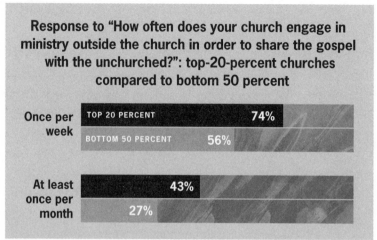

Source: Billy Graham Center Institute and Lifeway Research, Small Church Evangelism Study. We used 20 percent instead of 10 percent because of sample size.

Figure 9.2. Response to "How often does your church engage in ministry outside the church in order to share the gospel with the unchurched?": top-20-percent churches compared to bottom 50 percent

Figure 9.2 shows that top-20-percent churches reach out in their broader community more often. Through statistical analysis (called regression analysis, wherein each individual factor can be isolated and then its direct impact measured), we found this factor *predictive*. Reaching out to meet needs and share faith in the local community characterizes churches that become conversion communities. In other words, it is right, it is good, and it works for both people *and* congregations to pursue this blesser vision of mission. Churches that bless their communities through service and seek to communicate the good news about Jesus see more new people reached *and* more local communities influenced for good.

A New Paradigm of Evangelism: BLESS

An innovator of this paradigm of blessing as evangelism, Pastor Dave Ferguson developed an acronym to help his congregation live this out in their community. Located in the western suburbs of Chicago, Community Christian Church needed a way to make evangelism focused on blessing others in practical and specific ways rather than focusing on the mechanical outreach methods that had become tired. Building on Genesis 12:1-3, Pastor Ferguson emphasized five missional practices that constitute the core of BLESS outreach. I have changed the wording so as to emphasize that these missional practices are not just a new to-do list but a fundamental pattern of being blessed ourselves and then turning around and giving out of what we have received. As with Abraham, God blesses us to bless others.

Begin with prayer. Jesus and others have blessed you through prayer. Bless others who don't know Jesus yet through prayer.

Listen. Listen with care. Jesus and others have listened to you and heard you. Bless others far from God by listening and hearing them.

Eat. Eat together. Jesus and others have accepted you and "invited you to their table." Accept and invite others who don't know Jesus yet to your table (or to your local fast-food or farm-to-table restaurant).

Serve. Serve in love. Jesus and others have served you in ways that changed you. Serve others far from God in ways that can change them. Receive their serving of you too! Nothing you do gives dignity to others or creates openness to your sharing like receiving their help.

Story. Share your story. Jesus and others have shared their story and God's story with you in a way that changed you. Share your story with others far from God to reach them.[3]

Here is a graphic of those practices that might help you picture them:

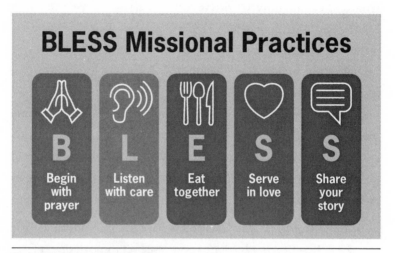

Figure 9.3. BLESS missional practices

As we engage these practices daily, we partner with God's Spirit to bless those who do not know God (and those who do). We practice these five simple steps with those in our spheres of influence, like friends, relatives, acquaintances, neighbors, and colleagues—especially unchurched and irreligious people—with the hope that we may love them well and help them travel further in their journey toward making faith commitments to Jesus and to a community that will love them well. As we seek to authentically BLESS others daily in the midst of our deepening relationships with the people in our lives, we trust that God will use each of us to bless our world like Christ. God's strategy of blessing others often helps people make progress on their journey toward Jesus.[4]

The Importance of Beginning with Prayer

Blessing those in our community begins with prayer, both for them and with them. Prayer immediately sets the tone for the relationship as simultaneously spiritual and other-centric. Through asking people what you can pray for and then following up, the act of praying helps believers in missional congregations attune to the specific ways they can love and serve their community. Tim Hawks is the lead pastor of Hill Country Bible Church in Texas, and during a cohort meeting, he repeatedly drew attention to how daily prayer for people made him more aware of opportunities for his church to bless the community.[5] That awareness spilled into all of his relationships, leading to many more opportunities to love the people in his world well.

Dan Weyerhaeuser, who is the pastor of Lakeland Church in Illinois, had the same experience. During a cohort meeting, Dan shared that he had been praying for opportunities to bless several people in his neighborhood.[6] One of the people he had left off his list was a Muslim neighbor who lived several houses away. He had tried to reach out to that neighbor, just to build a friendship, but he had felt that the neighbor was not open or interested. One day when Dan came home, he saw his neighbor clipping the bushes. His awareness had been heightened by his praying, even though this particular neighbor wasn't on his BLESS prayer list anymore. Dan went to wave and just say hi. Later this neighbor walked down to Dan, who had gone outside to get something from his car. The neighbor asked whether he could talk to Dan. They sat down together in Dan's backyard. One hour later, Dan's Muslim neighbor had shared his struggles in his family and had asked Dan for help, for encouragement, for advice, and for prayer.

In the cases of Tim and Dan, both pastors reported that praying for others attuned them to the needs of the community and over time opened opportunities for deeper relationships. Praying for and listening to the prayer requests of those in the community generated a space for conversation that both pastors had been desiring but unable to find and almost ready to give up on. One of the amazing things about seeking to bless all those around us is that it turns out this is exactly what God wants to do and is doing. Suddenly we get to be hands, feet, and voice for God's mission to bless everyone everywhere. God loves to bless us and others through us.

What's more, we don't just pray for people. Often we can pray *with* people, and especially at moments of pain and struggle in their lives. A simple and heartfelt pastoring prayer when people are hurting communicates love and presence to vulnerable people. Often I have experienced that they sense God's presence at those times, even people who are not sure they believe that there is a God.

Opening the Door for Sharing Your Story

As we listen to their story and affirm what we can, it becomes natural to meet for coffee or invite them to a meal. We eat together, a practice that communicates affection and equality. As our relationship then deepens, we find ways we can serve others and also ask for their help, opening the door for sharing our faith story. BLESS culminates in sharing our story of faith, relating to people how God has rescued and healed us through Jesus and set us on mission for his kingdom. While this is the more traditional component of evangelism, it is important to notice how this is the *culmination* rather than in *competition* with serving. Through praying, listening, eating, and serving, missional congregations are able to cultivate far more opportunities for sharing our story. We have invested in the people of the community and in doing so are granted opportunities and influence to share our own lives. In other words, we do not live our lives and then share our faith as some separate activity or component. Instead, we live our faith and share our lives with people.

We saw this dynamic consistently among conversion communities, those that were in the top 10 percent of conversion-growth churches. Through first meeting the needs of the community in relationship, they were able to verbally witness often and with high impact.

Likewise, in our "Unchurched Report," we saw that the top two actions that make unchurched people more open to hearing what Christians have to say about their faith are (1) <u>treating other people better because of their faith</u> (32 percent) and (2) <u>caring for people's needs because of their faith</u> (31 percent). In other words, <u>faith in action and expressed in everyday life makes a difference.</u>

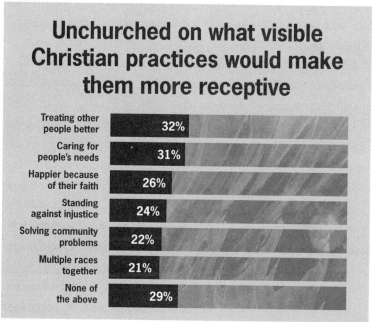

Unchurched on what visible Christian practices would make them more receptive

Treating other people better	32%
Caring for people's needs	31%
Happier because of their faith	26%
Standing against injustice	24%
Solving community problems	22%
Multiple races together	21%
None of the above	29%

Source: "Unchurched Report," Billy Graham Center Institute and Lifeway Research, April 24, 2019, www.billygrahamcenter.com/youfoundme/research

Figure 9.4. Unchurched on what visible Christian practices would make them more receptive

Pastor Jim's church illustrates how this kind of mutually genuine relationship develops opportunities for sharing faith stories.[7] Three days before the church's Christmas program, Jim was busy organizing last-minute details when a stranger walked into the church. From his looks, Jim guessed he might be homeless. Initially annoyed at the interruption, Jim still politely asked him, "How can I help you?"

The man explained, "I just came to give some money." This response caught Jim off guard, and all he could manage in response was "Really?" Casually, the man responded, "Yeah—sometimes I just do that," as he handed some money to the pastor. As they talked, pieces of the man's life unfolded. His name was Fred, and he was a believer but had been deeply hurt by the church in the past and had not regularly attended since. Before Fred left, Jim said, "Thank you for your gift. It means a lot! We're here for you too. I appreciate the ministry that you're sharing with people, and let us know if there's ever anything we can do."

A few weeks later, after New Year's, Jim received a phone call from Fred asking whether he believed in healing. Concerned at the line of questioning, Jim discovered that Fred was in the hospital due to a recent stroke and wanted to see whether the pastor would come and pray for him. When Jim arrived, he was able to pray with Fred, and over the following weeks he returned several times.

After getting out of the hospital, Fred dragged his friend John with him to visit Jim at the church. Over a dozen tamales that Jim purchased from a street vendor outside the church, Jim was able to engage both Fred and John on where they were in their spiritual journey. Reflecting on that conversation later, Jim noted how even the basic act of buying tamales from the vendor affected the two visitors and reemphasized, "Hey, we care about you." By the end of the conversation Fred expressed interest in visiting a church service. John chimed in, "Well, I want to come too, but I need a ride." He didn't have a car and was dependent on others for transportation. Jim was overjoyed that they both wanted to visit and arranged for the needed transportation. Jim later explained that it was a stretch for him to bridge the differences in cultural background and economic situation, "but they're people that Christ loves, and that's why we're in the business for doing this, salvaging broken lives."

Through this story you can begin to see the power of viewing evangelism as the process of organically and relationally blessing others. It is also a good way to reach activists and aspiring activists, including many millennials and younger people, as shown by the many stories we heard of younger people first connecting to congregations through the church's community-service efforts. But the depth, authenticity, and mutuality of these relationships are what opens the door to people coming to Christ and to congregations.

Conclusion

As I end this chapter, it is helpful to recognize again where we stand in this process of developing missional congregations. Having generated a sense of belonging within the community, a missional congregation begins the hard work of transforming it through BLESS. That means beginning with prayer, listening to responses, eating with

Figure 9.5. The process of developing a missional congregation

others, serving needs as they arise, and sharing your story about how Jesus has changed you.

Note that we are not creating a new list of do's and don'ts for you, though. We are asking that you realize and remember how you have been blessed and loved, and that you give only out of what you have received. Blessing others is rooted in first receiving from God, first being loved and chosen by God. We do not give out of a sense of responsibility or guilt. We give out of the grace we have received. Jesus lives in us, gives to us, and then gives us strength and wisdom to give to others. As Jesus taught so well, "I am the vine; you are the branches. If you remain in me and I in you, you will bear much fruit; apart from me you can do nothing" (Jn 15:5). The truth in this verse captures Jesus' pattern for blessing others.

What's more, as we enter into the lives of others far from God, we find that Jesus is already there, blessing them, drawing them, working in their lives to convict and convince them of his reality and his love. So our task is to discern where God is already at work and to join God in that work. We are assistant blessers, working for and with the Holy Spirit. That's encouraging. *amen!*

If we could gain a new vision for sharing our faith, be captivated by it, and know how to pursue it, we might all get involved. Based on the model of Abraham and Jesus, BLESS missional practices are a captivating practical vision. If we pursue it, beginning with prayer for people on our BLESS list, we can love people well, reach new people, and influence our communities.

As we serve and bless the broader community, as individuals and as a whole congregation, we remove barriers to faith and build on-ramps for people to connect. As we bless those we serve and then begin to make that all-important transition to genuine relationships and mutual partnering with those different from us, we can become a community of shared power and mission, lighting up the world, salting

[handwritten margin notes: So where should we focus? On Christ, not all my shortfalls. Change from the inside out. love this verse!]

our community, and reaching the unchurched. Let's recapture the ministry of Jesus, which combines compassion and verbal witness for our congregation and for the world.

Questions for Discussion

1. Does your church or small group emphasize compassion ministry or evangelism more? How could you take steps to achieve a better balance and integration?

2. What, if any, are your stereotypes of evangelism, and how do those stereotypes keep you from being an enthusiastic and effective witness in your world?

3. What stands out to you in the BLESS missional practices (Begin with prayer, Listen, Eat, Serve, Story) that could help you most grow in your own witness?

4. Consider using the BLESS Planning worksheet to grow as a congregation or small group in your BLESS missional practices. See the Billy Graham Center Resources in appendix one for information on how to access this online resource.

10

Bringing the Community to Church

There are two characteristics of top-10-percent conversion-growth churches that tower above all the other characteristics. First, conversion communities cultivate a culture of invitation, and second, they develop a culture of hospitality. These people are excited about their faith and excited about their congregation, so they naturally, regularly, and even passionately invite people to faith and to church. What's more, those congregations go out of their way to make people feel welcome. In particular, they make outsiders and first-timers feel welcome. In general, they make people who are different from them, who don't yet believe what they believe or live the way they live, feel right at home. Those churches make people feel loved and wanted.

This chapter will look at the invitational element of conversion communities, while the following chapter will explore the hospitality of conversion communities, but truthfully the two can't be separated. A strong invitational culture is very dependent on a strong hospitality culture. People will only invite friends, family, and acquaintances into a community where they feel assured that the people they invite will be wanted and welcomed. And a hospitality culture is not helpful in reaching unchurched people unless there is a very strong culture of invitation. These two qualities together are key components that churches must have in their journey toward becoming conversion communities.

On our picture of the life of a conversion community, we have come to the "Bring" part:

Figure 10.1. The process of developing a missional congregation

Belonging That Leads to Believing

Especially in our increasingly less Christian society, people today need time and a process to find their way to Christian faith and commitment. It is a journey. It does not happen overnight very often. And key to this journey today is that much of it happens in the context of community, a safe place for people to explore Christian faith and identity.[1] People need to check out Christian faith before they will commit. They need to belong before they can come to believe. So we need to be able to bring them into our community where they find acceptance and a safe place to explore their questions, concerns, and doubts. Bringing people is not just a self- and church-centered way to recruit new members. The primary motivation is not our need to fill the seats, meet the budget, and expand our reputation. The primary motivation is to fulfill the mission of Jesus "to seek the lost, restore the broken, and heal our community." Critical to conversion is providing community for the unchurched and then bringing the unchurched into that experience of community.

Missed Opportunities

But for or many Christians, false statistics, failed efforts, and a perceived lack of opportunity have led congregations into passivity in making friends and offering invitations. In our pastor cohorts and in countless seminars, Christians have told me they have few unchurched friends, so they don't really know who they would invite or even with whom they would have spiritual conversations. However, when we have helped people identify their actual opportunities, most have found many more than they thought they had.

Another challenge I have heard often is that many Christians are hesitant to invite friends and family members to their churches. Some have tried and failed. Others aren't sure how to extend such an invite or have too high of a cringe factor in their churches. The cringe factor is the number of times Christians would cringe at what happens in a service or event if they did bring a friend or family member who is still far from God.

On the whole, many opportunities to enrich and grow congregations, to strengthen communities, and to stimulate faith and connection for unchurched people are being lost and squandered. It is not just a few opportunities. It is forty-seven million receptive people, and another ninety-five million who might become receptive if engaged in a loving and non-stereotypical way. These are 143 million people, many who need purpose, meaning, and a sense of community, representing countless local communities that need vibrant congregations. These are my parents and your parents, my kids and your kids, and my friends and your friends. They are rich and poor, of many ethnic backgrounds, and all around us. There are so many missed opportunities.

The Impact of Personal Invitations

What could help us move from passivity and pessimism to optimism and action? One of the best places to start is in remembering that our invitations could be more effective than we think. Remember this statistic from chapter three? Fifty percent of unchurched individuals think receiving an invitation to church from a friend would be effective at getting them to visit, and even more, 55 percent, say they would respond positively to invitations from family members. When we realize that others are open to our invitations, we in turn become more active in inviting them.

The key to reaching most people is through the relational networks they have with people they trust. Donald McGavran wrote a book in 1955 called *The Bridges of God*, making the point that people come to faith and to congregations through relationships.[2] Relationships are the bridges of God. If our people are not active witnesses, inviters, and lovers of the people in their lives, those people will most often never wander their way into a church. This was true in 1955 when McGavran wrote it. It is, if anything, even more true today, in a culture where people are resistant to strangers they don't know coming up and "selling" them things they don't want.

But this relational and network approach is not new. All the way back in biblical times, Jesus told the people he sent to enter a town, find people of peace who welcomed them into their home, and then work through the trust and relationship networks of their hosts (Lk 10). Paul did the same. He would enter a city and start a business. He was a tentmaker by trade, so he started making and selling tents and thus building relationships in the marketplace. He also connected with religious seekers at synagogues. Because he was Jewish, he initially had trust and a hearing there, though he lost that bridge when he succeeded in pulling seekers away from the synagogue into the fledgling messianic movement he advocated.

These networks of trust are always the highways of relationship, communication, and influence that lead to faith and to congregational involvement. When people aren't building and being bridges, most of their friends and the people in their communities will never be reached. One of the great challenges in any place and time period for the church is to understand and then work through the networks of relationships in that particular culture. In American culture, those networks are often smaller and based around affinity. One of the major shifts in our culture that we need to respond to is that communities are more fluid, flexible, and flowing than they used to be. We live in a culture less connected through institutional hardwiring and more connected through microcultural affinity groupings. We live in a liquid culture of flow, of overlapping networks, more than a solid culture of discrete institutions, at least in the ways we form friendships and community.[3] Churches must respond by creating many more microcommunities to reach people in different affinity groupings. InterVarsity Christian Fellowship is one example of a ministry reaching the next generation on college campuses that has adapted to this social change by restating their vision as reaching "every corner of every campus." Microchurch is a very important dimension of missional communities of the future. My small group book club in my condo building is another simple example of microchurch expanding along affinity group networks.

Chris's story helps us see the significance of personal invitations through affinity networks more clearly. In spring 2014, Chris knew that his marriage with Diane was on the rocks.[4] In the midst of a strained relationship, he was growing increasingly desperate. Although he and his wife had never really attended church, their son was involved in the church's youth group, and one day his son told him, "Dad, you need to come to church, and you need to commit your life to Christ." His son's words broke loose something in his heart, and Chris's life began to take a 180-degree turn as he committed his life to Christ and began attending a smaller congregation.

As God continued to work in his life, Chris began sharing his story on Facebook. Tracy, an old high school friend with whom he hadn't spoken in over twenty years, saw his posts and reached out to him, explaining that she was about to leave her husband, Jim. She continued "He's really going to need a friend, and you could call him or something." So Chris reached out and invited Jim to church. Soon after, Jim committed himself to Christ and began experiencing dramatic changes in his life—so dramatic that even his wife took notice.

At the time, Tracy had no religious preference, though she had been raised Wiccan and had explored both the Mormon Church and Jehovah's Witnesses. However, the transformation in her husband's life piqued her interest, and so she came to church with her husband one week. In the middle of the service, she stood up and said, "You people don't know me, but my name is Tracy, and I am Jim's wife. Two months ago, I contacted Chris and told him that I'm leaving my husband, and it was over and we were done. After fifteen years of marriage, we were facing defeat and divorce." She continued, "I don't know what you did to my husband, but whatever has happened to him, I want that in my life. I want what he has, but I don't know how to get it."

Steve Colter, the pastor there, explained the gospel simply and told Tracy, "It's a matter of opening your heart to the Lord Jesus Christ."

There, in the middle of the service, she gave her life to the Lord. Reunited with each other, Tracy and Jim began coming to church every week and brought their teenage children along, one of whom was involved in Campus Crusade for Christ (now Cru) at her high school and had been praying for her parents as all of this unfolded.

Tracy's mom passed away the following year, and at the funeral Tracy was able to reconnect with her sister, who she had not seen in twenty years. Tracy discovered that her sister was searching for God, and so she invited her sister to their church's Easter service. Since then her sister has given her life to Jesus and has begun bringing her family to church as well. On top of that, Karen, Jim's sister, was amazed at the changes she saw in his life, and so she also came to Christ a few months later.

Through Chris's story, we see just how powerful a simple invitation can be, especially when it runs through preexisting relational networks of friends and family. Through the initial invitation of Chris's son, the lives of nine people were eventually affected. The beauty of it is that this is not just an isolated anecdote. The research findings clearly demonstrate the incredible influence of personal invitations by enthusiastic people. Personal invitations lead to changed lives and multiply throughout the relational networks of the people involved.

In conversion communities, this dynamic picks up momentum and impact as it unfolds. People invite people, who turn around and invite more people. Often the best inviters are the ones who have just experienced the life change and are still connected to networks of unchurched and irreligious friends and family members. Life change coupled with a culture of invitation often leads to countless people becoming interested in Christ and in congregations. We saw it again and again in our research. As people get excited about their faith and their congregation, invitations multiply, and so do followers and reproducers for Christ.

Recognizing Opportunities Around Us

Not only are our invitations more effective than we realize, but we also have more opportunities to invite others than we're aware of. From working with many pastors and congregation members, as well as professors at Christian colleges and businesspeople who seem to have only church friends, I have discovered a startling fact. Although most people don't think they have very many opportunities to reach out and invite others, they actually have far more opportunities than they think.

We must grapple with the fact that our lack of awareness of possible opportunities is often as big an issue as the lack of time and connections with unchurched individuals that create those opportunities in the first place. We have fallen asleep at the wheel. Keith Green makes a similar point in his poignant song "Asleep in the Light."[5] We have lost our sensitivity to opportunity. Both in our present relationships and life patterns and in our past relationships and opportunities, we often have far more connections than we have acted on.

Over the years, I've gotten to know Tim and have come to respect him a lot. He is a pastor of a very large church and can often feel like he has very low margin in his life. As we began meeting together in our cohort, he kept noting how surprised he was at the opportunities he already had that he had been unaware of and had let pass him by. This was a powerful realization for him. This is true of so many of us. He is a leader who was already seeing opportunities and acting on them before he ever came to the cohort, yet he still realized there were so many more.

If we stop and think about all the different arenas of our lives in which we have a measure of influence, we will begin to see all the opportunities we have to reach out to others. One source of such opportunities is people you've known in the past. Maybe it is time to rekindle a relationship, make a phone call, or send an email. Another source is extended family. So often God wants us to rekindle our prayer, our service, and our blessing of those in the extended family of which we are part. Often our opportunities lie in our everyday lives, as we come and go, walk through our neighborhood, or pick up coffee at Starbucks or wherever we are.

For Marge, an opportunity came during her aerobics class.[6] Marge was in her late eighties and had been a faithful member of her local congregation for several decades. Despite having deep roots of faith, she had never shared the gospel or her faith story with anyone. There were many reasons that made her feel uncomfortable talking about faith.

[handwritten margin note: I don't want to get to that age and say the same!]

That began to shift, however, when her church hosted a training called "Share Jesus Without Fear." Marge participated in the training event and began to believe that she could share the gospel with others.

Eventually Marge struck up a conversation with Mia, the twenty-something fitness instructor who led her aerobics class. Marge turned the conversation to spiritual matters and shared her faith with Mia. She then invited Mia to come to a block party that her church was hosting. When the block party rolled around, Mia showed up with her husband, Luis, and their son. It didn't take long to see that Mia and her son were thoroughly enjoying the party. Luis, however, seemed upset about something the whole time. He clearly didn't want to be there, or anywhere near the church for that matter.

During the block party, Jonathan, the pastor of the church who was hosting the party, and his wife, Sharon, met Mia and Luis. Mia and Sharon quickly connected over both having two kids, and their friendship grew from there. Sharon never pressured Mia to come to church, but as Sharon kept reaching out and investing in the relationship, Mia slowly began to visit the church every now and then.

Everything seemed fine on the outside. Luis had a great job, and they lived in a nice house. But as Sharon got to know them more, she realized that Mia and Luis were dealing with some significant challenges. Their marriage was struggling, and Luis was stuck in a serious drug addiction. With hearts of compassion, the church began to pray earnestly, asking God to intervene and transform the situation.

As an answer to prayer, Mia began attending the church more regularly and even committed her life to the Lord. A year later, Luis made his first appearance in church. He also showed up to a marriage class that the church was offering on Wednesday nights. The course lasted for six weeks, and Luis and Mia committed to working with Jonathan on some of their issues. Not long after the class ended, Luis reached a turning point in his life. He met with Jonathan and some other men in the church and gave his life to the Lord. Luis also let them know he was struggling with a drug addiction. He was met with love and support by the community. Over the following years, Luis grew in his faith and was able to come out of his addiction.

Marge's simple invitation turned out to be a gateway to transformation. Because Marge took the risk to share her faith for the first time ever, Mia and Luis and their children ended up getting connected to a vibrant church community, committing their lives to Jesus, and experiencing God's love to bind up the brokenness in their lives.

During a follow-up interview, Jonathan acknowledged that "all of this took time. It was conversation after conversation from several different people in the church, just to get to the point then where they accepted the gospel, to where they moved in to our community of faith." Nothing in this process happened overnight. It took love, prayer, and perseverance on the part of Sharon and the whole church community to see Mia and Luis experience that transformation. And it took Marge having the courage to recognize that she had an opportunity to reach out in the middle of the normal rhythms of her life.

We have more opportunities already built into the fabric of our lives than we often take advantage of. As we find ways to belong in our community and bless those around us, other opportunities will come our way. We may even begin to realize that we have more opportunities to reach out to unchurched individuals around us than we thought possible. For Marge it happened to be an aerobics class. Who knows what it might be for us?

Persevering Past Rejection

As we just read in the story of Mia and Luis, the process of transformation takes time, patience, and perseverance. It is challenging enough to persevere in our witness in the midst of the many demands of life, but it's even more difficult to reach out when we face the reality of rejection. In the midst of rejection, it's crucial for us to remember that we are simply called to be faithful in our outreach. We cannot control how people will choose to respond, but we can choose to love them regardless. God can use our invitations in the lives of others, even when they seem to fall flat in the moment and we don't see any results.

It can be surprising how an earlier invitation that was rejected can lead to a new openness and interest down the road. Sometimes the transition from a rejected invitation to an accepted one can even happen quite quickly. This was certainly true for Laura.

Walking up the street, an eighty-year-old Laura was lost in conversation with her friend.[7] As they walked by, a stranger interrupted them, inviting them to an evening of food and fellowship at a local church. Not paying much attention, she and her friend kept walking. "Don't hold your breath waiting," Laura muttered. Laura turned to her friend and said, "Are you going?"

"No," her friend responded.

"Me neither. I don't know what this guy's looking for, but he is not going to talk me into anything."

However, when 7 p.m. rolled around, Laura told her friend she was just stepping out for a minute and went down to the church to see what was going on. She soon fell into conversation with the pastor, and over hot dogs, popcorn, and coffee, Laura's story unfolded. She had attended church in the past but left over a disagreement in which members of the church had lied to her. The church also lost her trust because it "always said things would work out," but that was not the case in her life. She had lost several members of her family (father, mother, and two brothers), along with a friend who passed away from cancer. Through her many painful life circumstances, she had lost trust in God, thinking that God was doing these things to her. Consequently, she lived with, in her words, a bit of an attitude toward God.

Pastor Maner gently confronted her, asking whether it was really fair to blame God for the deaths in her family. Was God really doing that to her? Sadly, death is part of all of our lives. Before she knew it, the night came to an end, and as she prepared to leave, she found and thanked the person who had invited her. As she was on her way out, Pastor Maner took the opportunity to invite her to the Sunday worship service. "I'll see you on Sunday morning."

Laura responded, "I don't think so."

"No?" he replied.

"No, I don't think so."

At first she had been skeptical about what he was saying, but "when I sat back and thought about it, what he said was the truth. It wasn't nothing that was a lie. It was the truth." She confessed to her friend later, "I think he knows what he's talking about. Maybe I should give it a try." Her friend stayed home, but at 9 a.m. on Sunday, Laura found herself at church and has been going ever since. Reflecting on her journey, Laura is pretty convinced that "If I hadn't run into that man on the street somewhat randomly inviting people, I don't think I'd be

in church today.... I swear the Lord had something to do with it."
Two rejected invitations have turned into a life in a congregation and
in the faith. Although invitations work better when we know people
more deeply, even planting seeds with strangers can bear fruit if it is
done with care.

When others reject our invitations, it's tempting to think that
nothing has happened, but that is not true. With every invitation,
God's love can be extended to the other person, and God is continually at work in people's lives. We may give up, but the Spirit of God
does not.

Lest we give up too soon, persistence often pays off, as the next
story from our research illustrates.

As a salesman of a network marketing company, Miles began
reaching out in his different relational connections to generate sales,
and one person he invited to his home was Philip, a friend from his
childhood.[8] Miles soon discovered Philip was a committed Christian
and congregation member. Philip visited Miles, and instead of buying
his product, invited Miles to church. Although Miles didn't respond
to his invitation, the friendship was rekindled, and they connected
more often after that.

Every time Philip saw him, he asked, "Why don't you come to
church with me?" Miles explained he couldn't because he was too busy,
which was true. At the time he was working seven days a week at a
restaurant, a job he took after his time with the marketing firm.
However, soon after that restaurant closed, Miles and his girlfriend,
Sara, with whom he was living, lost $40,000. Miles was also strug-
gling with alcoholism and vividly remembers a night when he was
stopped by a cop for driving under the influence. He knew at that
moment that things had to change. Remembering Philip's invitation,
Miles went home and asked Sara, "Would you consider going to
church with me so he'll shut up about it? Because I'm tired of hearing

it, but he's not going to be quiet until we do." With that, they decided to give church a try.

The next week Miles and Sara found seats in the back of the church. He and his girlfriend heard different things from the same message as the pastor's words convicted them each in individual ways. When people were invited at the end of the service to give their lives to God, Miles deliberated how to respond, but he heard God speak to his heart, "Go, this is it." As he moved to the aisle, Sara took his hand, and they committed their lives to Christ together. After that, their lives began to change. They married a month and a half later, and they were baptized together the Sunday after that. The day he committed his life to Christ, his addiction to alcohol disappeared, along with his strong dislike for reading. Of course, changes in terms of issues such as addiction rarely happen overnight, but this time it did. Since then he has jumped into Bible studies with others as well as on his own.

Miles needed a friend like Philip who would be persistent and keep inviting him, even when he kept saying no. Because Philip persevered in reaching out to Miles, despite being repeatedly rejected, Miles eventually opened up his heart to God and experienced dramatic transformation in his life. Of course, Philip had no way of knowing this ahead of time, and neither do we. We don't know how God's love is going to transform people, but we know that it will. We must not lose sight of the transformation that God is inviting people into. As we keep that in mind, we will be able to endure both the rejection we might face and the discouragements we may deal with along the way. As the apostle Paul prays, "May the Lord direct [our] hearts into God's love and Christ's perseverance" (2 Thess 3:5).

Cultivating an Invitational Culture

Our top-10-percent conversion-growth congregations did not just have people who invited others and knew how to do so effectively. The

congregation as a whole had developed a culture of invitation. Many
people were inviting others to church, but the invitations didn't stop
there. Church members were consistently inviting others to join a
small group, to contribute in a ministry, and to commit to faith. Invitations were happening every step of the way along the journey to faith
for unchurched individuals.

Notice how this played out in Miles's story. Philip persistently invited Miles to visit the church. The pastor invited Miles to give his life
to Christ, and he made space and time for him to respond. After that,
a small group leader invited Miles to join a group and begin studying
the Bible. This church was a strong conversion community and had an
invitational culture on every level. Lives were being transformed as
a result.

In order to cultivate an invitational culture, it's important to recognize that there are different kinds of invitations. Conversion
communities have found ways to effectively invite people into:

- trust and relationship

- spiritual conversation

- Christian worship or entry-point opportunities

- small group community

- contribution of time to a ministry

- commitment to Christ as forgiver and leader

- inviting others to Christ and your congregation

This is not a purely linear process, where people have to go through
earlier steps to get to later steps. Sometimes people attend once and
already volunteer for something, and then go home and invite family
or friends because they were inspired or encouraged. So the bullet
points above are more like a spectrum than clearly defined and discrete steps. The key idea is seeing just how central this culture of

invitation is to every step an unchurched person takes toward connecting with a congregation and committing to Christ. Winsome and sensitive invitations shoot through the whole process of people's transformation. What's more, the point at which people commit to Christ as forgiver and leader can take place almost anywhere along the spectrum. Conversion-growth churches understand this process and are intentional about creating the steps so people can move seamlessly along the spectrum.

Interestingly, we found that none of the top-10-percent conversion-growth congregations had an invitational program or Invitation Training 101. Inviting was modeled by leaders and caught on with people. In contrast, I will never forget the pastor in one of our cohorts who designed a whole series so that his people would invite others. He exhorted them to invite unchurched individuals in their lives. He came up with catchy titles and made sure that every message addressed a question that unchurched and seeking people might be interested in. He printed up cards for people to give friends describing the series. The only thing he didn't do was invite anyone. He was quite surprised and dismayed when no one else did either. Sadly for this pastor, invitational cultures only begin and spread when leaders and laypeople actually start inviting others and enthusiasm starts growing. Again, imitation wins the day, every time.

The bottom line is that we just need to reach out in faith and invite someone. So how do we do it well? Good invitations need to be sender initiated but receiver oriented in the way they are phrased and communicated. Here are questions you can ask to determine whether you are being receiver oriented in your invitations:

1. What is the person's spiritual journey story, and how does my invitation relate to their journey and their needs and to how God has already been at work leading them in this direction?

2. What can I affirm about their life and openness, and why they would appreciate what might happen at the service or event? People sometimes will respond so much better when you invite them to something because they are very cool people who would love this kind of an opportunity than when you tell people, "Wow, your life is really on the rocks. You really need to come to church with me!"

3. What have I experienced at times of need that they could relate to? How can I invite them out of my own sense of need and vulnerability and not because I have it all together and they don't? When you can share your own need, then you can challenge them with theirs, and they will more likely be open to your challenge.

4. How can I let them know in a genuine and heartfelt way that they will not experience being judged or being pressured to be something they are not? Those two great fears are the speed bumps nearly every unchurched person has to get over in order to cross the threshold of a congregation. Our invitations need to disarm their defenses and fears. Often the best way to disarm is to mention how you felt afraid of those things yourself when you first attended, and the church accepted, loved, and wanted you. Hopefully, you can say that authentically.

There is one additional dimension of being receiver oriented. Sometimes the best place to initially bring someone is not your congregation. Sometimes you need to go the extra mile and start with a step the person you are inviting *can* take, not the step you *want* them to take. It might be an entry-point ministry rather than your Sunday service. It might be a social engagement opportunity. It might also be a different congregation or denomination. A Catholic couple in my neighborhood was very spiritually interested but had been turned off by Protestants and Protestant churches. So my wife and I looked for a renewed and alive congregation of Catholics in our area. We found a church that sponsored healing and renewal services and that was very globally connected. We invited our receptive neighbors to a healing service led by a visiting priest from India that genuinely communicated the good news about Jesus and demonstrated that good news by practicing pastoral healing prayer in special services. Our neighbors loved the service and began their journey back toward Christ and a congregation, even if not my congregation. Even though unchurched people are very receptive to invitations to congregations, what we invite them to matters a lot. I am not minimizing important theological differences here but rather challenging us to love people well and help them take the step toward Jesus that they are able to take.

I love how Jesus models being receiver oriented in his conversation with the Samaritan woman in John 4. When he asks, "Will you give me a drink?" he starts with a need he has, a way he is vulnerable (question three above), asking the Samaritan woman for service in a way that gives her dignity and boldness in addressing him (Jn 4:7). She responds by wondering how he, a Jew, can ask her, a Samaritan, for anything, much less even talk to her. He speaks about what he had to offer that can profoundly meet a spiritual need she has (question one above). "If you knew the gift of God and who it is that asks you for a drink, you would have asked him and he would have given you living water" (Jn 4:10). Then I deeply love how Jesus deals with issues of judgment and pressure. He asks her to get her husband, and she tells him she has none. Then he tells her about her life, but in the context of accepting her and offering her living water (and forgiveness). "You are right when you say you have no husband. The fact is, you have had five husbands, and the man you now have is not your husband. What you have just said is quite true" (Jn 4:17-18). It is not that we accept everything people do. It is instead that we know them, including their dark side, and we welcome them, accept them, and offer them hope. Finally, he reveals himself to her more deeply than he did to many other people he encountered (question two above). He invites her in. He affirms her dignity and welcomes her into his mission. The other disciples can't believe it when they return. She joins God's work, and a whole town is converted. Not everybody that Jesus reached joined Jesus' itinerant congregation. Some started their own, like this woman did.

Joining God at Work

I love how the Gospel writer John captures the invitational persistence of God in the words of Jesus. A lot of religious leaders tried to put Jesus in a box and tell him when it was time for God to work and when it was time for God to take time off, and how Jesus kept getting it wrong. In one instance, Jesus has just healed a man who had been crippled for thirty-eight years. Instead of being happy that this disabled man who had lain in one place for so long is now walking around and carrying his pallet with him, the religious leaders tell Jesus he sinned and did wrong because he told the man to carry his pallet on a Sabbath. They are clearly missing the point and rejecting the joyous news of such a changed life. Religious people, Jesus tells us, often miss the point.

Jesus' response in that moment is right on target. He says to them, "My Father is always at his work to this very day, and I too am working" (Jn 5:17). This captures beautifully the kind of expectation I am encouraging you to have. You are part of a team, with the Holy Spirit, who is already at work drawing people and preparing people for invitations in their lives. Not only is God at work, but other people are too. Often several of us, unknown to each other, are extending care and invitations to others. Sooner or later, the result can look like Holly's experience.

Holly grew up attending church with her mom.[9] After high school, she joined the Air Force and remained consistent with church for a while. However, as she began to make life choices that her parents didn't approve of, she also began to drift away from church. She observed that she was just as good as others who went to church, and so she came to the conclusion that "I can be just as good a person and stay here in my own home." In that way church essentially became unnecessary in her life.

Later in life, during her forties, Holly's mother continued to be a huge source of encouragement to her, and her mom let her know that she was consistently praying for her. Holly's sixteen-year-old son began attending church with a friend of his, and he consistently came home repeating, "Mom, you need to go to church." Through her mother and her son, Holly's desire to attend church began to resurface in her life, but because of her shyness, she hesitated to go without her husband.

One day, her husband had a conversation with a neighbor, who encouraged him to seek out God and "find out what it was all about." Also around that time, her husband's karate instructor (who happened to be a pastor but also a broker between a karate community and a congregation) invited them to church. They decided to visit and only then discovered that it was the same church that their son had been attending. During the service Holly was convicted by the message, convinced that the pastor was speaking directly to her. After visiting for four or five weeks, she decided to commit her life to Christ and began to grow in her newfound faith. With the help of others, she made it through early crises with her son and then with her finances, and today she is a powerful agent of the same kind of love and invitation she received.

People are more open and receptive than we think, and we have many more opportunities than we are capitalizing on. As we reach out and invite unchurched people to our church community and to faith, we must always remember that we are a part of something much larger than ourselves. We are part of an extended invitation team, including friends, family members, and others who love God, love their neighbor, and love their congregation. Beyond all that, God is already at work, preparing people's hearts for our invitations, long before we get involved in their lives. Jesus said it this way in John 6:44: "No one can come to me unless the Father who sent me draws them." It is very encouraging to realize that when we are inviting people, especially if we do so sensitively and after asking questions about where they are, we're often right in the current of the work of God's Spirit to draw people to himself.

Questions for Discussion

1. What entry points does your church or small group offer that you would be excited to invite receptive unchurched people to? If you don't presently have a good entry-point opportunity to invite people into, what could you offer?

2. As you look at the characteristics of being receiver oriented, what comes naturally to you, and where do you need help to grow?

3. What are some of the invitations you have offered that people have rejected? What did you learn, and what could help you keep persevering?

4. Where is your church strong on the spectrum of different invitations, and where do you need to be more intentional to provide a concrete step and action for people?

11

Building a Community of the Beloved Through Hospitality

The final step in the process of developing missional congregations is welcoming unchurched individuals to be the beloved. This is the capstone of the process, the ultimate goal of transforming those who were outside the church into not only friends but fellow followers and advocates for Jesus. As Christians, our primary identity is wrapped up in our faith. We are the beloved, as the apostle John calls us, because we know both that God lavishes his love on us as his children and that we then are to love one another (1 Jn 3:1). In light of this, we don't simply want unchurched people to become churched people; we want them to become children of God and experience belonging in the family of God and begin to invite others along too.

Among conversion communities, this new identity takes root and flourishes among visitors through the practice of hospitality. Top-10-percent conversion-growth churches have learned to be hospitable in the biblical sense, and it has made *all* the difference in their capacity for growing through conversions that stick. In *Saved by Faith and Hospitality*, theologian Joshua Jipp provides us with a perfect lens through which to understand hospitality within the broader arc of mission and evangelism. Hospitality, according to Jipp, is "the act or process whereby

the identity of the stranger is transformed into that of guest."[1] This is
exactly what God has done for us. He extended his love to us while we
were still sinners and welcomed us to experience his love when we were
still strangers (Rom 5:8). As we receive God's love and hospitality, it
changes our core identity from being a sinner to being God's beloved.

As Jipp points out, it is because the church has been a recipient of
God's generous hospitality that we can extend hospitality to each other
as well as those who are still estranged from the family of God. And
indeed we must. This practice of hospitality is a core component of our
witness and a key practice of missional congregations. As figure 11.1
illustrates, as we invite and bring others with us into our church
community, unchurched people can experience the love and hospitality
of God in ways that help them realize that they are beloved of God.

Figure 11.1. The process of developing a missional congregation

As we testify to the life-transforming love of God and welcome others to experience it as well, we will grow in becoming the conversion communities that God has always intended his church to be.

When Hospitality Is Missing

Too often hospitality is not one of the qualities people associate with their past experiences with church. Whether they attended church growing up or had only peripheral dealings with a local church at various times in their life, people rarely have a framework for understanding the kind of hospitality that conversion communities regularly practice. Instead, many express a sense of unwelcomeness at churches that pushes them to not stay long. Of even greater concern, many of these churches are completely unaware of this problem, expecting unchurched visitors to feel welcome through the same experience that draws church insiders to their services and ministries. This environment implicitly places an expectation on unchurched visitors to adapt to the existing church culture rather than creating bridges for new people unfamiliar with the idiosyncrasies of church life.

Over the past few years, I had the opportunity to be a witness to Chris, a friend who lives in another city on the West Coast. In one of our recent discussions, Chris recounted that he was thinking about visiting a church again for the first time in a number of years. While Chris has shown interest in spiritual things and is genuinely a loving person, his interest in a return to church was prompted by recent relational strife. His girlfriend recently let him know she is having second thoughts about their relationship and wants to take a break. In light of the difficult transition out of the relationship and because he had recently expressed a desire to revisit the issue of church, on a visit to Chris I invited him to take me along to a church he had seen nearby. Neither of us knew much of anything about this church as we walked into the sanctuary with a fairly small congregation. We saw a couple of parents with kids, and another younger couple standing off to the side of the sanctuary talking and drinking coffee. We chose a seat two-thirds of the way back, and people gradually found their seats. I was struck by how well everyone knew each other, warmly greeting each other and enjoying reconnecting after a week apart. As we had arrived fifteen minutes early, we both sat and watched as seemingly every person greeted everyone else. Yet over that span, no one greeted us. In a congregation where we stood out as the *only* visitors, everyone was content with their established relationships. If not for one woman waving at us from a distance and mouthing "Welcome," we would have entered and left without ever being acknowledged.

Although the sermon started fairly typically, with the pastor welcoming the congregation, it veered off track quickly when he went on a ten-minute tangent about the demon marijuana. For Chris, who had little experience with the church and was in the midst of a small congregation where drug use did not seem to be a pressing concern, the choice seemed to target him specifically. He later told me that it felt like the pastor singled him out, glancing at this newcomer frequently and menacingly as if to drive home his point. When the service ended, the pastor and church leaders remained up at the front. Sadly, we were able to slowly drift out from the church, with no substantive point of contact with anyone and what seemed like an oddly targeted sermon fresh in Chris's memory.

Needless to say, the event was damaging to the relational capital I had built with Chris. I had engaged him as a member of his community, developed a relationship with him through serving, and brought him to church where he could witness the body of Christ in worship, only to have the process stalled. Chris had finally taken a step back toward God, and it seemed like the hard work was being undone. Suffice it to say I would never make the mistake of taking inquiring people in my community to untested churches again. I will at least visit their website and look for clues as to their hospitality.

But what happened? Why was this visit so catastrophic? At its core this church had a hospitality problem. They would say they were warm and welcoming, but this affection was reserved for those *in* the community. When it came to their outreach, hospitality was missing. We think we are welcoming when we feel at home ourselves. But the test is when people different from us enter our community. Do they feel at home? Only they can tell you.

The example I recounted above might feel extreme, and readers might congratulate themselves on not being as closed off as this church. Yet our interviews uncovered many examples, among which I will cite just one more.

Liz is a waitress, Catholic by background. She is in that group of the one out of three emerging adults who still identify as Catholic in their early thirties. Liz occasionally attends a Mass on Christmas or Christmas Eve. When asked what her religious preference is, she says right away, "Catholic!" At one point she even further clarified, "I am not Christian, I am Catholic." This loyalty to a cultural version of Christian faith is common among Catholics who identify as Catholic without attending or connecting to any local church or parish. It also demonstrates the way in which the Protestant majority, particularly the evangelical majority, has often captured the designation "Christian" in many circles.

Liz expects to be attending church regularly in the future. When I first interviewed her, she was expecting her first child and talked about how much she feels the need for help in the area of values when it comes to bringing up kids in the world as it is. When I interviewed her a second time, she had given birth to her first child.

Catholic churches have the advantage in reaching out to Liz. But Catholic churches have struggled more than evangelical and non-denominational churches over how to reach people like Liz in a way that feels compelling, relevant, and easy for Liz to enter and engage. In the second interview, after the birth of her child, she related a story that emphasizes the difficulty people sometimes have in returning to the Catholic Church. When she called her local parish church to arrange for the baptism of her forthcoming child, she felt like the church put up a lot of hoops for her to jump through for her to reconnect. She needed the record of her Catholic affiliation, baptism, and first Communion, and she even needed the record of the Catholic affiliation of her godparents. She had trouble providing documentation, and no one at the church reached out to her, or invited her in, or tried to help her navigate the difficulties. It was as if they didn't really want her back. They seemed to Liz to be more concerned for their rules than for her. I know many Catholic churches are much more welcoming than what Liz experienced, including the parish church in our area of Chicago's South Loop, Old St. Mary's, but many more need to become so. The happy ending is that Liz did find a Catholic church that was alive and welcoming, and she is now involved. But too often that doesn't happen.

The reality is that many churches are simply unaware of how outsiders experience their Sunday morning services or their attempts to reconnect. Do you really know how people coming to church for the first time or the first time in a long time feel about what they experience at your church? Are you ready, through extending hospitality, to transform the stranger into a beloved member of the church, or are you more concerned with keeping that all in the family? Do you have unintended barriers to first-time visitors of which you might not even be aware? These are the questions of hospitality that face every church that wants to grow and reach out.

There are serious consequences for the lack of the practice of hospitality to the outsider, the seeker, the skeptic, or the stranger to the faith. People like Chris never come back. They leave more alienated than when they came, and the "lost" sheep becomes even more lost.

These consequences are felt not just by unchurched people but by all who visit a church whose culture is closed to the outsider. For instance, I have often spoken with churches that are ethnically homogeneous. They will tell me that they are committed to diversity and are always friendly when people of other ethnicities show up in church. So they can't understand why so often those people don't come back. When I visit the church, it is fairly easy for me to understand why people might not come back. They don't feel welcomed, expected, and addressed, including in the ways their ethnic background is important to them. They are outsiders to the culture and don't fit, and they know it. They don't feel at home.

That is often exactly how unchurched people can feel when they visit a church, whether they are seeking, skeptical, or merely strangers to the faith. They often <u>aren't expected</u>. They <u>don't feel welcomed,</u> given where they are spiritually, and they don't experience the fullness of God's love through the church. I would suggest that when this kind of dynamic happens, these churches have not taken the time to become truly hospitable to the other, the stranger. As a result, people can feel unwelcome, unwanted, excluded, and maybe even judged in the very place that ought most and best to usher people into a new identity as the beloved of God.

Understanding Biblical Hospitality

So how do churches learn to be hospitable to the seeker, skeptic, or stranger to the faith? How do churches continually cultivate that core identity of being beloved among both those who have never been to church before and those who have grown up in church but perhaps have never fully committed their lives and need acceptance through a rough time or a wrong decision?

It begins with <u>recapturing a biblical understanding of hospitality</u> and then <u>pursuing it</u>. Hospitality is welcome to the outsider, the stranger, the unlike. Especially in Scripture there is emphasis on the other as the poor, the needy, and the religiously disconnected. In *Making Room: Recovering Hospitality as a Christian Tradition*, Christine Pohl explains,

> [Biblical hospitality] included welcoming strangers into the home and offering them food, shelter, and protection. Providing hospitality also involved recognizing the stranger's worth and common humanity. Hospitality is an important theme in Scripture and is central to the gospel story itself. Both rewarding and challenging, hospitality remains an important expression of Christian faith today.[2]

Pohl goes on to say that "hospitality is a skill, gift, spiritual obligation, and also a practice."[3] It is this practice that conversion communities demonstrate, maybe as much as any other quality, especially to the unchurched, the seeker, the skeptic, the stranger, and the alienated. People who fear being judged find acceptance. People who fear being pressured to be something they're not discover that they are beloved just as they are. People who thought church was not really for them find out that they are included, accepted, addressed, and encouraged. In other words, the biblical tradition of hospitality practiced across various cultures and various times has long been understood to be intertwined with the proclamation of the gospel. It is a reenactment of our own faith and one of the most tangible manifestations to an unbelieving world that we have been brought close to God through God's Son.

In our culture, hospitality conjures up images of coziness, of family and friends, of those close to us coming into our homes and then reciprocating back toward us, having us into their homes. Churches that welcome friends and family, that emphasize those already close and inside, can feel to themselves like very warm and hospitable churches. But when outsiders enter, they can feel disconnected, unwelcome, and put off by the warmth, closeness, and impenetrability of the in-group. When people who are part of the in-group think a church is very warm and outsiders feel like it is off-putting, the church is exemplifying the opposite of Jesus' concept of hospitality and communicates that outsiders are unloved rather than beloved.

Jesus addresses what we often think about as hospitality when he talks about how the Gentiles invite their own friends and family over and get invited in return. So often in our churches we practice the same kind of hospitality, oriented to ourselves, the already found. If so, we already have our reward. Jesus emphasizes this point, saying,

> When you give a luncheon or dinner, do not invite your friends, your brothers or sisters, your relatives, or your rich neighbors; if you do, they may invite you back and so you will be repaid. But when you give a banquet, invite the poor, the crippled, the lame, the blind, and you will be blessed. Although they cannot repay you, you will be repaid at the resurrection of the righteous. (Lk 14:12-14)

It is also interesting to see where Jesus gets angry and judgmental. It is as a result of the exclusion of people from the community of God. It is when the blind and lame, foreigners and women, are excluded from being considered worthy of worshiping God. Jesus gets so angry at that exclusion that he goes into the temple and turns over moneychangers' tables because the court of the Gentiles is no longer a place of prayer for the nations (Mk 11:15-17). When eating at the home of the rich, Jesus includes and affirms a poor woman, possibly a prostitute, who crashes the dinner and wipes his feet with her tears out of love and gratitude (Lk 7:36-50). Jesus celebrates that she loves much, while the hearts of his rich hosts are cold and have little love. Again and again Jesus practices hospitality, radically welcoming those who are excluded and disconnected into a new identity as the beloved of God. Is that the culture of our congregation?

The Centrality of Hospitality

As the church, we are called to cultivate this kind of hospitality. It is what is biblical and right, and from our research it is also *the most important predictive factor of churches becoming conversion communities.* Figures 11.2 and 11.3 capture this finding from our survey of three thousand churches across the country.

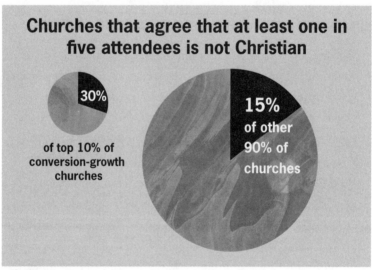

Source: Billy Graham Center Institute and Lifeway Research, Evangelism Survey of Three Thousand Protestant Churches.

Figure 11.2. Churches that agree that at least one in five attendees is not Christian: top-10-percent conversion-growth churches compared to other 90 percent

Figure 11.2 shows that top-10-percent conversion-growth churches, our conversion communities, attract and keep non-Christians at double the rate of other churches. As we interviewed pastors of these churches, we found that these churches practice hospitality that powerfully communicates God's love to people far from God who believe differently and are somewhat fearful about visiting congregations.

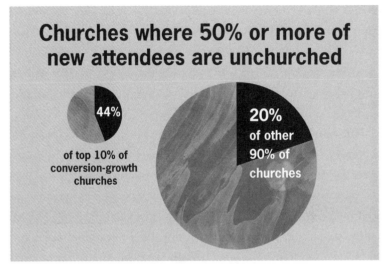

Source: Billy Graham Center Institute and Lifeway Research, Evangelism Survey of Three Thousand Protestant Churches.

Figure 11.3. Churches where 50 percent or more of new attendees are unchurched: top-10-percent conversion-growth churches compared to other 90 percent

Figure 11.3 reinforces the same point. For nearly half of all top-10-percent churches, more than half their new members were unchurched before they started attending. These churches attract, keep, and contribute to the needs and the lives of unchurched people in effective ways. They are profoundly hospitable to unchurched people and demonstrate love in ways that help the strangers and outsiders in their midst understand that they are beloved of God.

This factor of hospitality to the unchurched was the top predictive factor in our study of three thousand churches of every size plus an additional study of fifteen hundred small churches. Our qualitative interviews consistently emphasized this point as well and fleshed out what the statistics meant.

In our interviews we heard unchurched people express that they felt welcomed when they arrived and knew how to get to the places they were looking for (e.g., the kids' ministry rooms). Church members were attentive to the needs of those around them and went out of their way to care about first-time visitors. In these top-10-percent churches, the warm welcome extended beyond the greeting team. Many church members took the initiative to introduce themselves to visitors. This hospitality existed beyond the church building, as members invited visitors to connect outside the church context.

During our interviews we also found that the pastor, worship team members, small group leaders, and staff members were available and accessible to visitors. Previously unchurched individuals reported that the pastor was authentic and relatable in personal conversations as well as in sermons from the front. That sense of authenticity helped cultivate a safe place where people, both visitors and attenders, felt free to be themselves and ask any question they had. Over time visitors expressed that the church felt like home.

Hospitality can take a lot of different forms. There is not just one way to make people feel loved and valued, and people grow in their identity as God's beloved in different ways. You do not have to be a church full of extroverts to be warm and welcoming. Your church can identify its own strengths and what kind of unchurched people you might best be able to show hospitality to. Ask some of the people you feel you could best reach what they would respond to. Ask them to come to your church once as a favor to give you feedback on how you are doing. We don't have to be great at welcoming every kind of unchurched person, but we need to be great at welcoming some.

Hospitality in the Pulpit

It's important for a culture of hospitality to permeate the life of the church. Because the sermon is such a key component of Sunday worship services, it is not surprising that the pastor's ability to communicate with unchurched people through preaching is especially important.

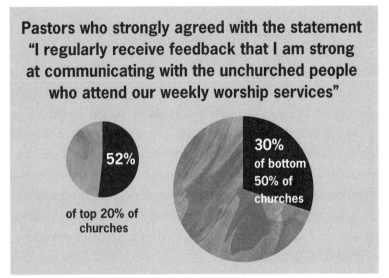

Pastors who strongly agreed with the statement "I regularly receive feedback that I am strong at communicating with the unchurched people who attend our weekly worship services"

52% of top 20% of churches

30% of bottom 50% of churches

Source: Billy Graham Center Institute and Lifeway Research, Small Church Evangelism Study. We used top 20 percent and bottom 50 percent in this graph because of sample size.

Figure 11.4. Pastors who strongly agreed with the statement "I regularly receive feedback that I am strong at communicating with the unchurched people who attend our weekly worship services": top-20-percent churches compared to bottom 50 percent

In fact, a pastor's ability to consider the reception of the sermon by unchurched people on Sunday mornings turned out to be one of our predictive factors in becoming a top-10-percent conversion-growth church. Over half of the pastors in top-20-percent churches (we used top 20 percent here because of sample size) strongly agreed that they regularly receive feedback that they communicate well with unchurched people during Sunday services. They expect unchurched people to be there, and they address them, applying the message in ways unchurched people can relate to. Crucially, pastors of missional congregations do not have to make the unchurched the *focus* of the sermon; rather, they only needed to *include* them in constructing the message. This means simple things such as avoiding or limiting Christian "insider" language that could make visitors feel excluded and suggesting applications for people who are not yet committed to Christ. In doing so pastors practice hospitality to these visitors by the way they preach. They welcome them by making the service and message of the gospel accessible.

This was the case for many previously unchurched individuals we interviewed, including Trevor.[4] He grew up going to church, as both of his parents were Catholic and deeply connected to their faith. Yet when he was eighteen or nineteen years old, Trevor left the church. In explaining his mindset at the time, Trevor remarked, "I wanted nothing to do with organized religion because it's all about money and it's all about sin, and how awful and evil you are as a person. I don't want anything to do with that. That's just not me." In the wake of this monumental decision, what struck home was the relative silence from the church. No one reached out or tried to understand why Trevor stopped attending.

Years later, Trevor's experience at the Good Shepherd Church was a stark contrast. "From the second that we walked into the door, it was a super warm and welcoming greeting." He and his family didn't even make it ten steps into the church building before a woman walked up and introduced herself. People were inviting and welcoming by sharing about the church and offering to help care for their baby daughter.

These expressions of hospitality left a deep impact on Trevor's family, yet what truly welcomed Trevor into the church was how this same theme of hospitality was communicated at the pulpit. Reflecting on his draw to the church, Trevor noted Pastor Al's "message of love and inclusion and acceptance and how we can, through our faith and through Jesus, how we can serve our community, what can we do to make this a better place. . . . That message just totally resonated with who I was." Pastor Al's preaching helped change Trevor's perspective of God from an angry, punishing deity to "more of a loving and understanding and compassionate God." The hospitality Trevor and his family experienced at Good Shepherd powerfully affected him in his faith journey and enabled him to begin to see himself as beloved by God.

Along with the core content of the messages, Pastor Al also shared illustrative stories from his own life that resonated with Trevor and helped him understand how the two-thousand-year-old text related to him now. Trevor acknowledged, "Sometimes it's hard to put [the Bible] in today's context, and I think he's really good at taking that message and bringing it to today."

Trevor experienced hospitality through a warm welcome as soon as he walked in the door. He felt expected, addressed, and included in the pastor's messages, and this significantly helped him to belong in the church community before fully believing. It cultivated a deeper identity in him and his family of being beloved.

Sustaining a Culture of Hospitality

In the case of Trevor, it wasn't long before Pastor Al asked him to begin to extend that same hospitality he had received to others. One Sunday the pastor identified a new couple to Trevor and asked him to introduce himself. This was the last thing that Trevor wanted to do, but having been received by others and welcomed as a beloved person of the church, he recognized the need to extend that same love to others. Despite his shyness, Trevor greeted the couple and worked to make sure they were welcome in the church. Later Trevor admitted that not only was it the right thing to do but that it was good for him. His faith became stronger, more real, and more generative toward others.

The thing about hospitality is that if only a few leaders are practicing it, it is neither sustainable nor effective. A small minority of people cannot be adequately hospitable to every visitor in the community. Rather, it takes a culture of hospitality. Leaders must consistently instill the value of hospitality in people, forging a community that understands itself as beloved by God and then extends that love to others through ongoing acts of hospitality.

Individuals can powerfully express love and welcome to outsiders, but in order for hospitality to shape church culture, it must be built into the structure of the church as well.

A key way that hospitality can be expressed through structured ministries is by having a clear and easy next step for visitors. As figure 11.5 reflects, the top 20 percent of evangelistically effective smaller churches had a monthly class for new attenders twice as often as other churches.

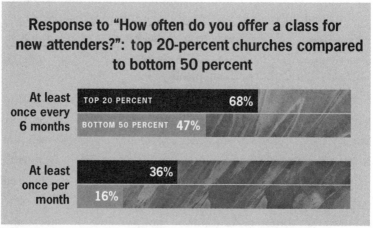

Figure 11.5. Response to "How often do you offer a class for new attenders?": top-20-percent churches compared to bottom 50 percent

Of course, it doesn't just have to be a class for new attenders. There are many other ways of effectively connecting with visitors, including hosting a lunch after church with the pastor or key leaders, or inviting visitors to an "after party" immediately after the service at which they can find out how to get more connected. Some churches organize small groups especially for newer people or launch programs specifically designed as orientations to Christian faith, such as Alpha, Christianity Explored, or Finding Your Way Back to God groups.[5]

These top conversion-growth churches often offer the next step much more frequently so that people have an opportunity to respond in one way or another, and these churches consistently communicate that they are offering it.

Using Hospitality to Overcome Fear and Bias

Strong conversion-growth churches know how to put people at ease in relation to the top two fears unchurched people have as they enter a church for the first time: (1) fear of being judged for their behavior or choices or beliefs, and (2) fear of being expected to be something they are not—in this case, committed Christians living a fully Christian life. They are not all the way committed, and they are afraid they will be expected to be.

Bailey is a great example of the need to overcome the fear factor.[6] She was first introduced to church in her childhood, when a friend invited her to come. She began playing the bells at church and had a generally positive experience. Later on, however, when she was attending church as an adult, she got the impression that they were more focused on building their membership numbers than investing in actual people. She often felt that churches "pressure you into becoming members right away, and that sometimes their ultimate goal is to gain members." One experience she noted was that she and her husband had been attending a nearby church for a while, and when a new pastor joined the church, the whole sermon was focused on either becoming members at that church or moving on to a different church. As she reflected on that, Bailey explained, "That rubbed my husband the wrong way and made him have reservations."

Time passed, and life began to get bumpy for Bailey. One of her daughters struggled with obsessive-compulsive disorder and a mood disorder, so there was extra strain on the family, and during that time she and her husband came close to filing for divorce. Then her daughters wanted to attend youth events at church, so Bailey started bringing them there. For about a year all she did was drop them off in the parking lot. Although she didn't step into church during that time, she began building relationships with the pastor and the youth leaders at the church. Because her kids were having a positive experience, Bailey's perspective of church began to change. She eventually began attending church as well, and she reflected on people who made her feel welcome there:

> Pastor Tim . . . always went out of his way and came over and talked to me, was friendly to me, but never pressured me. I would say that was another thing for me. I liked that I wasn't pressured into coming, because I feel like in the past if somebody was constantly knocking at my door and wanting me to come, it pushed me away more. But with Pastor Tim he gave me my space. Eventually he asked me to come sometime, but it was because I would talk positively about the experiences my kids were having there. He let me come on my own free will. He showed his love and care to me still to where I wanted to come on my own. I feel like Jesus worked through him to lead me there.

youth ministry goes beyond youth

Bailey was afraid of being pressured by the church to be something she wasn't. She kept her distance at first, not wanting to get too involved. Over time, her fears began to melt away as she received hospitality from that congregation in many forms and as she began to understand herself as beloved by God. In 1 John 4:18, John explains that "perfect love drives out fear." This was evident in Bailey's life and is true for countless others. As we demonstrate God's love and hospitality to the strangers in our midst, we can partner with God to overcome the fears that keep people from church and faith.

Balancing Hospitality with Depth and Clarity

I don't want to minimize the challenges in extending hospitality to unchurched people. Though this kind of hospitality is a fundamental biblical value and a central practice for churches that are growing through conversion, it is not easy to balance hospitality to unchurched with other important values and purposes the church has. Churches are called to worship God, apprentice people to become like Jesus, take countercultural stands on moral and ethical issues, and live a life that deeply and profoundly shapes believers into cultural change agents and difference makers wherever they live, work, play, and study. So churches are called to do much more than just extend hospitality to the unchurched. Sometimes these different purposes of the church are in tension with each other. How do we provide Christians with substantial and challenging biblical teaching, while at the same time making it accessible and inviting to people who are not committed to Christ yet? How do we worship God wholeheartedly when we come together, and still include people who are not yet worshippers of God?

I want to make a few suggestions that have come out of research and personal experiences with many churches.

First, God loves diversity and works in many ways through many different kinds of churches. Whatever you are best at and most committed to, keep pursuing as deeply and effectively as you can. Your path to becoming missional will be through your strengths and not apart from them. *Doesn't God use weaknesses though? Yet He equips w/ strength... how do we use our strengths not in self-reliance?*

Second, let God and your best thinking and discernment lead you into the most natural way for you to provide entry points of belonging before believing for unchurched people. Every church needs an entry point ministry. It could be Sunday. It could be recovery groups. It could be seeker groups or Alpha. It could be daycare. It could be after-school events. It could be small groups or missional communities. It could be so very many different avenues. Pick one or two and make that entry point fantastically hospitable. Don't let anything keep you from providing some pathway. And if it is not working yet, keep at it and get help from others until it is. If it is not working, either the people leading are not connecting to the unchurched enough yet or else when unchurched people visit, they are not feeling accepted and wanted and understood enough yet. People come to Christ in community most often. What entry point community do you provide? Is it working yet?

Third, practice communicating up front and with clarity about your moral and ethical boundaries. The last thing unchurched people need is to visit your church, feel accepted for who they are, and only later discover that because they are gay or divorced or whatever else, they can never contribute and lead in your church. Such experiences of rejection are profoundly alienating.

Becoming God's Beloved

For conversion communities, there is a missional engagement process captured by the prior three chapters. We belong out there as individuals and as the church; bless people where we live, work, study, and play; and then bring them into the community of our congregation. People then go through a cycle of becoming the beloved in community. They *connect* to Christians, *contribute* their gifts and abilities to the congregation, *commit* to Christ, and then *communicate* what God has done in their lives, inviting others into the same journey.

As part of this process, conversion communities regularly invite people to commit to Christ. Here is another predictive result of our research: pastors of top-20-percent conversion-growth churches invite people to commit to Christ once a week or more. In contrast, only 37 percent of pastors of bottom-50-percent churches make such regular invitations.[7] Sometimes few new people commit to Christ because we don't ask and invite such a response. But it is not just asking people to commit. It is having the process in place for people to become the beloved. Much of the conversion and life change process happens today not out there individually but within the congregation as people can belong until they believe. Kendra's story illustrates well this process of becoming the beloved.

Kendra's life was difficult growing up.[8] She and her mother lived out of a car for many years, and during that time she experienced ongoing abuse from her father. Although she had some experience with church as a child, she ended up leaving church "because I felt like if God loved me that much, then why would he want us to hurt the way we were hurting?" She couldn't reconcile a God who loved her but still let such traumatizing things happen to her, so she lost trust with God and found her own ways to cope. She started doing methamphetamines in order to stay up all night to protect herself from her dad, and it became a serious addiction.

Several years later, her mother started going to church once in a while and invited Kendra to join her. Kendra decided to give it a try but explained that "at that time we were using drugs, so we were like 'Oh my god! I don't want to be here.'" The drugs led her to get involved with gangs, and because she stayed up and ate all night, she became extremely overweight, with multiple, complex health problems. She reached a point where doctors didn't really know how to help her.

At that point a friend of hers, Rudy, invited her and her husband, Reggie, to visit a church. They decided to give it a try because they had nothing left to lose, and it ended up changing their lives. At this church they felt loved and not judged at all. Over the last two years that they've been attending, Pastor Stephen Hammond has bent over backward to help her walk the long road to healing. This has included ongoing prayer, practical help with health insurance issues, consistent counseling through the abuse she experienced as a child, helping her get to a place of forgiveness, and sharing prophetic words of encouragement and hope along the way. This holistic approach to healing and transformation has made all the difference in Kendra's life. She's lost a lot of weight, and although some health issues persist, she's also experienced physical healing in many areas.

Thinking back on the way Bethel Community Church welcomed her, Kendra gushed, "They showed us so much love, unconditional love. They didn't judge us on our past and what we did. They didn't judge us because of our tattoos or what we've gone through in our lives. But they loved us for who we are. And they don't ever treat us any different than they treat everybody else. Yes, and it's the most awesome feeling ever."

As we open our hearts to unchurched individuals and are intentionally hospitable to them in our churches, we demonstrate God's love in powerful and tangible ways. When we accept others just as they are and welcome them into the community of God's people, we will find ourselves with front-row seats to witness the power of God's love transform both individuals and the communities around them.

Developing a culture of hospitality and welcoming unchurched people into the identity of being God's beloved brings us full circle on the conversion community equation (fig. 11.1 above). In 1 John 4:19, John explains, "We love because he first loved us." The more we receive God's love, the more love we have to give. It is out of our identity as God's beloved that we can step out in faith to belong, bless, and bring others into our community. As unchurched individuals enter into a welcoming church community and are transformed by God's love, they are then able to return to their community and belong, bless, and bring others as well.

Questions for Discussion

1. How do you understand hospitality, and how does the biblical picture expand your understanding?

2. Do first-time visitors feel cared for or invited to become beloved in your congregation or small group, and what could help you strengthen the experience for them?

3. How do the various communicators in your church, its ministries, and your small group do at including unchurched people in their messages and communication?

4. Consider using the Church Warmth Assessment to assess the hospitality of your church. Many churches have found it wonderfully revealing and helpful for identifying some specific steps to take. See Billy Graham Center Resources in appendix one for information on how to access the online resource.

12

Conclusion

From a Conversion Community
to a Conversion Movement

Many churches in America are stalled in their conversion growth, but it doesn't have to stay that way. This book is the culmination of several different research projects focused on how unchurched individuals perceive the church and how the top-10-percent conversion-growth churches are effectively reaching nones, millennials, and irreligious around us. As we surveyed unchurched individuals, we found that they are more open to faith and to congregations than we expect. As we grab hold of this new narrative, may it infuse hope back into our hearts that our efforts in evangelism and outreach will bear good fruit, and may it help us see that the fields are indeed ripe for the harvest (Jn 4:35).

Our research on how churches are effectively reaching out has led us to the equation illustrated by figure 12.1. Missional leaders must set the pace for their congregation by first modeling outreach in their own lives. When leaders consistently find ways to live on mission with God in their daily lives, it sets the stage for missional living to become a defining element of their broader church culture. As missional leaders tell stories of both their success and failure and as they offer

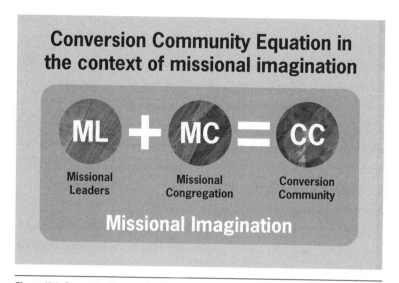

Figure 12.1. Conversion Community Equation in the context of missional imagination

inspiration and accountability to others in their church, they empower their leaders to sharpen their missional focus and raise up new missional leaders.

But it takes more than just missional leaders to become a conversion community. It also takes a missional congregational culture. Missional congregations belong in their broader community, bless unchurched and irreligious people in their spheres of life, and bring them into their congregations, where they can experience hospitality and love from the church and can grow in their faith and their identity as God's beloved. Because they have been welcomed, served, and changed, they begin to bless their friends and bring them as well.

These changes in leadership and congregational culture are motivated by a vibrant missional imagination that becomes reenchanted by the mission of Jesus, realizes the receptivity of the unchurched, and recovers a vision for the beauty and destiny of the church.

As this process takes place, congregations become conversion communities, where unchurched nones, irreligious, millennials, nominals, and others encounter the love and truth of God in transformative ways. Although conversion communities can come in all shapes and sizes, they are congregations where outreach is one of the top three priorities, where outreach is integrated into everything the congregation is doing, where at least 10 percent of the attenders are people who have made new commitments to faith in the last year, and where the congregation is growing by at least 5 percent per year. We found that through interviews with leaders and with previously unchurched people in those communities, lives are changing and communities are being influenced for good.

This conversion community equation has been at work historically and is continuing in congregations today. Many times the growth and multiplication of conversion communities leads to a conversion movement. Here is one such story from history.

A History of Dynamic Growth

In 1776, a small religious group known as the Methodists claimed a total of sixty-five churches sprinkled throughout the colonies. Over the next seven decades, they experienced explosive growth, and by 1850, Methodists had expanded to thirteen thousand congregations that engaged more than 2.5 million people.[1] Methodists towered in numbers over all other denominations; one out of every three Christians in the United States was Methodist. Figure 12.2 documents this growth by comparing the religious adherents of the most prominent denominations between 1776 and 1850. This represents the most explosive growth in the church in American history at the time.

It is interesting to note that this growth took place during a time when a lot of religious leaders thought that America was at its darkest hour religiously. For instance, Lyman Beecher, the most prominent Congregationalist pastor of his time, had many disparaging viewpoints on the religious attitudes of Americans and on the value of

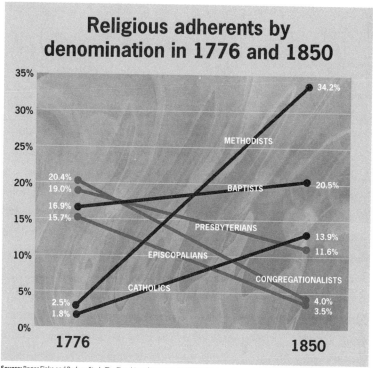

Religious adherents by denomination in 1776 and 1850

METHODISTS — 34.2%

20.4%
19.0%
16.9%
15.7%

BAPTISTS — 20.5%

PRESBYTERIANS — 13.9%
11.6%

EPISCOPALIANS

CONGREGATIONALISTS

CATHOLICS

2.5%
1.8%

4.0%
3.5%

1776   1850

Source: Roger Finke and Rodney Stark, *The Churching of America 1776-2005: Winners and Losers in Our Religious Economy* (New Brunswick, NJ: Rutgers University Press, 2005), 56.

Figure 12.2. Religious adherents by denomination in 1776 and 1850

Methodists and Baptists.[2] During this seventy-five-year period, Congregationalists went from 20 percent of all religious adherents (one out of five) to 4 percent, or one out of every twenty-five. Not surprisingly, Congregationalists in general—and Lyman Beecher in particular—felt Americans were very anti-Christian and trending rapidly in the wrong direction.

Their narrative was not that dissimilar to the negative narrative we discussed in part one of this book. At the time many thought that religious interest and receptivity were at a low point in the twenty years after the Revolutionary War. People weren't spiritually interested or open. Bars were opening on every street corner, and churches were shrinking in every county.

In the midst of this, however, the Methodists grew dramatically. How did they do it? In their book *The Churching of America: Winners and Losers in The American Religious Economy*, Rodney Stark and Roger Finke tracked demographics of the major denominations between 1776 and 2000 and reflected on why some churches grew and others dwindled.[3] Stark and Finke discovered several key reasons for the explosive Methodist expansion.[4]

Although Methodists had a strong hierarchy of authority throughout their denomination, the local congregations were largely led by laypeople. No special education was required to become a Methodist minister, and so the Methodists had a large supply of preachers who lived and worked alongside the other members of the congregation.

Because of their approach to cultivating leadership from within the existing community, Methodists experienced significant growth across ethnic and class distinctions. Methodists grew quickly among African Americans for the same reasons that they grew overall, but especially because they sought and embraced growth among African American congregations and the emergence of gifted African American preachers. While many denominations expressed a desire to reach African Americans, Methodists were uniquely successful in engaging them and in developing leaders.[5]

Methodist preachers also preached a conversion message wherever they went. You might think I have used the word *conversion* too much in this book. But our research and the sweep of history have shown that once the church drifts away from a focus on conversionism and changed lives, movements lose vitality and evangelism loses its focus and purpose. And once the church loses its priority for evangelism, mission drift and congregational decline will not be far behind. Methodist preachers also often used metaphors and stories that connected with people's hearts and engaged people's emotions in ways that were unique at the time. There was a strong message of spiritual reality that was focused on conversion and transformation in the lives of hearers. They cared about the physical and social needs of the people they reached, but they prioritized evangelism in the mission of God.

They also provided an entry point for people that was designed to welcome newcomers and seekers. This entry point was the class meeting. Classes were small groups that met weekly, where people could belong before they believed and find their way to Christ and then into the Christian life and community. When people were regularly attending the classes, their next natural step was to be involved in the larger society, made up of a number of classes. Here leaders and preachers taught sanctification and routine personal dedication to God. In this way they cultivated interest and excitement for the revival meetings that were conducted every quarter or so at district gatherings. Thus the Methodists offered people many opportunities to have their spiritual vibrancy and commitment restored.

Camp meetings, which often lasted a week at a time, offered people the opportunity for deep connection and community as well as significant biblical teaching and spiritual experience, all of which were hard to come by on the isolated, rural frontier. Methodists were able to maximize their use of camp meetings by publicizing them through circuit riders, who spanned both the towns and the frontiers. With this rhythm of mass gatherings at least annually, people had a sense of being part of a larger movement.

In these ways Methodists grew primarily through reaching unchurched people and establishing new congregations in the process of the westward expansion of the nation. There are clear threads of our conversion community equation at work throughout this example from history.

Early Methodists excelled at raising up <u>missional leaders</u>. Because their professional clergy were circuit riders and traveled to many congregations, there was a clear need for lay leaders to stand in the gap. They <u>cultivated lay leaders</u> based on deeds done and gifts experienced rather than education, class, race, or background. Everyday people in churches became missional leaders who had opportunities to first lead class meetings, then preach, then possibly become a circuit preacher. <u>Fruitfulness</u> was the key criterion and not anything of lesser relevance.

In addition, <u>evangelistic preaching</u> and <u>engagement with many</u> <u>non-Christians</u> was <u>highly valued</u> and <u>effectively practiced</u>. The needs and politics of churches did not push out the primary missionary energy and focus of the leaders. Messages shared by Methodist preachers <u>focused on conversion</u>, and <u>invitations to accept and believe in Jesus were commonplace</u>. These missional leaders created conversion communities because <u>conversion and life change</u> was at the <u>center of everything they did</u> in their <u>practice</u> of church life.

These missional leaders led their communities to become missional congregations. They <u>embraced many innovations to connect to the needs and cultural practices</u> of American society. In this way Methodists found ways to belong to and bless their broader community <u>without compromising their holiness, surrender, and sense of being set apart</u>. They lived a <u>countercultural Christian lifestyle</u>, but they embraced the emotionalism, camp-meeting structures, and preaching styles that <u>fit, appealed to, and worked with the unchurched</u>.

Methodist churches <u>also</u> had a clear strategy and structure for reaching and incorporating many people who were unchurched. They encouraged their members to bring people from their broader community with them to their church's classes. These weekly classes provided an entry point for most people who became Methodists— by being a safe place for people to belong before they believed and to be held accountable for seeking God and assurance of salvation.

Methodism founder John Wesley taught the achievability of entire sanctification in this life. By this he did not mean sinlessness, but he did mean <u>freedom from conscious sin and freedom for perfect love</u>. This vision for a potent Christian life and experience gave Methodists a longing, urgency, and hope for being passionately faithful and for living a dedicated life. By <u>accepting and engaging people where they were</u>, Methodists <u>demonstrated</u> the <u>love and acceptance of God</u>, which led unchurched individuals into a new identity as the beloved of God.

As people grew in their faith and surrendered to God, on fire with their faith and their outreach, new missional leaders were born who then went out as circuit riders to plant new churches and reach ever-increasing numbers of people. Methodism, like movements before it, focused on both <u>spiritual passion and structural and strategic connections</u>. This is what made the movement so effective at developing missional leaders, becoming missional congregations, and experiencing the joy and rapidly multiplying effect of being conversion communities.

Becoming a Conversion Community Today

In the years following 1850, Methodists started to decline in relation to population growth. As congregations became middle class and could afford their own pastors, circuit riders began to fill the long-term positions previously held by lay leaders. Churches became more established organizations, and organizational politics became a more central focus for Methodists. As a result the <u>church turned inward toward its structures rather than maintaining its outward, missional momentum</u>.

In addition, <u>mission</u> became <u>broadly defined</u> and <u>more about social uplift than about evangelism</u>. Status in society and academic success became more central in Methodist circles, and practices of honoring wealth and status infected the ways churches were structured. For instance, Methodist churches started charging rent for specific pews at church. The better the seat, the more expensive it was. Sermons also became more focused on social conscience than on conversion and changed lives.[6] The Methodist church in 1850 started a long trajectory toward decline, leading to a great need for renewal and refocusing. Interestingly, now the torch the early Methodists carried for cultivating conversion communities across the country is more often being carried by the descendants of Methodism, denominations such as the Wesleyans, the Nazarenes, and a multiplicity of Pentecostal movements. Churches, denominations, and networks must always guard missional integrity and evangelistic focus if they are to survive, thrive, reach people, and renew their communities and context.

Despite the general decline of the Methodist Church, along with other mainline denominations in the United States, there are signs of hope among congregations that learn from history and revitalize so that they can again become long-term conversion communities. One of those congregations from our top-10-percent conversion-growth churches is Valley Creek United Methodist Church.[7] It is a small church in the Virginia district of the Methodist Church led by Pastor Patrick. He has a vision for reaching new people and seeing his people deepened and revitalized in their faith. This church has been beginning to live out those dynamics and has grown with the help of its denominational leaders. As a church of 160, it saw fifty-five people make new commitments to Christ over the year of our study, and it acted intentionally and strategically to make that happen.

The church realized it needed help to become a missional congregation and to develop missional leaders. Patrick attended a district function where his church was invited to attend a daylong conference led by the group Reaching New People. He and some of his people attended a missional leader–equipping conference with two other Methodist churches from his district. After the training the churches were invited to become part of a coaching and conferencing plan to equip each church to reach new people. The denomination kicked in $1,500 for each church, and then the churches each invested $500. About ten churches committed, including Valley Creek. The coaching has been extremely helpful, as has the accountability for reaching out and sharing stories.

Missional leaders are developed through coaching, training, and accountability, and Patrick has been passing that on to his church members as well. He preached on the importance of being ready to share your faith story using the apostle Paul's story as a model, and he took time in a Sunday morning church service to help church members begin writing down their stories of how they came to faith. As a church, it has pursued a number of paths to equip and inspire its leaders and people to be more evangelistic and to be able to tell their story whenever they have opportunity.

The church has also found intentional ways to belong in and bless the community around it. It held a massive yard sale that drew six to seven hundred people and created the opportunity for connections with people from the church. The church also has a group of mall walkers, who after studying the Bible together walk malls, pray for people, and invite them to join them each week on their walk. They have especially reached people who were dones and had drifted away from the church. The mall walkers are not quite circuit riders, but they have found a way to turn their passion for reaching new people into a practical pattern of outreach.

But Patrick has been concerned about not just the early Methodists' conversionist dynamics and calling people to new faith. He has also pursued their version of revivals and camp meetings to deepen faith and the reality of Jesus in people's lives. Valley Creek has prioritized getting its people to a retreat they call "The Walk to Emmaus," based on Luke 24:13-35, where two unnamed disciples meet the resurrected Jesus, search the Scriptures about the death and resurrection of the

Messiah, and begin to have their hearts burn within them. Their faith comes alive. Many people from Valley Creek have attended this three-day renewal and revitalization retreat and have come alive in their faith. As individuals gain a deeper understanding of their identity as God's beloved, they have much more excitement about Jesus and their church to share with others. Word has spread about the retreat, and Valley Creek is partnering with other churches to broaden and multiply the impact.

Valley Creek United Methodist is pressing the pedal to the metal in growing missionally and inviting people to faith and to the church as well as deepening their people through renewal so that their passion for Jesus and for the church is ignited. They are implementing the conversion community equation of raising up missional leaders who then catalyze a missional congregation, and Valley Creek is moving toward becoming an ongoing conversion community as it facilitates life transformation by the power of God and for the glory of God.

Conversion communities can change cities. We need this to happen, and it cannot stop there. When conversion communities spread the passion for outreach either by planting new churches that are conversion communities or by banding together with other churches to cultivate conversion growth together, they begin to form conversion movements, which have the potential to impact our nation. The early Methodists were a conversion movement made up of multiplying conversion communities. It will take a movement of churches recapturing the vision of Jesus to multiply apprentices through conversion growth for us to see every individual and community in the United States affected by the gospel—and it's possible!

We are seeing this conversion movement happen in other parts of the globe more than in America. I recently taught in the Philippines and then visited a number of churches that are at the center of international conversion movements. I want to tell you about one.

Faythe Santiago is one of four daughters of Reverend Manny Santiago. Reverend Santiago planted a church in 1993 in his garage and called it Jesus the Lifegiver Church. He started outreach in a number of places but saw very little church growth for the next fourteen years, living much of his pastoral life very poor and through real hardship.

Growing up as a pastor's kid, Faythe had many dreams. She sang well, was creative and artistic, and longed to become a director of films and musical productions. Her plan was to go to the United States to get schooling to become a film director. She was on the path and ready to go.

During these years she also had one consistent fear. She did not want to sacrifice all that her parents had sacrificed to do ministry. She did not want to struggle like that. She did not want to live hand-to-mouth like that. God could call her to whatever God might want to call her to—except to work with her parents and to work in the church.

In 2008, before she had the chance to leave to go to America, God began to work in her to tell her that the very things she feared were exactly what God was calling her to do: to work with her parents, to work in the church. She struggled. She wept. She fought. Finally she surrendered to the will of God for her life.

She describes what happened next. Fire fell. She had an Acts 2 Pentecost-type experience and encounter with the presence of God. She wept again, not because of resistance but because of the fiery and overwhelming presence of God, which brought conviction, submission, and awe. She prayed constantly, gave her life fully, and gave up the things that had held first place in her heart: her dreams for success, for going to America, for directing films, and for leaving her country and her struggles behind. As she describes it, she repented of her idols, those things that had supremacy in her heart over Jesus.

After several weeks of prayer and revival in her own life, she preached in the little church that her father led, and to the sisters and family with whom she had grown up. The fire fell on others and on the little church. Her sisters gave their lives to Christ, as did others in her church.

The church increased its ministry and presence at local campuses in Manila and began to see students come to Christ, become committed, experience the fire, gather in small groups, and take steps in following Christ.

As the church started growing and followers started multiplying, emerging leaders created small groups and then clusters of small groups. When there were enough clusters of small groups, these leaders planted new churches, first in Manila, soon in other cities and areas of the Philippines, and then later in some other countries as leaders moved to new countries for business or school. When I met with Faythe and the leaders in Manila, we heard from her experience and then skyped with her father, Bishop Manny Santiago, who was in Canada meeting with a new Lifegiver church plant there.

In the last ten years, eighty-four churches have been started out of this revival. What's more, Faythe, her sisters, and her father have launched a youth movement called History Makers in the Philippines through worship gatherings and discipleship materials. The first youth gathering drew eight thousand young people, and it has continued to grow from there. The revival and multiplication of disciples, small groups, clusters, and new churches is continuing to increase. One of the most striking characteristics of this movement is that it is being fueled by many sons and daughters of pastors rededicating their lives to Christ and committing to working with their parents to build churches. It has been overwhelming and powerful for parents to see their kids captured and enraptured by God and joining them in their lifelong calling to build the church.

Other churches are now asking for help. History Makers and Life-giver churches are responding to requests from one thousand churches for help in revival and revitalization. All this began with college students giving their lives to Christ and surrendering to God's vision and call for their lives. Then the fire fell. It is burning, catching up young people across the Philippines, igniting churches in every region of the country, and now beginning to spread like wildfire to other nations through Filipino diaspora networks.

This movement is multiplying missional leaders, strengthening missional congregations, seeing multitudes of people come to Christ and surrender to Christ, and starting churches through small groups that are migrating to other cities and other nations. This movement has become a conversion movement, a network of multiplying conversion communities.

It can happen again in America. Our greatest barrier is not the shift in secular culture but the silent and secularized church.

How do conversion communities become conversion movements? How do churches that are reaching people and lighting up communities endure and multiply over time?

Conversion movements develop missional leaders and missional congregations, and they do so animated by spiritual dynamics that are vibrant and go viral. These spiritual dynamics include passion for Jesus, enduring theological and moral boundaries, and contextual potency. Let me unpack these three underlying spiritual drivers of enduring conversion movements.

My study of history and research into the contemporary church has led me to some counterintuitive conclusions about what makes for strong conversion movements over time. Strong moral and theological boundaries are crucial. Movements need a sense of boundaries and a sense of strong identity. When they shift those boundaries to meet the standards of the culture, they may succeed for a while. But in the long run they will lose their identity and their countercultural presence in the world. That <u>countercultural presence</u> is absolutely crucial for maintaining a long-term impact as a conversion movement. But having moral and theological boundaries is not enough. There are many cold-hearted movements that have succeeded at having strong moral and theological boundaries. The other underlying spiritual marker for many conversion movements that we have looked at is <u>spiritual</u> <u>passion for Jesus</u>. That <u>spiritual passion is contagious</u>, and it is the fire that fills the structures that multiply for conversion movements. These movements <u>worship with intensity (whatever that may look like</u> <u>culturally</u>); challenge members to go above and beyond in their expressions of devotion, such as by pursuing practices of silence, solitude, prayer, and fasting; and <u>challenge their people to surrender fully</u> <u>to Christ</u> and not let other idols of the culture, whether the old idols of wood and stone or the new digital and pop-culture idols of celebrities and style, replace God as first in their heart.

Finally, you can have moral and theological boundaries and spiritual passion for Jesus and yet lack cultural bridges and connections. Fortress movements at least for a while can maintain high passion, be quite countercultural, but not have the bridges and connections in the culture for people to walk across. Those <u>bridges might be people, practices, language, symbols, or methods of communication</u>. Conversion movements have those in spades. Billy Graham was a force for revival behind the Iron Curtain as well as in America. He had profound spiritual passion, strong but not narrow moral and theological boundaries, and used cultural methods and means of organizing and communicating in powerful and effective ways. He sparked conversion movements in many cities in the United States but also in China, Korea, and many other countries in the world.

So those three dimensions—spiritual passion, countercultural moral and theological boundaries and identity, and cultural bridges—are the

three animating factors for missional leaders and missional congregations that especially stand out for conversion movements that endure
and expand over time. That is what characterized the Methodist
movement at least through 1850. It is what characterizes the movement
that Faythe Santiago helped spark in the Philippines. It is also evident
in movements such as the Church of the Highlands in Alabama. It is
the second-largest church in the nation and has grown primarily
through multiplication of small groups and campuses across the whole
state. Church of the Highlands focuses on Jesus, has maintained theological and moral consistency in its stances, and effectively bridges
culture in its worship, preaching, and especially small group structures
that have fanned out across the state and helped develop the disciples
who then become core at each new campus they plant.

Hillsong is another example of a movement that has multiplied to
many places in the world that were considered resistant to the gospel.
Worship and passion for Jesus drives the expansion of the movement.
Consistency in moral and theological boundaries characterizes the
movement. And cultural expression, especially in areas of music and
experiential faith, has provided the vehicles through which the passion
and call to Christ have been fueled.

These are just a few examples, across different church sizes and
spiritual traditions, that give hope of a new day for American congregations. Revitalization is possible, maybe even likely. Fueled by missional imagination to see the receptivity and harvest that is truly out
there and to develop missional leaders and orient our churches as
missional congregations, we could see conversion movements once
again rise up and influence culture and communities. We could
witness our churches becoming conversion communities and even
conversion movements that can change the trajectory of our nation.
May conversion communities like Valley Creek United Methodist,
Church of the Highlands, History Makers and Lifegiver churches,

Hillsong, and many others multiply across our country and world; may your congregation become one of them; and may God visit us with another renewal of religious life in America.

Questions for Discussion

1. What inspires or challenges you most about the story of the Methodist Church?

2. Rick suggests that what animates the multiplication of enduring conversion movements is spiritual passion for Jesus, strong moral and theological boundaries and identity, and contextual potency. Where is your congregation strong, and where do you most need to grow in these three underlying areas of passion, conviction, and cultural connection?

3. Spend some time in prayer for your church and your group to become a conversion community and ultimately a conversion movement. Spend time praying for the renewal of the life of the church in America.

Acknowledgments

Although I have often had help here and there on other books I have written, this one truly felt as though it took a whole village of people to produce!

If I was the mayor of this book-bearing village, undoubtedly Kerilee Van Schooten was the deputy mayor. Her patience, perseverance, intelligence, wit, and wisdom were always available and ever crucial. She served from beginning to end in roles of researcher, organizer, editor, sounding board, and keeper of the deadlines. Without her, I certainly would never have made it all the way through.

I am also indebted to Andrew Macdonald for stepping in at key points when I felt stuck and helping me get unstuck and on the move again. His ability to effectively hear and then suggest structure and flow ideas was quite valuable to me.

I am deeply grateful to Billy Graham Center colleagues who carried some of my other responsibilities in order for me to focus and finish this book, including Christina Walker, Jim Lundgren, and others. The whole Billy Graham Center and Wheaton College teams of which I am a part provide a community of learners and leaders who are inspiring and stimulating. I am especially thankful for a leader like Ed Stetzer, who provides an organizational context that values theological integrity, evangelistic faithfulness, action-oriented research, and entrepreneurial creativity.

My partners at InterVarsity Press, including Al Hsu, Cindy Bunch, and Jeff Crosby, have shown dedication and commitment to this project and provided insightful feedback along the way. I am also indebted to my "anonymous" readers Doug Schaupp and Jessica Fick for strong encouragement and insightful critique to strengthen the book. They represent a part of my former and present extended family in InterVarsity, with whom I still feel connected.

Our partners at Lifeway Research, including Scott McConnell, Lizette Dillinger, and Casey Oliver, provided solid survey research and helpful insights and analysis. Wayne Kriemelmeyer also helped immensely in the additional analysis of that data we did at the Billy Graham Center.

My team members for the Church Evangelism Initiative, including Jim Lundgren, Terry Erickson, Ron Mangin, and Kerilee Van Schooten, have been wonderful partners in kingdom innovation as we have tested together the best practice ideas I discovered in research and through networking. I also cannot adequately thank the many pastors and leaders who have become friends and partners through the cohorts we lead. I cannot name them here, as I would no doubt forget someone who was very important, but you know who you are, and you have been my muse! My partnership with colleague and cohort curriculum coauthor Beth Seversen at the Evangelical Covenant Church has also been generative of best practices and solid research insights that have found their way into these pages. My friend Kevin Harney and his Organic Outreach International team have also been very encouraging and helpful in contributing to the material in this book.

My dear friends in our reading group, the Mead Men—Lon Allison, Jerry Root, Walter Hansen, David Henderson, and our friend with Jesus now, Chris Mitchell—sat through wonderfully helpful readings of chapters and gave encouraging and incisive critique. You are also partners on the evangelism journey.

I am profoundly inspired by and thankful for my wife, Mary Kay, principal of an early childhood school in a largely Hispanic Chicago neighborhood and my partner in living out what we believe and what I write about in our everyday urban Chicago life. And for my beloved sons Chris, Steve, and Colby, who are still awaiting my promised science fiction / fantasy book . . .

Above all I am truly thankful to God, Father, Son, and Holy Spirit, who cares a lot more about what I long for in the church than I ever could and has blessed me more in this project than I would ever have believed possible.

Appendix 1

Billy Graham Center Resources

This book launches a line of resources that will be produced and published in partnership with InterVarsity Press.

Our vision at the Billy Graham Center is to be a *world hub of inspiration, research, preaching, and training that will glorify Christ and serve every church and organization in preaching and teaching the gospel to the world.* We seek to be a Switzerland among evangelism- and mission-oriented churches and ministries, bringing together other leaders and organizations for conversation, problem solving, and resource sharing, and generating strategies to influence the world with the gospel. Under the leadership of Ed Stetzer, we are publishing and making available world-class resources to revitalize churches, reinvigorate mission and evangelism, and stimulate creativity and engagement of the gospel with the world.

For resources for your use in churches and ministries related to *You Found Me: New Research on How Unchurched Nones, Millennials, and Irreligious Are Surprisingly Open to Christian Faith*, visit our research institute website at www.billygrahamcenter.com/youfoundme /resources and enter the code YFM.

Resources that you can download on this site include:

- An inspiring and instructive chapter on leading missional change in your church, based on how this change occurred in a larger and older evangelistically challenged organization. You will be given the key principles for leading missional DNA change.

- A simple repeatable exercise you can use to help raise the evangelism temperature of your team and your church.

- A Warmth Assessment for your church that will help you and your team assess the entry point experience of your unchurched visitors.

- A fuller description of the research projects that were conducted for this book.

- And others!

For information on how to get involved in pastor and leader cohorts, go to the Church Evangelism Initiative website at ceicohorts.com.

For further information on publications that come out of the Billy Graham Center / InterVarsity Press partnership, visit our website at billygrahamcenter.com/research.

For our general resources on evangelism, visit ceicohorts.com /evangelism-resources.

Appendix 2

Contributing Research Projects

Research Project Part A: Measuring Evangelism in Protestant Churches Study

This study was commissioned by the Billy Graham Center and conducted by Lifeway Research. The phone survey of one thousand Protestant pastors was conducted August 29 to September 11, 2018. The calling list was a random sample stratified by church size drawn from a list of all Protestant churches. Each interview was conducted with the senior pastor, minister, or priest of the church. Responses were weighted by region to more accurately reflect the population. The completed sample is one thousand surveys. The sample provides 95 percent confidence that the sampling error does not exceed plus or minus 1.8 percent (this margin of error accounts for the effect of weighting). Margins of error are higher in subgroups.

The interviewers asked questions in the survey related to present total attendance, new commitments to Christ as Savior in the last year that were retained by the congregation, and attendance three years prior. Thus two primary factors of interest were examined in the survey: the increase of retained new commitments to Jesus over the last year, and attendance growth over the last three years. Cross-tabulation for these factors enabled us to determine the percentage of Protestant churches that have grown at least 5 percent per year for the last three years and also are seeing at least 10 percent of their worship attendance this year who are new commitments to Christ. Those are the two key standards we have used in this project to define characteristics of conversion communities.

Research Project Part B: Unchurched Study

This study was designed by the Billy Graham Center Institute in partnership with Lifeway Research. Between May 23 and June 1, 2016, Lifeway Research surveyed over forty-four hundred individuals. Survey respondents were screened to include only those who had not attended a religious service in the past six months except for a holiday or special event such as a wedding or funeral. This left a total of two thousand unchurched individuals who completed the survey.

Overall, this study revealed that unchurched individuals are more open to faith conversations and the church than the dominant narrative in society has led us to believe. The data also demonstrates that unchurched individuals also perceive the church and the Christian faith more positively than is generally expected.

The Billy Graham Center Institute also conducted further analysis of the data by exploring how specific subgroups responded to survey questions.

Regarding the methodology and margin of error, a demographically balanced online panel was used for interviewing American adults. Slight weights were used to balance gender, age, ethnicity, income, region, and religion. The sample provides 95 percent confidence that the sampling error from the online panel does not exceed plus or minus 2.7 percent. This margin of error accounts for the effect of weighting, and margins of error are higher in subgroups.

Research Project Part C: Evangelism Survey of Three Thousand Protestant Churches

This study was sponsored and designed by the Billy Graham Center Institute in partnership with Lifeway Research. The phone survey of Protestant pastors was conducted in three waves: July 2015, September 2015, and January 2016. With one thousand respondents in each wave, the completed sample is three thousand surveys. The calling list was a stratified random sample, drawn from a list of all Protestant churches. Each interview was conducted with the senior pastor, minister, or priest of the church called.

Once the surveys were complete, the top 10 percent of evangelistically effective churches were determined based off their score for the following eight variables:

1. New commitments per attendee, to factor in the conversion-growth rate so that larger churches wouldn't automatically be considered more evangelistically effective due to their size

2. Age of new commitments score, so that churches with many conversions of children who have grown up in the church wouldn't automatically be considered more evangelistically effective

3. Retained new commitments per attendee, to factor in ongoing discipleship as part of successful evangelism

4. Percentage of weekend attendance who are non-Christian, to factor in effective ongoing engagement with non-Christians as part of effective evangelism

5. Level of agreement to "I intentionally spend time building friendships with non-Christians for the purpose of sharing Christ with them," to factor in the personal evangelism of the church's leadership because the leaders impact the effectiveness of the whole

6. Level of agreement to "We are consistently hearing reports of members of our congregation engaging in evangelistic conversations, where people share their faith with people who are not Christian," to factor in broader congregational involvement in evangelism rather than only a select few who are particularly effective in evangelism

7. Level of agreement to "How often does your church specifically pray together as a congregation for the spiritual status of people known to members who are not Christians?" to factor in the role of prayer in evangelism because dependence on God affects the effectiveness of evangelism

8. The population growth or decline of the surrounding area, so that churches in areas that have an increasing population overall wouldn't automatically be considered more evangelistically effective than churches in areas with declining population

Quotas were used for church size, and responses were weighted by region to more accurately reflect the population. The sample provides 95 percent confidence that the sampling error does not exceed plus or minus 1.8 percent. This margin of error accounts for the effect of weighting, and margins of error are higher in subgroups.

Research Project Part D: Qualitative Interviews of Pastors and Previously Unchurched

The Billy Graham Center at Wheaton College conducted interviews of pastors from the most evangelistically effective churches identified in the Evangelism Survey of Three Thousand Protestant Churches Study. The qualitative pastor interviews also included referrals to new believers in their church. Additional phone interviews were conducted by the Billy Graham Center among these new believers. Analysis of the interviews was conducted by the Billy Graham Center and

Lifeway Research. During the first phase of the project, churches ranking among the top-10-percent of evangelistically effective churches who also agreed to be contacted again for research were invited to participate in in-depth interviews.

A total of fifty-seven pastors and forty-one previously unchurched individuals were interviewed in this study. The research for this project was directed by Rick Richardson, and the research team comprised twenty individuals, including faculty, staff, and students affiliated with the Billy Graham Center Institute and students participating in a doctoral seminar at Trinity Evangelical Divinity School (TEDS). The day-to-day management of the project was shared by Kerilee Van Schooten and Robyn Keller.

Research Project Part E:
Small Church Evangelism Study

This study was designed by the Billy Graham Center Institute in partnership with Lifeway Research and the Caskey Center for Church Excellence at New Orleans Baptist Theological Seminary. The purpose of this study was to explore the practices of small churches (up to 250 attendees) that are predictive of rates of new commitments to Christ and the retention of these new commitments within congregations. The phone survey of pastors of churches in evangelical and black Protestant denominations was conducted from March 16 to March 31, 2017. The calling list was a random sample, stratified by church membership and denominational groups, drawn from a list of all evangelical and black Protestant churches. Each interview was conducted with the senior pastor, minister, or priest of the church called. The completed sample is fifteen hundred surveys. Responses were weighted by region and denominational group to more accurately reflect the population. The sample provides 95 percent confidence that the sampling error does not exceed plus or minus

2.7 percent (this margin of error accounts for the effect of weighting). Margins of error are higher in subgroups.

Out of twenty-nine factors included in the survey, ten factors were shown by statistical analysis to be *predictive* for churches experiencing more retained new commitments to Jesus as Savior in churches of 250 or less. The results were obtained by regression analysis, wherein individual factors are identified, all other factors are controlled for, and the variance caused by each particular factor can be determined. The key issue these factors predict is the number of people who commit to Christ as Savior *and* are retained. Since we are called to make disciples and aim to grow, these predictive factors are our most important findings from the study.

However, these factors together predict 20 percent of the variance between churches, which means that there are other factors as well that have not yet been identified.

The study was sponsored by the Billy Graham Center, the Caskey Center, the Assemblies of God, the Associate Reformed Presbyterian Church, the Church of the Nazarene, the Conservative Congregational Christian Conference, Converge Worldwide, the Evangelical Covenant Church, the Evangelical Free Church of America, the Foursquare Church, The Missionary Church, the Southern Baptist Convention, Vineyard USA, and the Wesleyan Church.

Together, these five different but connected research projects have given us rich and full-orbed data that has informed the identification of best practices and their application in groups of pastor cohorts and the churches these pastors lead.

Notes

1 Introduction: The Challenge Congregations Face in America

[1]Exponential, which conducted the survey, used a convenience sample to estimate that 80 percent of churches in America are plateaued or declining, 16 percent are growing, and only 4 percent are multiplying. They are working with Lifeway Research to confirm this statistic with a more random sample of churches across America.

[2]Billy Graham Center Institute and Lifeway Research, Measuring Evangelism in Protestant Churches Study. Refer to appendix two, part A, for more information on this study.

[3]Billy Graham Center Institute and Lifeway Research, Measuring Evangelism in Protestant Churches Study. This 10 percent includes Protestant churches that have grown at least 5 percent per year in attendance over the last three years and also have experienced at least a 10 percent conversion growth rate over the last year. What that 10-percent conversion-growth-rate statistic means is that these churches have had at least 10 percent of their present attenders make new commitments to Christ as Savior over the last year. In other words, their growth focuses on conversion growth, not transfer growth.

[4]John Stuart Mill, "Inaugural Address," February 1, 1867, St. Andrews University, printed in E. Littell, *Littell's Living Age*, fourth series, vol. 4 (Boston: Littell and Gay, 1867), 664.

[5]Martin Luther King Jr., "Letter from a Birmingham Jail," April 16, 1963, https://kinginstitute.stanford.edu/chapter-18-letter-birmingham-jail.

[6]Pew Research Center, "America's Changing Religious Landscape," Religion and Public Life, Pew Research Center, May 12, 2015, www.pewforum .org/2015/05/12/americas-changing-religious-landscape/.

[7]Michael Lipka, "Millennials Increasingly Are Driving Growth of 'Nones,'" FactTank, Pew Research Center, May 12, 2015, www.pewresearch.org /fact-tank/2015/05/12/millennials-increasingly-are-driving-growth-of -nones/.

[8]Rodney Stark, *The Rise of Christianity: A Sociologist Reconsiders History* (Princeton, NJ: Princeton University Press, 1996).

[9]Stark, *Rise of Christianity*, 93.

[10]David, interview by Rick Richardson, Qualitative Interviews of Pastors and Previously Unchurched, April 19, 2016. For more information on this study, refer to appendix two, part D.

[11]"Unchurched Report," Billy Graham Center Institute and Lifeway Research, April 24, 2019, www.billygrahamcenter.com/youfoundme/research. For more information on this study, refer to appendix two, part B.

[12]The 100 percent figure is drawn only from the CEI cohort surveys and does not include data from the cohorts led by the Evangelical Covenant Church.

[13]The 35 percent figure is drawn only from the CEI cohort surveys and does not include data from the cohorts led by the Evangelical Covenant Church.

[14]Elizabeth Drescher, *Choosing Our Religion: The Spiritual Lives of America's Nones* (Oxford: Oxford University Press, 2016), loc. 5616, Kindle.

[15]Conversion, as Lewis Rambo defines it, "is a process of religious change that takes place in a dynamic force field of people, events, ideologies, institutions, expectations, and orientations." It can begin in a sudden flash of insight, or it may unfold gradually. It is sometimes emotionally and interpersonally dramatic; other times, shifts in affiliation occur with little immediately noticeable effect on self-understanding or primary relationships. For Christians, the blinding conversion of the apostle Paul on the road to Damascus and the extended philosophical explorations and moral transformation of Augustine of Hippo are paradigmatic. See Lewis R. Rambo, *Understanding Religious Conversion* (New Haven, CT: Yale University Press, 1993), 5.

2 Exposing Common Myths
About Unchurched Americans

[1]Daniel McGinn, "Marriage by the Numbers," *Newsweek*, June 4, 2006, www.newsweek.com/marriage-numbers-110797.

[2]Megan Garber, "When Newsweek 'Struck Terror in the Hearts of Single Women,'" *The Atlantic*, June 2, 2016, www.theatlantic.com/entertainment/archive/2016/06/more-likely-to-be-killed-by-a-terrorist-than-to-get-married/485171/.

[3]"Soul Has Weight, Physician Thinks," *New York Times*, March 11, 1907, https://timesmachine.nytimes.com/timesmachine/1907/03/11/106743221.pdf.

[4]Lana Burgess, "What Percentage of Our Brain Do We Use?," *Medical News Today*, updated February 27, 2018, www.medicalnewstoday.com/articles/321060.php.

[5]Crimes Against Children Research Center, "Online Victimization: A Report on the Nation's Youth," June 2000, www.unh.edu/ccrc/pdf/Victimization_Online_Survey.pdf.

[6]Naomi Wolf, *The Beauty Myth* (New York: Anchor, 1992).

[7]Dave Mosher and Skye Gould, "How Likely Are Foreign Terrorists to Kill Americans? The Odds May Surprise You," *Business Insider*, January 31, 2017, www.businessinsider.com/death-risk-statistics-terrorism-disease-accidents-2017-1.

[8]Benjamin Radford, "How Much Does the Soul Weigh?," Live Science, December 1, 2012, www.livescience.com/32327-how-much-does-the-soul-weigh.html.

[9]Robynne Boyd, "Do People Only Use 10 Percent of Their Brains?," *Scientific American*, February 7, 2008, www.scientificamerican.com/article/do-people-only-use-10-percent-of-their-brains/.

[10]Crimes Against Children Research Center, "Online Victimization: A Report on the Nation's Youth."

[11]Tetyana, "Naomi Wolf Got Her Facts Wrong. Really, Really, Really Wrong," Science of Eating Disorders, June 7, 2012, www.scienceofeds.org/2012/06/07/naomi-wolf-got-her-facts-wrong/.

[12]Christian Smith, "Evangelicals Behaving Badly with Statistics," *Books & Culture* (January/February 2007), www.booksandculture.com/articles/2007/janfeb/5.11.html.

[13]Ed Stetzer, "Curing Christians' Stats Abuse," *Christianity Today*, January 15, 2010, www.christianitytoday.com/ct/2010/january/21.34.html.

[14]"Chicken Little," World Story (accessed December 1, 2018), www.worldstory.net/en/stories/chicken_little.html.

[15]"Chicken Little," Merriam-Webster.com (accessed December 1, 2018), www.merriam-webster.com/dictionary/Chicken Little.

[16]John R. Landry, "Can Mission Statements Plant the 'Seeds' of Dysfunctional Behaviors in an Organization's Memory?," *Proceedings of the Thirty-First Hawaii International Conference on System Sciences* (1998): 169.

[17]Xinghua Li, "Communicating the 'Incommunicable Green': A Comparative Study of the Structures of Desire in Environmental Advertising in the United States and China" (PhD diss., University of Iowa, 2010), 81.

[18]National Education Association of the United States Dept. of Audiovisual Instruction, *Audio Visual Communication Review*, nos. 3-4 (1955): 226-27.

[19]Barna, *Spiritual Conversations in a Digital Age*, Barna Report, 2018, www.barna.com/spiritualconversations/.

[20]Barna, *Spiritual Conversations in a Digital Age*.

[21]A recent and popular work that explores how churches can retreat from culture into local-oriented communities is Rod Dreher's *The Benedict Option: A Strategy for Christians in a Post-Christian Nation* (New York: Penguin, 2017). While Dreher's work is often mischaracterized as a return to the isolationist tendencies of early twentieth-century fundamentalism, he does advocate for Christians adopting a far more internally focused perspective rather than broad public engagement.

[22]Michael Lipka, "Five Key Findings About the Changing U.S. Religious Landscape," FactTank, Pew Research Center, May 12, 2015, www.pewresearch.org/fact-tank/2015/05/12/5-key-findings-u-s-religious-landscape/.

[23]Ed Stetzer, "If It Doesn't Stem Its Decline, Mainline Protestantism Has Just 23 Easters Left," *Washington Post*, April 28, 2017, www.washingtonpost.com/news/acts-of-faith/wp/2017/04/28/if-it-doesnt-stem-its-decline-mainline-protestantism-has-just-23-easters-left/?utm_term=.ee2d594b32e9.

[24]Pew Research Center, "America's Changing Religious Landscape," Religion and Public Life, Pew Research Center, May 12, 2015, www.pewforum.org/2015/05/12/americas-changing-religious-landscape/.

[25]This data is from the additional analysis that the Billy Graham Center Institute conducted on the data collected in the unchurched study. See "Unchurched Report," Billy Graham Center Institute and Lifeway Research, April 24, 2019, www.billygrahamcenter.com/youfoundme/research. For more information on this study, refer to appendix two, part B.

[26]The US Census Bureau reports an estimated total US population of 318,558,162 in 2016. Of this total, 244,945,724 are adults above the age of eighteen. The "Unchurched Report" conducted by the Billy Graham Center Institute and Lifeway Research reports that 45 percent of the US population is unchurched, which corresponds to 143,351,173 unchurched individuals in the United States and 110,225,576 unchurched adults.

[27]George Barna and David Kinnaman, *Churchless: Understanding Today's Unchurched and How to Connect with Them* (Carol Stream, IL: Tyndale House, 2014), viii.

[28]Pew Research Center, "America's Changing Religious Landscape," Religion and Public Life, Pew Research Center, May 12, 2015, www.pewforum .org/2015/05/12/americas-changing-religious-landscape/.

[29]Lydia Saad, "Catholics' Church Attendance Resumes Downward Slide," Gallup, April 9, 2018, https://news.gallup.com/poll/232226/church -attendance-among-catholics-resumes-downward-slide.aspx.

[30]Pew Research Center, "America's Changing Religious Landscape."

[31]Pew Research Center, "America's Changing Religious Landscape."

[32]Elizabeth Drescher, *Choosing Our Religion: The Spiritual Lives of America's Nones* (New York: Oxford University Press, 2016), 51.

[33]Pew Research Center, "'Nones' on the Rise," Religion and Public Life, Pew Research Center, October 9, 2012, www.pewforum.org/2012/10/09/nones -on-the-rise/.

[34]Ed Stetzer, "No, American Christianity Is Not Dead," CNN, May 16, 2015, www.cnn.com/2015/05/16/living/christianity-american-dead/index .html.

[35]Ed Stetzer is working on a forthcoming book on this phenomenon, its significance, and how it happened, to be published by InterVarsity Press.

[36]From an article titled "Why Do 80% of Youth Leave Church After High School?," anonymous personal communication with Ed Stetzer, September 15, 2017.

[37]Ed Stetzer, personal communication, November 15, 2016.

[38]Jon Walker, "Family Life Council Says It's Time to Bring Family Back to Life," SBC 2002 Annual Meeting, June 12, 2002, www.sbcannualmeeting .net/sbc02/newsroom/newspage.asp?ID=261.

[39]Stetzer, "Curing Christians' Stats Abuse."

[40]Stetzer, "Curing Christians' Stats Abuse."

[41]Smith, "Evangelicals Behaving Badly with Statistics."

[42]"Most Teenagers Drop Out of Church as Young Adults," Lifeway Research, January 15, 2019, https://lifewayresearch.com/2019/01/15/most-teenagers -drop-out-of-church-as-young-adults/.

[43]"Reasons 18- to 22-Year-Olds Drop Out of Church," Lifeway Research, August 7, 2007, https://lifewayresearch.com/2007/08/07/reasons-18-to -22-year-olds-drop-out-of-church/.

[44]Lance Ford, *Revangelical: Becoming the Good News People We're Meant to Be* (Carol Stream, IL: Tyndale House, 2014), 126.

[45]Alan Hirsch and Michael Frost, *The Shaping of Things to Come: Innovation and Mission for the Twenty-First-Century Church* (Peabody, MA: Hendrickson, 2003), 186.

[46]Scott McConnell, personal communication, October 4, 2016. This data came from the unchurched study, conducted in partnership with Lifeway Research. It is also corroborated by Barna's "State of the Church" report in 2016. See Barna Group, "The State of the Church 2016," September 15, 2016, www.barna.com/research/state-church-2016/.

[47]"Choosing a New Church or House of Worship," Pew Research Center, August 23, 2016, www.pewforum.org/2016/08/23/choosing-a-new-church -or-house-of-worship/.

[48]"Most Teenagers Drop Out of Church as Young Adults."

[49]Stetzer, "No, American Christianity Is Not Dead."

[50]"Unchurched Report," Billy Graham Center Institute and Lifeway Research, April 24, 2019, www.billygrahamcenter.com/youfoundme /research.

[51]"Tina," interview by Kerilee Van Schooten, Qualitative Interviews of Pastors and Previously Unchurched, April 5, 2016.

[52]Rodney Stark and Byron Johnson, "Religion and the Bad News Bearers," *Wall Street Journal*, August 26, 2011, www.wsj.com/articles/SB10001424053 111903480904576510692691734916.

[53]Lawrence O. Richards and Gary J. Bredfeldt, *Creative Bible Teaching* (Chicago: Moody, 1998).

[54]Stetzer, "Curing Christians' Stats Abuse."

[55]Kara Powell, *Growing Young: Six Essential Strategies to Help Young People Discover and Love Your Church* (Grand Rapids: Baker Books, 2016), 17.

3 Embracing a New Narrative About the Unchurched

[1]Pew Research Center, "'Nones' on the Rise," Religion and Public Life, Pew Research Center, October 9, 2012, www.pewforum.org/2012/10/09/nones -on-the-rise/.

[2]Kate Lyons and Garry Blight, "Where in the World Is the Worst Place to Be a Christian?," *The Guardian*, July 27, 2015, www.theguardian.com/world /ng-interactive/2015/jul/27/where-in-the-world-is-it-worst-place-to-be -a-christian.

[3]This data comes from the additional analysis conducted by the Billy Graham Center Institute on the data from the "Unchurched Report." See "Unchurched Report," Billy Graham Center Institute and Lifeway Research, April 24, 2019, www.billygrahamcenter.com/youfoundme/research.

[4]Rick Richardson, "When Questions Reflect Issues of the Heart: A New Evangelism for a New Day," *The Exchange* (blog), April 7, 2017, www .christianitytoday.com/edstetzer/2017/april/when-questions-reflect-issues -of-heart-new-evangelism-for-n.html.

[5]In answer to a question to nonevangelicals about whether perceptions of evangelicals had improved, stayed the same, or worsened since the 2016 election, 5 percent said improved, 64 percent said stayed the same, and 31 percent said worsened. This result of political polarization has to be taken into account in invitations we make. See Ed Stetzer, *Christians in an Age of Outrage: How to Bring Our Best When the World Is at Its Worst* (Carol Stream, IL: Tyndale House, 2018), 284-85.

[6]North Point Ministries (accessed December 4, 2018), http://northpoint ministries.org.

[7]"What Is Starting Point—New Site Landing Page," North Point Ministries (accessed December 4, 2018), https://vimeo.com/219575604.

[8]"Fresh Start with God," Saddleback Church (accessed December 4, 2018), https://saddleback.com/connect/ministry/freshstart.

[9]See "Next Steps," Calvary Fellowship (accessed December 4, 2018), https://
westhartfordchurch.com/next-steps/; and "Plan a Visit," Lakeland Church
(accessed December 4, 2018), https://lakeland.org/plan-a-visit/.

[10]Aaron Smith and Monica Anderson, "Social Media Use in 2018," Internet
& Technology, Pew Research Center, March 1, 2018, www.pewinternet
.org/2018/03/01/social-media-use-in-2018/.

[11]Q Place (www.qplace.com) is a great example of a neighborhood group.
Missional communities come in many varieties. 3DM and Mike Breen
(https://3dmovements.com) pioneered missional communities in the 1990s
in Sheffield, England, when they got kicked out of their worship space and
had to decentralize into minichurch clusters of house groups that focused
on reaching their communities. The Soma churches in Washington (https://
wearesoma.com) are churches made up of missional communities, driven
by their mission to reach new people and to improve the quality of life in
their communities.

Mothers of Pre-Schoolers (MOPS) often gathers Christian mothers during
the day together to pray and support each other, but it can become a very
effective outreach strategy.

Northpoint Church offers Starting Point Groups as the place for seekers to
belong and learn the fundamentals of Christian faith (www.startingpoint.com).

Alpha (https://alphausa.org) is a ten-week introduction to Christian faith that
is designed for seekers and explorers of Christian faith. It is intended to witness
to people through good apologetics, verbal explanation of the basics of the
faith, and powerful encounters with the Holy Spirit in healing and hearing
from God. It came out of the Anglican Holy Trinity Brompton in London
and has spread around the world and into many segments of society.

Christianity Explored (www.christianityexplored.org) is a biblically based
inductive and teaching curriculum aimed at introducing people to Jesus and
the Scriptures. It came out of All Souls Church in London, where John
Stott, a well-known evangelical pastor, presided for many years.

[12]One-third of 143 million = 47.6 million. Thirty-three percent of 143 million
unchurched adults and children represents 47 million people, 36 million of
whom are adults.

[13]Hartford Institute for Religion Research, "Fast Facts About American Religion" (accessed April 5, 2018), http://hirr.hartsem.edu/research/fastfacts
/fast_facts.html.

[14]"Most Teenagers Drop Out of Church as Young Adults," Lifeway Research, January 15, 2019, https://lifewayresearch.com/2019/01/15/most -teenagers-drop-out-of-church-as-young-adults/.

4 Engaging the Receptive Millennials, Nones, and Nominals in Your Life

[1]Barna Group, "What Non-Christians Want from Faith Conversations," February 19, 2019, https://www.barna.com/research/non-christians-faith -conversations/. A sample from Barna Group, *Reviving Evangelism: Current Realities That Demand a New Vision for Sharing Faith* (Ventura, CA: Barna Group, 2018).

[2]Michael Lipka, "Millennials Increasingly Are Driving Growth of 'Nones,'" FactTank, Pew Research Center, May 12, 2015, www.pewresearch.org/fact -tank/2015/05/12/millennials-increasingly-are-driving-growth-of-nones/; Pew Research Center, "Religious Landscape Study," Religion and Public Life, Pew Research Center (accessed April 5, 2018), www.pewforum.org /religious-landscape-study/.

[3]"Most Teenagers Drop Out of Church as Young Adults," Lifeway Research, January 15, 2019, https://lifewayresearch.com/2019/01/15/most -teenagers-drop-out-of-church-as-young-adults/.

[4]Christian Smith, Kyle Longest, Jonathan Hill, and Kari Christoffersen, *Young Catholic America: Emerging Adults, In, Out of, and Gone from the Church* (Oxford: Oxford University Press, 2014). See, for instance, Smith's six categories of emerging adults and the interviews they did with people from each, summarized on page 91.

[5]This data comes from additional analysis conducted by the Billy Graham Center Institute on the data from the unchurched study. "Unchurched Report," Billy Graham Center Institute and Lifeway Research, April 24, 2019, www.billygrahamcenter.com/youfoundme/research.

[6]Pew Research Center, "America's Changing Religious Landscape," Religion and Public Life, Pew Research Center, May 12, 2015, www.pewforum .org/2015/05/12/americas-changing-religious-landscape/.

[7]The widespread use of the term *none* in the press has helped construct the category. It has given people a term to use as a descriptor they did not have before, and one that has an element of being iconoclastic but not necessarily anti-God. It is anticategory more than anti-God, and it avoids the negative

associations that *atheist* and even *agnostic* can have. See Elizabeth Drescher, *Choosing Our Religion: The Spiritual Lives of America's Nones* (Oxford: Oxford University Press, 2016), loc. 745, Kindle.

[8]"The new survey finds that the atheist and agnostic share of the 'nones' has grown to 31%. Those identifying as 'nothing in particular' and describing religion as unimportant in their lives continue to account for 39% of all 'nones.' But the share identifying as 'nothing in particular' while also affirming that religion is either 'very' or 'somewhat' important to them has fallen to 30% of all 'nones.'" Pew Research Center, "America's Changing Religious Landscape."

[9]"A majority of the religiously unaffiliated clearly think that religion can be a force for good in society, with three-quarters saying religious organizations bring people together and help strengthen community bonds (78%) and a similar number saying religious organizations play an important role in helping the poor and needy (77%)." Pew Research Center, "'Nones' on the Rise," Religion and Public Life, Pew Research Center, October 9, 2012, www.pewforum.org/2012/10/09/nones-on-the-rise/.

[10]This data comes from the additional analysis conducted by the Billy Graham Center Institute on the data from the unchurched study.

[11]This data comes from the additional analysis conducted by the Billy Graham Center Institute on the data from the unchurched study.

[12]"As the ranks of the religiously unaffiliated continue to grow, they also describe themselves in increasingly secular terms." Pew Research Center, "America's Changing Religious Landscape."

[13]"Unchurched Report."

[14]Pew Research Center, "Religious Landscape Study."

[15]This data comes from the additional analysis conducted by the Billy Graham Center Institute on the data from the unchurched study.

[16]See Jared E. Alcantara, *Crossover Preaching* (Downers Grove, IL: InterVarsity Press, 2015), chap. 1.

[17]Pew Research Center, "America's Changing Religious Landscape."

[18]This data comes from the additional analysis conducted by the Billy Graham Center Institute on the data from the unchurched study.

[19]This data comes from the additional analysis conducted by the Billy Graham Center Institute on the data from the unchurched study.

[20] According to the additional analysis conducted by the Billy Graham Center Institute on the data from the unchurched study, 36 percent of unchurched Hispanics agree that the Christian faith is good for society. This is significantly lower than 52 percent of unchurched African Americans and 42 percent of the overall unchurched population.

[21] This data comes from the additional analysis conducted by the Billy Graham Center Institute on the data from the unchurched study.

[22] Her friend is from one of the African American denominations that emphasizes Wesley's entire sanctification and focuses on certain marks of holy living. Many of those denominations became Pentecostal after the Azusa Street revival in California in 1906, but some churches, like the one Danita's friend went to, remained in the holiness tradition, not accepting speaking in tongues as a third work of the Holy Spirit, in addition to salvation and sanctification.

[23] For years now I have been reflecting on the model Paul gave us of doing just this, of discovering and capitalizing on receptivity, as he did in his speech to the Athenians in the Areopagus. The event is recorded in Acts 17, and I explored his basic approach first in my book *Evangelism Outside the Box* (Downers Grove, IL: InterVarsity Press, 2000). Later Doug Schaupp and Don Everts developed their approach from the same Acts 17 passage in their book *I Once Was Lost* (Downers Grove, IL: InterVarsity Press, 2008).

[24] Schaupp and Everts, *I Once Was Lost*.

[25] The following text is lightly adapted from pages 77-78 of *Evangelism Outside the Box*, with permission from Rick Richardson.

[26] For instance, see Tim Keller, "Tim Keller—North American Mission: The Outward Move," Redeemer City to City, October 18, 2018, www.facebook.com/RedeemerCTC/videos/462093247614418/, minute 56 to the end, and Tim Keller, "Tim Keller—North American Mission: The Inward Move," Redeemer City to City, October 19, 2018, www.facebook.com/RedeemerCTC/videos/699476167094172/, minute 55 to the end. These are brilliant lectures on engaging people in our culture today.

[27] I think I first heard this turn of phrase from my friend Becky Pippert, author of *Out of the Saltshaker and Into the World*, rev. ed. (Downers Grove, IL: InterVarsity Press, 1999).

[28] See Tim Keller, "Tim Keller—North American Mission," Redeemer City to City, October 18, 2018, and October 19, 2018.

5 Exploring the Conversion Community Equation

[1]Steve Beirn and George W. Murray, *Well Sent: Reimagining the Church's Missionary-Sending Process* (Fort Washington, PA: CLC, 2015), 63.

[2]The term *conversion community* comes from Doug Schaupp, national evangelism director for InterVarsity. In their book *Breaking the Huddle: How Your Community Can Grow Its Witness* (Downers Grove, IL: InterVarsity Press, 2016), Doug, Don Everts, and Val Gordon outline how Christian communities need to progress from "huddled" communities, where witnessing is merely an idea or concept, to "conversion" communities, which are aligned around a common witness.

[3]Curt Coffman and Kathie Sorensen, *Culture Eats Strategy for Lunch: The Secret of Extraordinary Results, Igniting the Passion Within* (Cork: BookBaby, 2013), 2. As Coffman and Sorensen admit, the quote is thought to originate from the famed business author Peter Drucker, although it may be apocryphal.

[4]Chacon, interview by Rick Richardson, Qualitative Interviews of Pastors and Previously Unchurched, April 8, 2016.

6 Modeling Outreach Others Can Imitate

[1]Harvey Mitchell, interview by Johwa Lee, Qualitative Interviews of Pastors and Previously Unchurched, April 5, 2016.

[2]Quoting Dave Ferguson's talk at an Evangelism Leaders Fellowship (ELF) gathering in December 2017 at the Billy Graham Center at Wheaton College.

7 Multiplying Missional Leaders

[1]Mike Breen first put me on to the field of mimetics as a helpful way to understand discipleship as the process of imitation and to begin to grapple with how preaching could much more effectively influence others. Books such as *The Master and His Emissary* by Iain McGilchrist, on the difference between left- and right-brain function, along with the implications for communication and imitation, are very helpful. Iain McGilchrist, *The Master and His Emissary: The Divided Brain and the Making of the Western World* (New Haven, CT: Yale University Press, 2009).

[2]"Mimetic," Merriam-Webster.com (accessed December 1, 2018), www.merriam-webster.com/dictionary/mimetic.

[3]Richard Dawkins coined the expression "memes" in *The Selfish Gene* (Oxford: Oxford University Press, 1976). Susan Blackmore has written one of the most helpful books on memes and mimetic replication in *The Meme Machine* (Oxford: Oxford University Press, 2000). Genes carry the genetic code to reproduce life. Memes carry the memetic or imitation code to reproduce thinking and behavior. As a brief description: "A meme is a cognitive or behavior pattern that can be transmitted from one individual to another one. Since the individual who transmitted the meme will continue to carry it, the transmission can be interpreted as a *replication* [or reproduction]: a copy of the meme is made in the memory of another individual, making him or her into a *carrier* of the meme. This process of self-reproduction (the memetic life-cycle), leading to spreading over a growing group of individuals, defines the meme as a replicator, similar in that respect to the gene." F. Heylighen, "Memetics," Principia Cybernetica Web, November 23, 2001, http://pespmc1.vub.ac.be/MEMES.html.

[4]Haikarate4, "Where's the Beef Commercials – Wendy's 1984," May 2014, www.youtube.com/watch?v=riH5EsGcmTw.

[5]Kenneth T. Walsh, "6 Best 'Zingers' From Past Presidential Debates," *USNews*, October 1, 2012, www.usnews.com/news/blogs/ken-walshs-washington/2012/10/01/6-best-zingers-from-past-presidential-debates.

[6]Steve Carter, *This Invitational Life: Risking Yourself to Align with God's Heartbeat for Humanity* (Colorado Springs, CO: David C. Cook, 2016).

[7]"Stories," Granger Community Church (accessed December 1, 2018), https://grangerchurch.com/stories/.

[8]Jerry Root, personal communication, July 18, 2018.

[9]Chris McChesney, Sean Covey, and Jim Huling, *The 4 Disciplines of Execution: Achieving Your Wildly Important Goals* (New York: Free Press, 2016).

[10]Kevin Harney, *Organic Outreach for Churches: Infusing Evangelistic Passion in Your Local Congregation* (Grand Rapids: Zondervan, 2018), 118.

8 Belonging to the Broader Community

[1]Steve Corbett and Brian Fikkert, *When Helping Hurts: How to Alleviate Poverty Without Hurting the Poor . . . and Yourself* (Chicago: Moody, 2009).

[2]See "CCD Philosophy," Christian Community Development Association (accessed December 1, 2018), https://ccda.org/about/philosophy/. This page gives a great overview of the values of an organic and relational approach to meeting needs that then creates relational bridges across which the gospel and invitations can travel.

[3]Jay Pathak and Dave Runyon, *The Art of Neighboring: Building Genuine Relationships Right Outside Your Door* (Grand Rapids: Baker Books, 2012), 18-21.

[4]"Shawn," interview by Christina Walker, Qualitative Interviews of Pastors and Previously Unchurched, April 21, 2016.

[5]My colleague Beth Seversen also calls them brokers and has discovered in her research ways that brokers are key in reaching emerging adults today. Beth Seversen, "From Foreign to Familiar: Distinctive Elements and Evangelistic Approaches of Evangelical Covenant Churches Reaching and Incorporating Western Emerging Adults," (PhD diss., Trinity Evangelical Divinity School, 2017).

[6]Thom Rainer goes as far as to say the next major staff position for churches looking to the future and toward combining service and verbal witness will be a pastor of community evangelism. "The Next Future Church Staff Position: Pastor of Community Evangelism," Thom Rainer, April 18, 2016, https://thomrainer.com/?s=Community+Evangelism. Although I love this idea, we found many examples of brokers who were not hired by the church but wanted to play this role as a bridge between the church and the community.

[7]Craig Watson, interview by Kerilee Van Schooten, Qualitative Interviews of Pastors and Previously Unchurched, March 10, 2016.

[8]Carter, interview by Kerilee Van Schooten, Qualitative Interviews of Pastors and Previously Unchurched, March 10, 2016.

[9]Carter, interview by Van Schooten.

9 Blessing the World to Reach the World

[1]Barna, Reviving Evangelism, Barna Report, 2019, www.barna.com/research/non-christians-faith-conversations/.

[2]Mark Russell, *The Missional Entrepreneur: Principles and Practices for Business as Mission* (Birmingham, AL: New Hope, 2010).

[3]Dave Ferguson, "Five Ways to Bless Your Neighbors," The Verge Network, December 27, 2012, www.vergenetwork.org/2012/12/27/five-ways-to-bless

-your-neighbors-dave-ferguson/; "BLESS Intentional Evangelism Initiative," Evangelical Covenant Church, accessed August 2, 2018, https://covchurch.org/evangelism/bless/.

[4]See also the Evangelical Covenant Church website on BLESS resources: https://covchurch.org/evangelism/bless/. The Billy Graham Center and the Evangelical Covenant Church have been in an informal partnership over these last several years, and we have used their graphics and adapted their descriptions with permission.

[5]Shared in a January 2018 cohort meeting through the Church Evangelism Initiative.

[6]Shared in an October 2017 cohort meeting through the Church Evangelism Initiative.

[7]Jim, interview by Nathaniel Mullins, Qualitative Interviews of Pastors and Previously Unchurched, March 31, 2016.

10 Bringing the Community to Church

[1]Beth Seversen has done insightful work on the ways in which emerging adults in her study developed a Christian identity through their involvement with churches, meaning that they belonged and behaved as Christians on the way to believing and becoming Christians. Her upcoming book published by InterVarsity Press will explore these issues and many others in relation to millennials' conversion process and congregational commitments. Beth Seversen, "From Foreign to Familiar: Distinctive Elements and Evangelistic Approaches of Evangelical Covenant Churches Reaching and Incorporating Western Emerging Adults," (PhD diss., Trinity Evangelical Divinity School, 2017).

[2]Donald McGavran, *The Bridges of God: A Study in the Strategy of Missions* (Eugene, OR: Wipf & Stock, 2005).

[3]Pete Ward, *Liquid Church* (Eugene, OR: Wipf & Stock, 2013).

[4]Steve Colter, interview by Kerilee Van Schooten, Qualitative Interviews of Pastors and Previously Unchurched, April 26, 2016.

[5]Keith Gordon Green, "Asleep in the Light," *No Compromise* (Brentwood, TN: Universal Music Publishing Group, 1978), https://genius.com/Keith-green-asleep-in-the-light-lyrics.

[6]Jonathan, interview by Joshua Gregerson, Qualitative Interviews of Pastors and Previously Unchurched, March 28, 2016.

[7]Laura, interview by Kerilee Van Schooten, Qualitative Interviews of Pastors and Previously Unchurched, March 21, 2016.

[8]"Miles," interview by Kerilee Van Schooten, Qualitative Interviews of Pastors and Previously Unchurched, April 20, 2016.

[9]"Holly," interview by Kerilee Van Schooten, Qualitative Interviews of Pastors and Previously Unchurched, April 20, 2016.

11 Building a Community of the Beloved Through Hospitality

[1]Joshua W. Jipp, *Saved by Faith and Hospitality* (Grand Rapids: Eerdmans, 2017), 2.

[2]Christine D. Pohl and Pamela J. Buck, *Study Guide for Making Room: Recovering Hospitality as a Christian Tradition* (Grand Rapids: Eerdmans, 2001), https://practicingourfaith.org/pdf/MakingRoomStudyGuide.pdf, 1.

[3]Pohl and Buck, *Study Guide for Making Room*, 2.

[4]"Trevor," interview by Kerilee Van Schooten, Qualitative Interviews of Pastors and Previously Unchurched, April 28, 2016.

[5]Alpha (https://alphausa.org), Christianity Explored (www.christianity explored.org), and Finding Your Way Back to God (www.rightnowmedia .org/Content/Series/157704?episode=1) are resources that help people understand the foundations of the Christian faith. They facilitate open discussions about the Christian faith in a way that allows people to be honest about their questions and hesitations and also invites people to explore and accept the truth of the Christian faith.

[6]"Bailey," interview by Darryl McAuley, Qualitative Interviews of Pastors and Previously Unchurched, March 31, 2016.

[7]Small Church Evangelism Study, Billy Graham Center and Lifeway Research.

[8]Kendra Smith, interview by Rick Richardson, Qualitative Interviews of Pastors and Previously Unchurched, April 4, 2016.

12 Conclusion: From a Conversion Community
to a Conversion Movement

[1]Roger Finke and Rodney Stark, *The Churching of America, 1776–2005: Winners and Losers in Our Religious Economy* (New Brunswick, NJ: Rutgers University Press, 2005), 57.

[2]Finke and Stark, *Churching of America*, 59.

[3]Their analysis is sociological but has many connections to good theology—that is, theology based on Scripture. Such theology unpacks the nature of the church on mission as it grows in influence and numbers, the nature of churches that add "to their number daily," as the book of Acts puts it (Acts 2:47). Stark and Finke have adapted concepts related to religious capital (the value of religious involvement for life and for other social and economic benefits), market share (the share of the religious market that churches have been able to attract), and "rational choice theory" (explaining the reasons people choose one congregation over another). I realize there are limitations to this economic and demographic approach to religion and to evaluating its success, but it is one important indicator of relevance and certainly the ability to reach new people and have an impact on local communities. See Finke and Stark, *Churching of America*, 160-82.

[4]Finke and Stark, *Churching of America*, 72-116.

[5]Finke and Stark, *Churching of America*, 99-101.

[6]Finke and Stark, *Churching of America*, 170, 172.

[7]"Patrick," interview by Kerilee Van Schooten, Qualitative Interviews of Pastors and Previously Unchurched, April 19, 2016.